The US Government Case Study of Human Manipulation

Intelligence Science Board

I0407142

INTELLIGENCE INTERVIEWING

TEACHING PAPERS AND CASE STUDIES

A Report from the Study on Educing Information

ISBN-10: 1468117149

ISBN-13: 978-1468117141

Compiled & Published by

www.MindControlPublishing.com

Acknowledgments

Many professionals have contributed to the thinking presented in the teaching papers and case studies in this booklet. These persons come from intelligence, law enforcement, military, academic, and research organizations. All share the belief that the United States can increase and improve our knowledge in intelligence interviewing – a critical national security area.

The ISB Study on Educing Information has received support from many organizations. Those of us working on the Study have appreciated the assistance and encouragement of senior government leaders as we have tried to craft a way forward.

To each and all, thank you.
Robert A. Fein, Ph.D.
Chairman, ISB Study on Educing Information

Contents

Introduction

For the past five years, an extraordinary amount of worldwide interest has focused on U.S. interrogation activities. However, the United States has made little systematic effort to develop a knowledge base that could underlie effective interrogation policies, practices, and procedures for the future.

In 2004 the Intelligence Science Board (ISB) established the Study on Educing Information[1] to examine the current state of scientific knowledge regarding interrogation and learn about training programs that prepare individuals to conduct custodial interrogations. In December 2006, the study team delivered its Phase I report to the Director of National Intelligence.[2] The report contained three major findings:

•The study team's extensive investigations determined that the U.S. Government had funded significant research efforts on interrogation during the 1950s, but revealed no government research programs on interrogation-related topics in the past forty years.

•The study team could not discover an objective scientific basis for the techniques commonly used by U.S. interrogators.

•The study team could not find an Intelligence Community (IC) organization with the current responsibility, authority, capability, and accountability to develop the range of intelligence interviewing operational, training, and research activities needed in the near and distant future.

The Phase I Report recommended that the IC initiate a research program to develop a foundation for future interrogation research, systems, and practices. The Deputy Director of National Intelligence for Collection requested the ISB's Study on Educing Information to continue its work and pursue this goal. Two premises underlay the effort:

1) For the foreseeable future, the United States will need information from persons in custody who may know about matters critical to our national security.

The U.S. Government Case Study of Human Manipulation

[1] The Phase I study team chose this unusual term to signify a broader focus than that suggested by the emotionally loaded term "interrogation."

[2] See Intelligence Science Board, *Educing Information— Interrogation: Science and Art, Foundations for the Future* (Washington, DC: National Defense Intelligence College, December 2006). The book is also available on line at www.fas.org/irp/dni/educing.pdf.

2) Intelligence interviews with persons in custody are likely to be most effective if based on knowledge-based theory and analysis.

The Phase II study brought together skilled interviewers, interrogators, former case officers, psychologists, law enforcement professionals, academic researchers, and negotiation experts. Over a period of two years, these professionals met to review cases and scientific research, learn from effective intelligence interviewers, and discuss strategies and practices. This booklet reflects one outcome of that research and those discussions,[3] and captures suggestions for the future of what has increasingly come to be called "intelligence interviewing."

The study chair chose the term "intelligence interviewing" for Phase II for two reasons. First, "interrogation" may have different technical meanings in various defense and law enforcement settings. Second, as noted previously, "interrogation" now carries with it a range of (often highly coercive) stereotypes. "Intelligence interviewing," by contrast, is a term not previously used in intelligence, military, or law enforcement settings. As used in this booklet, it signifies the gathering of useful and accurate information by professionals questioning detainees.

The emphasis of this booklet is on non-coercive intelligence interviewing. The study chair has followed the arguments as to the moral, social, and possible military costs of coercive interrogations, as well as the debates about the possible utilitarian value – and limitations – of coercive interrogations. The chair was also aware of considerable success that skilled interviewers, using a systems approach, achieved through non-coercive interrogations of prisoners of war during World War II and in Vietnam, and in the 1990s and since 2001 with members of al-Qa'ida. This report reflects the contributors' view that the United States and other democracies can benefit from exploring and learning more in the area of non-coercive intelligence interviewing.[4]

Intended Audience

In recent years, U.S. Government organizations with interrogation responsibilities have operated programs that vary with regard to specific purposes, professionalism, ages of personnel, expected length of service of interrogators, and approved approaches and techniques. Some individuals and organizations distinguish among tactical, operational, and strategic interrogation. This booklet may be of interest to the full range of persons involved with interrogation and intelligence interviewing. However, it is written primarily for individuals concerned with "high-value" detainees and those who focus mainly on strategic interrogation.

> [3] See also *Interrogation: World War II, Vietnam, and Iraq* (Washington, DC: National Defense Intelligence College, September 2008). The book is also available on line at http://www.ndic.edu/press/12010.htm .
>
> [4] During Phases I and II, contributors could find no studies that compare the results of "coercive" interrogations with those of non-coercive intelligence interviews. It is also difficult to imagine how such studies might be conducted in a scientifically valid, let alone morally acceptable, manner.

Organization

The first section of this booklet contains six papers on topics central to interrogation and intelligence interviewing: persuasion, power, interests and identities, stress, resistances, and memory. Each paper reviews some conventional beliefs as well as current behavioral science perspectives about the topic. Since a short booklet could not encompass all "conventional beliefs," the papers refer only to those described in U.S. Army Field Manual, 2.22-3, *Human Intelligence Collector Operations*.

These papers also do not include complete literature reviews, but instead draw on behavioral science theory, articles, and books in each area. Each paper includes some key points and questions for future research. The papers are drawn solely from open source materials.

The second section presents two brief case studies. The first case reports on a 14-day interrogation of Mohammed Rashed Daoud al-'Owhali, a key participant in the attack on the U.S. Embassy in Nairobi, Kenya, on August 7, 1998. The second case describes the interrogation of a senior North Vietnamese intelligence officer during the Vietnam War. The case studies include short teaching notes. The cases are meant to be read in the context of the six papers. While military, law enforcement, and intelligence organizations have produced various kinds of after-action reports on interrogations,"thick" cases for analysis and teaching are rare to non-existent. These cases and notes therefore illustrate only a few possible approaches to developing teaching materials for intelligence interviewing professionals.

A Framework for Intelligence Interviewing

Discussions of interrogation often involve consideration of "techniques." For example, FM 2-22.3 describes seventeen approved techniques for interrogation. This booklet is meant to provoke discussion of a somewhat different framework, especially in the context of high-value detainees in custody. Intelligence interviewing, as described here, is based on four related ideas:

1) consideration of the multiple contexts in which intelligence interviews occur

2) a team approach
3) the team's constant need to widen and deepen its knowledge about each detainee and his[5] circumstances

4) the importance of developing an"operational accord" with the detainee

Intelligence interviewing, if done professionally and with the benefit of current and emerging knowledge, occurs *in context*. Context includes the physical environment or setting in which the detained person resides and in which interviews take place. It also includes the interpersonal environment established by the interviewer and the intelligence interviewing team. Further, *context* encompasses the informational environment; it includes all the facts and perspectives about the detainee possessed by the intelligence interviewing team.

All this calls for an "integrated systems" perspective. The expectation that an interrogator could walk into a room with a high-value detainee and simply employ "techniques" to gain accurate and important information significantly underestimates the complexity of effective intelligence interviews. Ideally, an interviewer will know everything that is affecting the detainee inside and outside the interviewing room. What have guards been saying to him? What are his relationships with other detainees? What discussions has he had with them? What information is known, or being developed, about the detainee and the accuracy of his statements?

The interviewing "framework" suggested in this booklet incorporates both the physical setting and the overall plan for working with *a particular detainee*. The framework also includes ongoing observation and assessment of a detainee's stress levels, sources of power, interests, identities, memory, and resistances. In this framework, observations from the team (and consultants) aid the interviewer to create a productive interpersonal environment with the detainee. Interactions with others – guards, other officials, collaborating detainees – and the living conditions within the detention environment likewise may contribute to the detainee's willingness to furnish information.

As interviews and interactions take place, information from other intelligence systems is immediately provided to the team. Communications intercepts, and immediate efforts to verify the detainee's statements and to follow up on leads, increase the "information power" of the team. Information power in turn aids interviewers to develop a productive operational accord with the detainee. This integrated systems approach may increase the likelihood that the detainee will provide useful and accurate information and also that he will provide more of the information that he has.

[5] For simplicity this document uses male pronouns to refer to detainees and to intelligence interviewing professionals. There is of course no implication that only men are or will be detainees, or that only men are or will serve as interrogators and intelligence interviewing

professionals.

The Importance of an Operational Accord

Intelligence interviewing, as presented in this booklet, involves carefully developed, consistently reviewed relationships between interviewer(s) and detainee. Where the Army Field Manual and conventional thinking about interrogation advocate building "rapport," these papers suggest a different concept: operational accord.

"Rapport" means different things to different people. To some it implies friendship or an increasingly informal relationship between interviewer and detainee. Others may view rapport building as a task to be completed in the first five to ten minutes of the interview (for example, by asking the detainee how he is feeling), with little explicit attention paid to "rapport" thereafter.

By contrast, "operational accord" denotes a special "working" or "professional" relationship between the interviewer and the high-value detainee. It is characterized by the detainee's willingness to supply accurate information, at least some of the time, in response to the interviewer's questions. The concept also implies that the interviewer has an individualized and effective strategy for interactions with the detainee. Once an operational accord develops, it may allow an intelligence interviewer to engage with, challenge, and debate with the detainee, or agree with him if appropriate, without shutting down the relationship or causing the loss of important information.

According to the framework suggested here, an intelligence interviewing team works to develop and support an environment that gives the interviewer(s) opportunities to develop an operational accord with a detainee. The team seeks to provide information to the interviewer, and analyzes what the detainee says and how he behaves. The intelligence interviewing team works to provide and support both a physical and an interpersonal context that promote productive discussions with the detainee.

Longer Term Goals

This ISB study has recommended that the U.S. Government establish a specialized, professional cadre of government intelligence interviewers.

The U.S. Government Case Study of Human Manipulation

This cadre should be given the responsibility, authority, capability, and accountability to develop the range of operational, training, research, and liaison activities required. Such work might permit the United States to become a world leader in non-coercive intelligence interviewing within five years.

An encouraging first step took place on January 22, 2009, when President Barack Obama issued an Executive Order, "Ensuring Lawful Interrogations." This order limits interrogation techniques and approaches to those authorized by U.S. Army Field Manual 2.22-3. It permits the FBI and other law enforcement agencies to continue to use "authorized, non-coercive techniques of interrogation that are designed to elicit voluntary statements and do not involve the use of force, threats, or promises." The Executive Order also establishes a Special Inter-agency Task Force on Interrogation and Transfer Policies "to study and evaluate whether the interrogation practices and techniques in Army Field Manual 2-22.3, when employed by departments or agencies outside the military, provide an appropriate means of acquiring the intelligence necessary to protect the Nation, and, if warranted, to recommend any additional or different guidance for other departments or agencies…"

Much remains to explore and learn in the area of non-coercive intelligence interviewing. The papers, case studies, and teaching notes in this booklet may be useful in several ways. The booklet may provide experienced and successful interviewers a more formal understanding of the approaches they may have used instinctively. It may also help them to communicate their expertise to their colleagues. In addition, ideas in the booklet may aid students and trainees to formulate a better framework for building intelligence interviewing relationships. The concepts presented here may encourage researchers to pose and find ways to answer questions about intelligence interviewing.

This booklet is intended to foster thinking and discussion and to encourage knowledge-based teaching, research, and practice. It does not, and cannot, offer doctrine or prescriptions. It is a start, not an end.

Section I Teaching Papers

Persuasion

How Can an Intelligence Interviewing Professional Persuade a High-Value Detainee to Provide Information?

The central challenge facing intelligence interviewing professionals is to obtain accurate, timely, and useful intelligence from detainees. A companion challenge is "completeness" – to gather as much of the useful information known by each detainee as reasonably possible.

Highly effective intelligence interviewers constantly seek the most promising means – tangible or intangible – to persuade a particular detainee to provide information. However, many feel that their ability to persuade just"comes naturally" to them – that these skills are difficult to understand fully, or to study, or teach to others. Behavioral science research on persuasion, changing minds, and understanding core concerns helps to explain the effectiveness of skilled intelligence interviewers. Behavioral science research may also be used to suggest practical ideas, both in terms of practice and research. There are, of course, no formulas or quick solutions to the challenges of persuasion: Persuading a detainee to provide useful information requires planning, commitment, and on-going objective assessment.

Conventional Beliefs

Historically, a segment of the interrogator community has focused on using some level of psychological, emotional, and physical force to"gain" the detainee's cooperation. Others have employed a variety of imaginative "ploys" or"tricks" to achieve the same outcome.

Army Field Manual 2-22.3, *Human Intelligence Collector Operations*, defines interrogation as follows:

1-20. Interrogation is the systematic effort to procure information to answer specific collection requirements by direct and indirect questioning techniques of a person who is in the custody of the forces conducting the questioning.

The U.S. Government Case Study of Human Manipulation

The Field Manual outlines two primary categories of techniques: *control* and *rapport*. It then describes an array of approaches designed to establish and maintain one or both of these elements (with emphasis on maintaining control at all times). Underlying all these approaches is the effort to undermine the detainee's interest in resisting while encouraging cooperation:

8-5. The HUMINT collector's objective during this phase is to establish a relationship with the detainee that results in the detainee providing accurate and reliable information in response to the HUMINT collector's questions. The HUMINT collector adopts an appropriate persona based on his appraisal of the detainee but remains alert for verbal and nonverbal clues that indicate the need for change in the approach techniques... At the initial contact, a businesslike relationship should be maintained. As the detainee assumes a cooperative attitude, a more relaxed atmosphere may be advantageous. The HUMINT collector must carefully determine which of the various approach techniques to employ.

FM 2-22.3 makes clear that no single method of persuasion will prove effective across the broad range of detainees an interrogator might encounter:

8-6. Detainees will cooperate with the HUMINT collector for various reasons ranging from patriotic duty to personal gain, such as material gifts or money. They may also respond to emotion or logic. Regardless of the type of detainee and his outward personality, every detainee possesses exploitable characteristics that, if recognized by the HUMINT collector, can be used to facilitate the collection process. These characteristics may be readily apparent or may have to be extrapolated from the detainee's speech, mannerisms, facial expressions, physical movements, involuntary responses (perspiration, changes in breathing, eye movement), and other overt indications that vary from detainee to detainee. From a psychological standpoint, the HUMINT collector must be cognizant of a variety of behaviors.

Behavioral Science Perspectives

Behavioral science research affirms elements of these conventional beliefs. Behavioral science theory and research may offer guidance on how to adapt one's persuasive style to an individual detainee –and on the range of persuasion strategies available to an intelligence interviewing professional. Additionally, behavioral science perspectives may suggest a more nuanced and sophisticated framework for persuasion, particularly for those working with high-value detainees.

Research findings provide compelling evidence that most people, even"resistant" people, can be persuaded to act in fairly predictable ways whether or not they intended to do so. Persuasion is often a subtle and carefully crafted process tailored to each individual. Skillful persuasion may bring a detainee to view his situation and the information he holds differently than before; he may even believe he came to these conclusions largely on his own.

Knowledge from behavioral science may increase effectiveness in interviewing an individual detainee; it also provides powerful questions for future research. Although little research has been found that examines persuasion in the context of intelligence interviewing, the studies available have produced practical findings that may be adapted to the detainee population. In particular, the concept of a strategic plan or "persuasion framework" designed for each individual detainee may be more useful than the idea of trying one or another standard"approach."[1]
*

People are constantly bombarded by messages designed to influence their thinking and behavior. Everyone can recall being persuaded to act in ways they had not intended, perhaps even against some of their own interests. A person living on a fixed income might buy a car he had only planned to look at. (The generous deal was just too hard to resist, especially after talking to the salesman– a great guy who grew up in the neighborhood and played baseball on the old field.) Or he might keep lending money to a friend who is chronically broke…telling himself that this time his friend really will keep his promise to pay back the loan.

Why do people allow themselves, or agree, to behave in ways they may not have initially intended? Psychologists, especially social psychologists,[1]have long studied the science behind the art of persuasion, dissecting the subtleties of both verbal and nonverbal behavior, that persuade individuals to feel, think, and act in certain ways. In addition, researchers in behavioral economics[2]have discovered that *understanding* an "irrational" decision-making process – such as paying more for a certain product because the higher price must mean it is better – often makes this irrational human behavior fairly predictable. Research in neuroscience further helps to explain why people make the decisions they make, including decisions that seem to be made "automatically,"or without much conscious thought.

Many of the researchers in these fields have studied people in the Western world. However, some research, and much anecdotal information, suggests that the research findings are applicable to a range of people from various backgrounds and cultures. In fact, research in the field of neuroscience suggests that at least some of the concepts below are"hard wired" in the brain.

Further research is needed to determine whether some or all of the principles of persuasion discussed below indeed have universal relevance, including how they may apply to a range of high-value detainees.

[*] FM 2-22.3 practice requires HUMINT collectors to develop an "Interrogation Plan" to guide interactions with a detainee. The concept of a "persuasion framework" builds on this idea, affirming that such interactions should be carefully planned. It also encompasses additional analysis and additional factors, such as the other people with whom the detainee interacts, the physical setting, the detainee's sources of power, etc.

Why Might an Intelligence Interviewing Professional and Team Want to Understand Persuasion?

Many detainees are willing to provide *some* information, and some of this information may have value. However, detainees will less commonly reveal information they consider especially valuable: information that prevents the next attack, leads to the head of their organization, or directly implicates the detainee or his family. This is particularly true if the detainee believes the intelligence interviewing team does not know what valuable information he holds.

Ulrich Straus notes in his book, *The Anguish of Surrender*[3]: "Silence is by far the best weapon a prisoner determined to divulge no information can wield. It seems clear, however, that virtually none of the Japanese POWs availed themselves of it."

It follows that the first challenge facing many intelligence interviewing teams is to move the detainee from silence to providing a little information to providing more information. There is a second vital challenge: that of"completeness." Ideally, the team would persuade the detainee *to provide all or most of the important information he holds*. These goals may not be achievable or practical with every detainee. However, persuasion can often open doorways: a) through careful planning to seek specific information and b) serendipitously and incidentally.

How Can Extremists Be Persuaded to Provide Information?

Convincing people to change their minds is rarely easy. Intelligence interviewing teams may deal with detainees who have deeply held extremist beliefs, and many experts have suggested that such ideas are difficult to change. However, the team's goal is to obtain useful information, not to convert the detainee to a new belief system.

The team therefore might focus first on assessing the detainee's interests (what does he *really* want, compared with what he may be saying) and sources of power (what kinds of strengths and influence may he have). The objective here is to start by building an operational accord[*](see *Interests and Identities* and

[*] "Operational accord" denotes a special "working" or"professional" relationship between the interviewer and the high-value detainee. It is characterized by the detainee's willingness to supply accurate information, at least some of the time, in response to the interviewer's questions. The concept also implies that the interviewer has an individualized and effective strategy for interactions with the detainee. Once an operational accord develops, it may allow an intelligence interviewer to engage with, challenge, and debate with the detainee, or agree with him if appropriate, without shutting down the relationship or

causing the loss of important information.

Power). The team would also focus on ways of avoiding or dealing with resistances (see *Resistances*). Over time – several hours to several days – a persuasive interviewer may lead the detainee to develop enough doubt about the ideas and preconceptions he brings to the interview that the detainee becomes amenable to persuasion and provides useful answers to questions. In addition, in the context of these discussions, the interviewer may pick up incidental and unexpected information.

While altering fundamental values and ideas may not necessarily be the goal, almost any interaction with a detainee is likely to influence a detainee's beliefs in some way. Some of these shifts may be very helpful.

Take a detainee who views all Americans as bigoted, uneducated, and ignorant of Islam. Then consider an American intelligence interviewing professional whose family came from the detainee's region of the world. Imagine that the interviewer is fluent in Arabic. He also is happy to exchange ideas and stories about family, religion, and sports, and he does all this, conversationally and nondefensively.

Even if the intelligence interviewing professional does not use these conversations primarily to change values and ideas, this type of interaction may create chinks in the defensive armor of even a highly resistant detainee – and may begin to change the rigid thinking that steels the detainee against any sort of accord with an "ignorant enemy." It is these subtle shifts in thinking that may nudge a detainee toward providing information. Therefore, each interaction with a detainee might best be carefully thought out and implemented. Unintended, contradictory messages – for example, a guard's snide comments to a detainee– could quickly damage an operational accord (see *Interests and Identities*).

How Might an Intelligence Interviewing Team Persuade a High-Value Detainee to Provide Useful Information?

As in all aspects of intelligence interviewing, no one strategy or "approach" will prove effective with all detainees. Intelligence interviewing professionals and teams can benefit from thinking about an individualized "persuasion framework" for each detainee. A detainee's susceptibility to persuasion, and the persuasion framework that is most likely to succeed, depend on many factors, including:

•The overall context of the intelligence interviewing environment, including a carefully designed detention and living environment, the timing of interactions, and the food, reading materials, etc., made available to the detainee

An intelligence interviewing team works to develop and support an environment that gives the interviewer(s) opportunities to develop an operational accord with a detainee. The team seeks to provide information to the interviewer, and analyzes what the detainee says and how he behaves. The intelligence interviewing team works to provide and support a physical context and an interpersonal context that promote productive discussions with the detainee.

•The treatment the detainee experiences from all persons with whom he interacts, including prison guards, intelligence interviewing professionals, translators, and other detainees (if any)

•The individuals with whom the detainee talks, both inside and outside the intelligence interviewing room

•The extent to which an intelligence interviewing professional and the detainee can identify and explore shared social identities and mutual interests (see *Interests and Identities*)

•The methods the intelligence interviewing team uses to manage sources of power and to avoid or deal with resistances (see *Power* and *Resistances*)

•The detainee's ability and willingness to consider perspectives other than his own
•The detainee's intellectual capacity and curiosity
•The range of beliefs and views to which the detainee was exposed while growing up

While the intelligence interviewing team might try to understand the last three factors on this list and take them into account, they are largely outside of the team's control. In contrast, the team might strive to influence the first five factors with careful planning. The team might plan which topics to discuss, and also how certain interactions might affect a detainee's attitudes, behavior, and emotions. The way a detainee feels about his situation, and those around him, can greatly impact the amount and value of the information he provides.

What Principles Guide Effective Persuasion?

Robert Cialdini, a social psychologist, formulated six principles of persuasion after conducting experiments and studying highly persuasive people and the tactics they used when interacting with others. These principles[*] are:

- Liking
- Authority
- Reciprocity
- Commitment/Consistency
- Social Validation (Proof)
- Scarcity[4]

[*] See Cialdini's book *Influence: The Psychology of Persuasion* for a more in-depth description of these principles and the research behind them.

Tactics based on these principles are particularly powerful because they are often subtle and hard to detect. These tactics often cause people to respond in fairly automatic ways without much (or any) thinking. The tactics are, therefore, often difficult to resist.

These principles of persuasion may serve as a useful guide for intelligence interviewing professionals as they plan a persuasion framework for each detainee.

Liking

People prefer to say "yes"to individuals whom they like. Several factors may enhance a detainee's liking for an interviewer – even if the detainee *tries not to like* this "enemy." These factors include physical attractiveness, similarity to the detainee, a complementary social style, and a feeling that there is an association between the intelligence interviewing professional and something or someone the detainee already knows and values. Certain behavior, such as offering convincingly genuine praise, or a warm blanket on a cold evening, may also contribute to the interviewer's likeability.

Research has uncovered increasing empirical evidence for the importance of a complementary style sometimes called "mirroring," "mimicry," "pacing," or "matching."Some psychologists theorize that subtle mimicry is effective because it elicits an unconscious, physiological response in the brain. According to these findings, mirroring someone's posture, movements, voice tone, pitch, etc., during an interchange may create an immediate social bond, even between strangers. Effective mirroring must be done in a non-obvious way.

Authority

Most cultures include strong pressure to comply with, or at least pay attention to, the requests of an authority. An intelligence interviewing professional has many options for establishing authority when working with a detainee (see *Power*). Using information skillfully, following culturally relevant reasoning and logic, drawing upon research, and making reference to relevant historical events may enhance persuasion. This principle of persuasion may resonate best with well educated detainees who value rationality and have at least a partially Western mindset. Or it may be that the principle of authority is important across *all* cultures, but the ways of establishing authority may differ.

During interviews of an admitted al-Qa'ida member detained in a Middle Eastern country just after 9/11, an intelligence interviewing professional realized that the detainee was well educated and well versed in the doctrinal aspects of his religion. The detainee stated that he believed without qualification in the cause of al-Qa'ida and Bin Laden's leadership in "fighting the enemies of Islam." While discussing the depth of his religious beliefs and exhibiting much pride in his knowledge of all aspects, he asserted that he could not abide the killing of innocent civilians.

During this interview session, the intelligence interviewing professional exhibited deep familiarity with the structure of al-Qa'ida, though feigning some limits in that knowledge. He also indicated that he had made efforts to learn about Islam, including Islam's injunction against killing innocent civilians. The detainee demonstrated an apparent respect for the interviewer's "expertise" and in the course of subsequent sessions helped to fill in some knowledge gaps.

Research has demonstrated that symbols– including titles such as "Dr." and the clothing people wear – can often enhance authority. A group of intelligence interviewing professionals working in Guantanamo Bay, Cuba, received a clear demonstration of this. Some members of the interviewing team "dressed down" in shorts and Hawaiian shirts during their interactions with detainees. An analyst wearing a business suit accompanied one intelligence interviewing professional to an interview. The foreign detainee instantly appeared more attentive and cooperative when they entered the room, and soon asked the interviewer, "Is this your boss?" The interviewer was taken aback, since he was older than the analyst and had many more years of experience. Yet he had never seen the detainee so alert and ready to talk.

Reciprocity

The need to return favors may be "hard-wired" into the human brain. In fact, sociologists have found that all human societies follow the rule of reciprocity.[5] If one person gives something to another, even if the giver is not especially likable, the recipient often feels an uncomfortable sense of imbalance and indebtedness if he cannot reciprocate. (The impulse to reciprocate is not necessarily a conscious thought, but is often based on a *feeling* of indebtedness.) The impetus for reciprocity is powerful, since it applies even to uninvited gestures and can spur unequal exchanges. To rid himself of the feeling of indebtedness, or to express gratitude, a person might agree to a request for a substantially larger favor than the one proffered and received.

Many intelligence interviewing professionals have noted the effectiveness of using reciprocity with detainees. The initial favors may be subtle and intangible, such as listening to a detainee talk or acknowledging his beliefs, or tangible, such as offering a drink of water with a meal. When a detainee begins to feel the pull to reciprocate, he may have little to offer in exchange other than the information he holds.

Commitment/Consistency

The U.S. Government Case Study of Human Manipulation

Almost all people wish to appear consistent in their words, beliefs, attitudes, and deeds. Especially if they have openly committed themselves to a position, most people tend to behave in ways that are stubbornly consistent with that position –to do otherwise may suggest a person is unsure of himself, or even worse, untrustworthy. The drive to be, and to seem, consistent may even lead people to act in ways clearly contrary to what they would see as their best interests.

Aware of this tendency, persuasion professionals – from academics such as social psychologists, behavioral economists, and negotiation experts to salespersons and con artists – often seek to induce people to take an initial position consistent with the behavior the professional will later request. An intelligence interviewing professional would therefore try to move a detainee toward a cooperative interaction, or at least not a wholly resistant one. He might also try to forestall an overt declaration of commitment to an uncompromising position. For example, an interviewer might find it useful to deter a detainee from stating aloud that he is unreservedly dedicated to jihad. One way to do this might be to change the subject: the detainee will have an opportunity to discuss jihad in the future, but first the intelligence interviewing professional would like a chance to talk with the detainee as a person, discussing family, studies, sports, etc.

Illustration: The Difficulty of "Backing Down"

Soon after capture a detainee moderately committed to jihad sought to demonstrate his status by "confessing" that he had sworn *ba'yat* to UBL, when in reality he had made no such commitment. The detainee later came to form an operational accord with the intelligence interviewing professional, and bonded with other detainees who were less extreme in their views. Over time – especially as he saw how fellow detainees who expressed their less radical beliefs received benefits ranging from better living conditions to being sent home – the detainee began to doubt the wisdom of his initial false statements. Despite his misgivings, however, he struggled with how he could now possibly change his story– he had consistently talked to the other detainees, and behaved throughout the interrogation sessions, as if he were wholeheartedly committed to al-Qa'ida's cause.

The U.S. Government Case Study of Human Manipulation

Social Validation (Social Proof)

Social proof occurs when individuals look to other people to determine how to think and behave. This psychological phenomenon most often occurs in unfamiliar and uncertain situations when people find it difficult or impossible to determine appropriate behavior. This situation often creates a feeling of discomfort, and causes people to look for a quick way to "fit in" and feel comfortable once again: "Should I wear slacks or a dress?" "Should I accept an alcoholic drink or not?" In these circumstances people often assume that the others around them know more about the situation and the appropriate response, and therefore imitate what they see the others doing.

Everything is relative. Like an airplane pilot landing in the dark, we want runway lights on either side of us, guiding us to the place where we can touch down our wheels." (Dan Ariely, *Predictably Irrational*)

Social proof is especially influential under two conditions, both of which can apply in a custodial setting:

•*Uncertainty* – When a person is unsure of his surroundings and when the situation is ambiguous, he may be more inclined to pay attention to the actions of others and to accept those actions as correct.

•*Similarity* – People are more inclined to follow the lead of others who seem similar to themselves.

This principle can have an especially strong effect on detainees who are new to a particular custodial setting and have never been detained before. Here the importance of the interviewer's confederates becomes apparent. The interviewing team might pay careful attention to who shares the detainee's environment and the detainee's possible interactions with others.

This principle of social proof also explains the power behind informing a detainee, or casually letting him know, that many other detainees have already provided information of value. The persuasive power of "social proof" increases even further if the interviewer can offer examples of multiple detainees, particularly those who are "famous" or admired, who have provided intelligence of value. For example, mentioning to a detainee that a well-known terrorist leader revealed the attack that had been planned in city X might subtly influence the detainee to provide more useful information.

Scarcity

People typically perceive things that are rare or difficult to obtain as more valuable than items that are plentiful. They also respond to losses (for example, the loss of freedoms) by wanting the lost item more than before. Scarcity of a desirable item may invoke a feeling of yearning, and the thought"I must have that." An intelligence interviewing professional might influence a detainee to provide information by using both tangible and intangible incentives that the detainee perceives as "scarce." The interviewer can enhance scarcity by using"deadline" tactics.

The scarcity principle operates most powerfully when something may become newly scarce, for example, the detainee might no longer receive the special meals he has been given all along. The idea of scarcity may also arise when one has to compete with others. For example, "The USG is willing to cut a deal with you so that you can see and talk with your family via video conference, but they can offer this to only five detainees over the next couple of days." "Scarcity" activates emotions that may blur clear thinking; many people find it difficult to steel themselves against this tactic.

As with all behavioral tactics, the intelligence interviewing professional must follow through, on time, with any promised reward; otherwise effectiveness diminishes.

What Are "Core Concerns,"and How Do They Affect Persuasiveness?

Daniel Shapiro, a psychologist and negotiations expert, and Roger Fisher, also a negotiations expert, have described five "core concerns,"believed to apply to all persons to varying degrees.[6] They are:

•Appreciation
•Affiliation
•Autonomy
•Status

The U.S. Government Case Study of Human Manipulation

•Role

Planning carefully to understand and respond appropriately to a detainee's needs in each of the five core areas could help an intelligence interviewing professional persuade a detainee to provide information (see **Power**). It is likely that each detainee will have stronger needs in some areas than others. For instance, one detainee may have a strong desire to feel respected, for example, as an elder with wisdom. Another may have a strong need to feel a sense of companionship with people who understand him. All five core concerns might be continuously assessed for each detainee, as they can change over time.

Appreciation

People often feel appreciated when they learn someone understands their point of view. Appreciation may be communicated verbally or by actions such as giving something (which also may lead to some reciprocity). To enhance this feeling, an intelligence interviewing professional can communicate through actions and words that he empathizes with many of the detainee's experiences, thoughts, and feelings.

An interviewer tells the story of having inadvertently let a detainee sit in freezing temperatures, for hours, in the back of a Humvee. When the condition of the detainee was discovered, the team hastened, obviously apologetically, to provide warm blankets, a warm place in an otherwise cold room, hot food, and hot tea. The detainee rewarded the team with very useful information.

Affiliation

Feeling connected to others can be emotionally comforting. An accord can result more easily and quickly when people believe they have something in common. The intelligence interviewing professional might seek to find links with a detainee, perhaps by discussing family, work experiences, religious backgrounds, sports, or hobbies (see also *Interests and Identities*). In some cases, treating the detainee as a colleague and emphasizing the shared nature of the intelligence interviewing task may also enhance the detainee's sense of affiliation.

The U.S. Government Case Study of Human Manipulation

An expert intelligence interviewer tells the story of connecting with a hard-boiled detainee who had been very reticent. The interviewer was able to start a long, self-disclosing discussion about his own children, and asked about those of the detainee. He then got the detainee to think about the kind of world that each of them would want for their children. They found much common ground between them, as they both hoped for their children to have better lives than their fathers. The discussion ended with the detainee providing vital information – and with his tearfully embracing the interviewer who had forged an important emotional connection.

Autonomy

The need for autonomy varies across cultures and among individuals. It also may vary with respect to different aspects of one's life, but almost all people wish to feel they possess some control over some part of their lives. Detainees who have a strong need for autonomy are likely to find detention particularly disagreeable, and to become even more resentful if they are constantly told what to think, what to talk about, and how to behave – in addition to being told what to wear and what and when to eat.

Since control is *built into* a detention setting, the intelligence interviewing professional may be able to reduce resistances to some degree by creating the perception that the detainee has at least small areas of control. The interviewer could negotiate minor aspects of an intelligence interview by discussing options with a detainee: for instance, "Would you prefer to stand or sit while talking?" "Would you rather eat alone or together with me?" "Would you prefer to talk about, or to draw, what you know about X?"

Psychological research has also demonstrated another key element of autonomy: people are more likely to change their beliefs if they feel that they reached a new conclusion on their own. Thus, a detainee is more likely to change his mind – for instance, about whether he will talk with the intelligence interviewing professional – if he feels he made the decision on his own, rather than being browbeaten into accepting another's opinion.

There may sometimes be additional benefits to sharing control; sharing control over a conversation may be a way to gain important information. For example, one master intelligence interviewer notes: "From my point of view, the detainee who seeks to take control by asking questions can be quite useful to a savvy interviewer – one can learn a great deal from the questions that are asked."

Status

Acknowledging a detainee's status– as a professional person, a leader, a parent, etc. – may provide a way for an intelligence interviewing professional to gain respect and possibly some leverage to persuade; almost all individuals enjoy feeling that they are respected and viewed as important. No matter how much the interviewer may dislike a particular detainee, it is often easy to discern the qualities and capacities the detainee values in himself. If asked, many detainees will in fact tell what they are most proud of, or how important they were prior to detention. The interviewer might look for and acknowledge sources of status related to family background or social skills, educational achievement, professional or technical expertise, life or business experience, intellectual capacity such as "big picture thinking," emotional insight, moral standing, physical strength or athletic ability, and so on.

Recall the example of the analyst in the business suit. In this instance, the detainee probably responded to the presence of someone he perceived as an authority figure. He may also have viewed the analyst's presence as a tribute to his own importance, and thus experienced a boost to his sense of status.

Role

People are used to playing many roles in life, and may find it hard to give up these roles, particularly while detained (see *Interests and Identities*). If a detainee is used to playing the role of jihadist, and is then treated in detention *only* as a jihadist, he will probably persist or even grow in all of the behaviors and beliefs that accompany this role. The intelligence interviewing professional can reduce the detainee's resistance by understanding and drawing out the *other roles* that the detainee has played. Perhaps this detainee also enjoys his roles as an educator, a student, a father or father figure, or a member of a sports team. The interviewer can therefore enhance his ability to persuade by acknowledging the detainee's more desirable roles, as well as by thinking carefully about the roles that he himself and the other members of the intelligence interviewing team might convey (see *Interests and Identities*, on "cross-cutting identities").

Japanese POWs hardly knew what to make of the "nice" way they were treated. "Weren't the interrogators still the enemy?" The enemy's unwillingness to assume the proper "enemy role" made it difficult for the prisoner to adopt the correct role prescribed by the Bushido code. (Ulrich Straus, *The Anguish of Surrender*).

How Can an Intelligence Interviewing Professional Create an Environment for Persuading a High-Value Detainee to Provide Information?

Research by psychologist Howard Gardner suggests that it is easier to change people's beliefs when the individuals find themselves in a new environment, are surrounded by peers with new ideas, or encounter "luminous" personalities.[7] All of these elements come into play when working with detainees, and skillful intelligence interviewing professionals can apply them in a well-thought-out, well controlled, long-term custodial setting.

How Might the Custodial Environment Aid Efforts at Persuasion?

The overall detention environment plays an essential role in the success (or failure) of intelligence interviewing. The experience of Japanese prisoners of war (POWs) during World War II (see box) highlights the importance of considering how a detainee might have viewed his world prior to detention, and how the conditions of detention could influence his beliefs.

Ishii Shuji, one of the few Japanese survivors of the Battle of Iwo Jima, wrote a memoir of his experiences. His account exemplifies how a detainee's perspective might shift, and even shift unusually quickly, when encountering a new, unexpected environment.

According to Ulrich Straus: "A sense of relief overcame Ishii when he saw that the POW camp already held dozens of his countrymen. Shame would be a little easier to endure when shared. In his memoir, Ishii went on rapturously about the cleanliness of the field hospital, the clean drinking water, soap, medicines, and his soft bed, while only hours before he had been starving and drinking his own urine simply to survive. Now he had food in quantities he could only have dreamed about earlier in the day. Then he smoked his first cigarette as a prisoner, a moment lovingly described. Truly, as Ishii wrote later, it was the 'difference between heaven and hell'."

- As noted, intelligence interviewing teams might help shape the detention environment. Before conducting an intelligence interview the team might explore:
  What environment would help persuade a detainee to tell what he knows?

- Should all detainees be placed in a specified environment, or would an individually designed environment increase the chances of success with this particular person?

- Which guards, intelligence interviewing professionals, interpreters, debriefers, imams – and which clan, tribe, or family members (if any) –might be permitted to interact with this detainee? Which individuals is this detainee likely to find most appealing, or "luminous,"so that they can increase the possibility of persuasion?

- If this detainee is permitted to interact with other detainees, who should the other detainees be?

- How might it affect this detainee if he were placed with others who formerly held beliefs similar to his, but have now somewhat modified their views?

In a 2008 article in the *Los Angeles Times*, "Fighting terrorism with terrorists,"Joshua Kurlantzick reported that Indonesia, Saudi Arabia, Egypt, Singapore, Malaysia, Jordan, Yemen, and the Netherlands have launched"deradicalization"programs in an effort to convince jihadists to change their radical perceptions of their religion. Saudi Arabia's program reportedly offers shorter jail sentences to militants who agree to undergo intense classroom sessions designed to convince them that Islam does not condone terror. Kurlantzick cites General David

Petraeus, then commander of U.S. forces in Iraq, as stating that the Saudi initiative may be one reason for the recent sharp decline in the number of foreign fighters coming into Iraq.[8]

The International Crisis Group reported in November 2007:

One Indonesian initiative, focused on prisoners involved in terrorism, has won praise for its success in persuading about two dozen members of Jemaah Islamiyah (JI) and a few members of other jihadi organisations to cooperate with the police. Key elements are getting to know individual prisoners and responding to their specific concerns, often relating to economic needs of their families, as well as constant communication and attention. One premise is that if through kindness, police can change the jihadi assumption that government officials are by definition thought (anti-Islamic), the prisoners may begin to question other deeply-held tenets.

Once prisoners show a willingness to accept police assistance, they are exposed to religious arguments against some forms of jihad by scholars whose credentials within the movement are unimpeachable. Some have then accepted that attacks on civilians, such as the first and second Bali bombings and the Australian embassy bombing, were wrong. The economic aid, however, is ultimately more important than religious arguments in changing prisoner attitudes.[9]

How Can a Team Identify Persuasive Arguments?

Someone who can share information in a way that "resonates" with another person is more likely to be effective in influencing that person's thinking. To enhance persuasiveness, the intelligence interviewing team might seek to identify which ideas and which interviewer(s) might resonate with a particular detainee. Intelligence interviewing professionals may find it helpful to engage in perspective-taking exercises, such as "stepping into the detainee's shoes," observing the situation from different points of view ("mine," "his," "fly on the wall"), and reversing roles and role-playing among the members of the intelligence interviewing team.

A team might routinely assess the known and likely circumstances of the detainee's upbringing and recent life experiences in order to tailor the persuasion framework around them. The team might explore such questions as:

- Was the detainee born into a family with extremist beliefs? If not, when and how did he acquire his radical religious or other motivations?

- Did he (and possibly his peers) take an apparently unwavering route to his current beliefs and circumstances

- Which leaders, doctrine, dogma, and social groups appear to have influenced and motivated him?

- Did the detainee experience profoundly important events such as a family member's death "at the hands of the enemy," a diaspora existence, chronic poverty, or life in a totalitarian or police state?

The results of such perspective-taking exercises can enhance the team's understanding of who might meet with the detainee and what demeanor and questioning style(s) to use during the interaction.

The interviewing team might also evaluate a range of interview formats and discussion topics, as well as the use of famous metaphors, inspiring catch phrases, and references to religiously significant literature. In addition, the team might consider the most effective format for presenting information, based on estimates of how the detainee best processes information.

Preparation questions might include: "Does this detainee think in numbers? Should we show him statistics?" "Does he think graphically? Would pictures help?" "Is there any appropriate 'hands-on' task for a detainee who has particular skills and training, or belongs to a profession such as engineering, that might aid him to feel understood and appreciated?" "Has he responded in the past to charisma? Moral authority?"

The U.S. Government Case Study of Human Manipulation

How Have Intelligence Interviewing Professionals Put these Ideas into Practice?

Many leading intelligence interviewing professionals seem to understand intuitively how to persuade a detainee to provide accurate information. However, few of them have so far captured all their insights in writing or trained others to develop and apply their special skills. In addition, they may not always use these skills systematically.

Even so, master intelligence interviewing professionals consistently refer to many of the concepts discussed above (although they often use different words) when they describe intelligence interviewing successes. Many report that they carefully observe the detainee, and that they are keenly aware of how the detainee is likely experiencing them. They understand that the detainee may be constantly analyzing the situation and the interviewer. They often model the behavior they desire from the detainee, such as critical thinking and openness to another's point of view. They use many of the persuasion strategies with ease, and in doing so have found ways to build an operational accord with a range of different detainees. They seem almost instinctively to recognize and deal appropriately with a detainee's core concerns to enhance persuasion. They often seem intuitively to make multiple adjustments *in the course* of an interview, often without an explicit examination as to why they are shifting tactics.

Recent research findings in the field of neuroscience may help to explain, at least in part, why master intelligence interviewing professionals are so good at what they do, and how building an accord seems to come so naturally to them. These findings suggest that much of our decision-making may be less"rational" than originally believed, and may actually occur more or less outside of our conscious awareness. As we go through life, gain experience, and pay attention to our successes and our mistakes, we often learn a great deal both consciously and subconsciously. Throughout this learning process, constant observation and practice of skills, and explicit, diligent review of mistakes and successes, are vital, so that *in the immediate situation* we can both act and adjust appropriately without having to take the time to consciously "think it through."

The U.S. Government Case Study of Human Manipulation

How a Master Intelligence Interviewer Describes His "Intuition"

This was our first time with this particular high-value detainee. In preparation we pored over results of other interviews and all available information about him. His dossier indicated he felt he was deprived of due respect for his lofty position in his organization. Our plan therefore was to play to his ego and his sense of how important and successful he had been. We wanted him to tell us his story –almost as if we were correspondents, or historians. Our game plan called for rapt attention, and hanging on his every word. Approbation and compliments would be plentiful. So, we went in, and after introductions and ample greetings, and laying out our bona fides – where we've been, whom we've talked to, and so on –we transitioned into "tell us your story" mode.

Now, I tell you the following with the proviso that I know and understand what I am about to tell you *post interview*. It is hard to remember what, if anything, I was conscious of at the time...

So, in the moment, I got the sense he saw what we were doing and that we might quickly come off as patronizing and insincere. (This is one of the unintended consequences of an intelligence interviewer's being anything less than a master thespian!) So I cannot tell you that I noticed it consciously at the time, but as the interview progressed I sensed somehow that he had a highly developed perceptiveness. We had better be careful. We could lose him early, and thereafter have to work *very* hard to ever achieve a frank, sincere, man-to-man level of discussion.

Days later he actually told us that we came off at the very beginning as applying a "technique" that included hyperbole and overdone compliments. I believe that we caught it quickly, however, and shifted fairly smoothly to "less game plan" and more "reality-based discussion" of where he had been and what was going on with his organization at the time. This shift worked to good effect as he appeared to like us and he became more conversational... and he ultimately provided intelligence information of value.

Will These Ideas Always Work?

The ideas described above provide a framework for persuading detainees to provide at least some useful information. Intelligence interviewing teams might also bear in mind the question of "completeness." That is, a detainee may also provide *more* of the useful information he has if the entire interviewing environment and all interactions reflect what is known about persuasiveness.

As in all complex endeavors, there are no magic bullets in intelligence interviewing. Research findings highlight,[10] and leading intelligence interviewing professionals constantly reaffirm, that changing a person's mind usually results from a slow, almost unidentifiable alteration in viewpoint, rather than from any single argument or sudden epiphany. (A detainee is very unlikely to experience an abrupt shift in his thinking, and decide to reveal everything he knows, after hearing one or two well-crafted arguments.) Questioning, steps forward and backward, and emotional conflict will occur throughout the process. Future research might help to determine how to apply these principles to intelligence interviewing more effectively.

Key Points
Master Intelligence Interviewing Professionals Are Persuasive, Flexible, and Use a Dynamic Approach

Intelligence interviewers constantly seek just the right means to persuade each individual detainee to provide useful information. Many ideas may inform the persuasion process, for example, using the principles of "liking," "authority," "reciprocity," "commitment/consistency," "social proof," and "scarcity." An intelligence interviewing professional is likely to increase his effectiveness by systematically using these principles in ways appropriate to each individual detainee, on the basis of an individually planned "persuasion framework." These principles may help both to gather information of value and also to elicit more complete information from each detainee.

Understanding Core Concerns Enhances Persuasion

Like all people, detainees have needs. Understanding what is important to a detainee, and appropriately responding to a detainee's core emotional concerns, can increase the likelihood of persuading the detainee to provide information. The strength of each core concern varies from detainee to detainee; core concerns include needs to feel appreciated, affiliated, autonomous, and acknowledged for status and important roles.

The Custodial Environment Is Important

The detention context is likely to play a key role in the success or failure of persuasion. Research suggests that it is easier to influence people who find themselves in a new and fairly ambiguous environment, who are surrounded by people similar to themselves, and who encounter people capable of delivering a message that resonates. It therefore may be worth considering how to craft a carefully designed environment that considers factors such as the timing of interactions, the treatment a detainee receives from guards, and the import of every discussion the detainee has with anyone in his environment.

Use Persuasion Thoughtfully and Wisely

A "persuasion framework"might best be used with caution, with on-going review, and in the context of a team approach. Constant assessment of interviewing strategies, review of hypotheses about what a detainee knows, and vigilance about potential misunderstandings are essential if an intelligence interviewing professional is to gather accurate intelligence information from detainees. This is especially true for increasing the likelihood of gathering *complete* information.

Intelligence interviewing professionals and teams might also continuously review the possibility of false confessions and false information. In addition to attempts to deceive (see ***Resistances***), detainees may make false statements if they believe or know what information the interviewer wants or expects to hear.

Behavioral science research in the field of police interrogation has raised awareness that highly persuasive tactics may lead innocent persons to"confess" to acts they did not commit. While intelligence interviews are primarily intended to gather information on a variety of topics rather than to obtain admissions of guilt, the findings offer relevant parallels. Research shows that both guilty and innocent persons are more likely to confess to a crime when the interrogator presents false evidence. Another inducement is the use of "minimization" tactics, for example, normalizing the actions of the accused – "Look, everyone has stolen something at some point" – and implying that a confession will lead to reduced charges. Research suggests that certain populations of people, such as juveniles and persons of limited intelligence, seem especially vulnerable to making false confessions. In addition, people under duress may manufacture information to reduce the pressure on them or to stop pain.

Areas of Operational Interest That Merit Further Research

- What might be effective ways for intelligence interviewing professionals to deal with extreme beliefs expressed by the detainee?

- To what extent are each of the principles of persuasion, the core emotional concerns, and our ideas of how and why people change their perceptions, valid across cultures? How might principles of persuasion apply differently, if at all, for women, children, or other "non-traditional" detainees? How do these principles apply, *in practice*, to detainees from various different cultures?

- What might be learned from former POWs about how the conditions and treatment experienced in detention influenced their beliefs and perspectives? What interviewing strategies and conditions do they believe might have motivated them to provide more information to their captors?

- What is the most effective way to "plant seeds" between sessions (i.e., give the detainee something to think about at the conclusion of a meeting so he is more likely to provide more information at the next meeting)?

- What might be learned from cases where detainees provided useful information after initially refusing to engage in any dialogue or to respond meaningfully to questions, and cases where detainees *stopped* providing information after earlier offering some of what they knew?

Power

Who Has What Kinds of Power in Intelligence Interviewing?

Even though captivity would seem to place a detainee in a relatively helpless position, both the intelligence interviewing team and the detainee have various kinds of power in the intelligence interviewing process. The *sources* of power for each side may also be similar, although they will differ from individual to individual and from context to context. Effective ways of using various kinds of power may also differ for detainees and intelligence interviewing teams. No single type of power, or way of exerting it, will inevitably lead to a particular desired result, so the topic merits careful analysis.

Conventional Beliefs

In essence, the conventional view suggests that the interrogator must work to exhibit irresistible power by exerting constant control over the detainee. Several common beliefs about power appear to have informed the manner in which many interrogations with persons in custody have been conducted. These include:

- Interrogators hold *all* the power.

- *Control* is synonymous with *power.*

- *Control* must be *overt* and *maintained.*

- *Power* implies the threat of *negative consequences.*

When two or more people interact, the term "power" is generally used to describe the capacity to influence another person. By contrast, the term"control" in interpersonal contexts usually pertains to the capacity to restrain, direct, or dominate another person.

The revised Army Field Manual 2-22.3, *Human Intelligence Collector Operations*, reflects the emphasis on control in current interrogation doctrine. For example:

1-10. During the approach phase, the HUMINT collector establishes the conditions of *control* and rapport to gain the cooperation of the source and to facilitate information collection.

8-7. Each approach is different, but all approaches have the following in common. They *establish* and *maintain control* over the source and the collection effort. This does not equate to physical control. Rather, it means that the HUMINT collector directs the conversation to cover the topics that are of interest to him. In a very basic sense, the HUMINT collector is in control if he is asking questions and receiving answers. If the source is asking questions, refusing to answer questions, or directing or attempting to direct the exchange, he is challenging for control. *If the source challenges this control, the HUMINT collector must act quickly and firmly to reestablish control.* (Emphases added.)

Behavioral Science Perspectives

In contrast to conventional beliefs, negotiation theory and practice suggest that all parties in an intelligence interview have some sources of power, and that the nature of power is far more complex than just"control." The intelligence interviewing team and the detainee are each likely to have various, and changing, kinds of power during their interactions. The team will find different sources of power relevant at different times in seeking information of various kinds from each particular detainee. The relevance of different kinds of power will depend on the specific purpose and context of the interview – see box below on "The "detainee's information" is not a simple concept."

The Nature of Power Is Complex

The kinds of power that each party possesses, and the ways the parties may use power, vary considerably. For example, a captor might have physical control over a detainee and still treat that detainee with great respect, as evidenced by many interrogators who interviewed Japanese POWs during WWII.

Perceptions of power – the sources of power each party *thinks* he possesses and *believes* the other might have – may be as important as an actual source of power. Either party may deal with the other on the basis of perceptions. These perceptions might include both the *kinds* of power on each side and the *balance* of power. One subtle example derived from research on such perceptions suggests that "negotiators who see themselves as having fewer options in comparison to the opponent are more likely to resort to aggressive strategies as a way of seeking change in the relative control…of each party."[11]

Certain kinds of power may exist outside the realm of conscious perception, such as the reactions of a detainee to an interviewer whom he finds very likable. Some forms of power, such as charisma and moral authority, may be evident to the other party in the interview. On the other hand, the person who is affected may not necessarily understand his own reactions to charisma and moral authority. And some forms of power, such as a strong fallback position, may be hidden.

What Are the Primary Sources of Power?

Experts who study high-stakes negotiations – both adversarial and collaborative– have described several sources of power in human interactions. Different experts use different lists, and may define each source of power somewhat differently. In addition, the sources of power overlap – and may enhance or undermine each other. The list below is condensed, and short, and is intended only as a basis for the present discussion. Such a list is likely to develop considerably over time, as further research on intelligence interviewing and persuasion reveals new insights.

Information power: Information may be the most important kind of power in intelligence interviewing. Hanns Scharff, a famous German interrogator in World War II, painstakingly amassed significant amounts of information from every source available. He then used the information in seemingly casual ways in conversation with captured American and British pilots to gain significant intelligence information – sometimes, and perhaps often, without the pilots' ever realizing they had given up valuable information. The term *information power* in this booklet should be taken to mean all information from every source, plus expertise in analysis and in using the information.

Relationship power: The Intelligence Community (IC) has long recognized the power of "personal connection" and relationships: most people respond to those whom they like. The concept of relationship, as used here, is much broader than the conventional idea of "rapport," and includes all of what has been learned about persuasion. *Relationship power* in this booklet should be read to include concepts such as liking, an impulse toward reciprocity, responses to legitimate authority, moral authority, charisma, perceived trustworthiness, leadership, emotional and social intelligence, and empathy.

Together with information power, relationship power served as a major platform for Hanns Scharff's success. As a more recent example, a famous New York City law enforcement professional, when asked how to develop excellent interrogators, reportedly said, "Just give me someone to train that everybody likes." As another example, colleagues attributed the high effectiveness of a particular IC case officer to his "nearly uncanny gift of rapport with any stranger."

"Fallback" power: Fallback power means that the detainee and intelligence interviewing professionals perceive that they have alternatives in the interactions between them. They may commit to these alternatives temporarily or permanently. The alternatives may or may not be known to the other party. Each party might have several fallback positions and could use them in succession.

One way to understand the importance of a fallback position is to imagine asking your boss for a raise. Unbeknownst to your boss, you have just won the lottery. In this situation you know that you have unanticipated power because you now have another source of money if your boss refuses a raise (or if he or she takes offense and fires you). Research about negotiation practice suggests that simply *knowing* you have an excellent fallback position will on average make you a more successful negotiator. In negotiation theory a fallback position is known as a BATNA: the best alternative to a negotiated agreement. In this booklet, a *fallback* position means an alternative plan or action –for the detainee or intelligence interviewing professional – that is perceived to be or might become available.

The power of incentives and disincentives: Incentives serve as rewards or potential rewards for desired behavior. In addition to *tangible* incentives, such as better food or more comfortable living quarters, there are *intangibles*, such as engaging in conversation with a lonely detainee or simply behaving courteously. Obviously, there are tangible and intangible disincentives as well, such as withdrawing comfort items or ignoring a detainee who very much enjoys talking.

Each of these is discussed in more detail below.

What About Control as a Source of Power?

The list above does not specify"control" as a source of power. As noted, conventional thinking about control suggests that the intelligence interviewing professional must always exert direct and overt control over the detainee. However, behavioral science findings indicate that an intelligence interviewing professional may actually *lose* some power by focusing too much on control.

For example, attempting continuous dominance, and causing the detainee to feel as if he has little or no control over what he discusses (at a time when he has no control over where he sleeps, what he is given to eat, and when and where he may go) may make the detainee more resistant. Crafting an interpersonal environment in an intelligence interview where the detainee feels as if he has some control may in fact increase the likelihood of an operational accord,* and in turn decrease resistances (see **Resistances**).

Letting a detainee believe that he is controlling the conversation may sometimes be helpful in another way: an expert interviewer may pick up useful information this way. Skilled intelligence interviewers report that they have been able to assess the intellectual level of the detainee and perhaps his education, to "take the measure of the man," and to learn a good deal about his interests and what he knows, when the detainee thinks he is in charge of the discussion.

*Operational accord" denotes a special "working" or"professional" relationship between the interviewer and the high-value detainee. It is characterized by the detainee's willingness to supply accurate information, at least some of the time, in response to the interviewer's questions. The concept also implies that the interviewer has an individualized and effective strategy for interactions with the detainee.

Contemporary research in behavioral economics, social psychology, and the theory of negotiations may help intelligence interviewing teams to reassess earlier thinking about"control." The concepts of "autonomy" and"reciprocity" provide examples of useful ideas in this context (see *Persuasion*).

How Can the High-Value Detainee and the Intelligence Interviewing Team Use Information Power?

Information power involves not only possessing information, but also understanding how to use that information to good advantage. This could mean withholding the information completely or for a given time,"sharing" inaccurate information, or using information (accurate or not) to influence the other party's perceptions, behavior, or ability to remember.

Detainee

No matter what approaches the intelligence interviewing team takes, a detainee has some control over the information he possesses. Obviously, a detainee who knows that his most important information has a short shelf life may recognize that he need only outlast the intelligence interviewing professional for a relatively short period. A detainee with a plan for resistance may understand that he has considerable power. Such a plan might be based on prior training or designed in anticipation of capture or in response to detention.

The detainee has a number of *information-based ploys* available. They include presenting a layered resistance strategy by offering successive cover stories; employing bits of deception, perhaps mixed with fantasy and random bits of truth; responding to questions with elaborate disinformation or misleading stories; or casting blame on others. The detainee may make demonstrably false admissions of guilt to create difficulties for the captor by throwing all the detainee's responses into question. The detainee may provide partial and incomplete information that his captors already know, or feign loss of consciousness, physical illness, mental illness, or loss of memory. Many of these tactics might also be characterized as resistance techniques (see *Resistances*).

Case Example of Layered Resistance

After an initial interrogation and physical beating by South Vietnamese security personnel, Tai shifted to a fallback position to avoid being forced to reveal the location and identities of his personnel in the area. He"admitted" [falsely] to being a newly infiltrated captain from North

Vietnam. When the interrogation became more intense, he "confessed" [falsely] that he was really a covert military intelligence agent sent to South Vietnam to establish a legal identity and cover legend before being sent on to France for his ultimate espionage assignment (which he claimed to have not yet been fully briefed on). Each time he shifted to a new fallback story, Tai made an initial show of resistance and pretended to give in only when his interrogator "forced" him to make an admission. He did this to play on the interrogator's ego by making him think that he had "cracked" his subject's story and to divert attention from the information that Tai wanted to protect – such as the location of his headquarters, the identity of his communist contacts, and his own identity and position.[12]

If the detainee has information about the United States, can use a concealed skill in English or another language, or has a keen understanding of the nature of memory, he may be able to use this information power to manipulate the intelligence interviewing team and individual interviewers. For example, a detainee who is skilled in building relationships by using intangible incentives (see below) may deliberately seek to build credibility with an intelligence interviewing professional, while sharing only unimportant information. He may occasionally cooperate a little but may follow an overall strategy of prolonging the time the intelligence interviewing team invests in trying to draw information from him, an unproductive source. He may attempt to shape the course of questioning by providing seemingly constructive, but ultimately dead-end or minimally useful leads. And he may accomplish all of this in a likable and plausible way that keeps the intelligence interviewing professional from recognizing what is happening.

In most cases an intelligence interviewing team can only estimate a detainee's knowledgeability. The estimate may not be correct. The detainee may have very detailed information about a particular topic – a *depth* of information – that is not known to the intelligence interviewing team. The detainee may also have substantial information in areas *unknown* to the intelligence interviewing team.

For example, the team may know the detainee was involved with certain activities in country X, but may not know enough even to suspect that the detainee was involved in planning operations against U.S. interests in country Y with operatives from country Z. This latter point is one of the primary reasons for seeking to build a strong operational accord with the detainee. Such an accord may enable the intelligence interviewing professional to discover– perhaps serendipitously, and well beyond the"intelligence requirements" (IRs) – the depth and breadth of the detainee's knowledge.

The "Detainee's Information" Is Not a Simple Concept.

Throughout the IC, one conventional definition of the "purpose of intelligence interviewing" is "to meet the intelligence requirements– the IRs." The Army Field Manual says that the collector "directs the conversation to cover the topics that are of interest to him." Often the IRs determine these topics. The emphasis on IRs also leads to the idea of "pertinent" questions, that is, questions pertinent to the IRs. The focus on IRs has also led to the concept of gaining "conscious" cooperation. It may be worthwhile to reconsider these three ideas, especially in the context of high value detainees.

The Army Field Manual concept of"gaining the cooperation of the detainee" in order to obtain specific answers for IRs may sometimes be helpful, but often may be far too narrow. Conscious cooperation is indeed valuable. However, it is not essential for acquiring useful information, for several different reasons.

The first reason is that much of what might be called "cooperation" is not necessarily"conscious," since a good deal of decision-making may not rise to the level of conscious thought. For example, a detainee may not have thought about why he is providing information; he may simply feel drawn to talk about what he knows, perhaps in an effort to reciprocate respectful treatment by likable intelligence interviewing professionals who seem to value all that he has to say. Thus, providing information in the spirit of reciprocity might or might not be fully"conscious." This may be important, since a resistant detainee may not want to believe he is cooperating with the enemy.

The second reason is that agencies and interviewers may want to think well beyond "pertinent" questions, and the IRs, especially when dealing with high value detainees. There are different kinds of useful questions and useful information.

An effective operational accord –in which the interviewer and detainee engage in wide-ranging discussions and genuine dialogue, even if the dialogue is sometimes adversarial – may provide the intelligence interviewing team with *information the detainee might not recognize as important or might not remember that he knew*. Pools of information that may or may not have been known to the intelligence interviewing team may *serendipitously* become available. A team may also pick up *incidental* information that later proves of value, as Hanns Scharff did, *including significant names or facts*. That information in turn may allow the team to avoid or sidestep resistances (see **Resistances**). Sometimes the information may be useful with another detainee at another time.

Intelligence Interviewing Team

As Hanns Scharff demonstrated, optimal use of information includes continuous review and re-evaluation of everything the intelligence interviewing team knows about the source, including information about the source's various social identities, social networks, interests, and constituencies (see **Interests and Identities**). Preparation for interviewing, and continuous planning – together with role-playing to practice these plans and back-up plans – will help. This may include detailed planning to help the source to remember accurately (see **Memory**).

Intelligence interviewing professionals need extensive practice in listening, observing, and maintaining situational awareness, which includes collecting"serendipitous" and incidental information and noticing emotional and physiological cues. Analysts on an intelligence interviewing team who have real time access to a detainee's information, and real-time ability to compare this information to all-source intelligence and investigative information, greatly increase the team's information power. In addition, an environment that includes monitored cells, confederates, and guards who listen closely can add to the team's sources and power of information.

MIS-Y

The U.S. Government Case Study of Human Manipulation

At Fort Hunt, during WWII, the United States was able to garner useful information from high-value German POWs: "As EPWs [Enemy Prisoners of War] were returned to their rooms upon the conclusion of each interrogation session, explicit instructions were issued to the...staff that these individuals were not to be disturbed for an extended period. The objective was to create an environment conducive to capturing potential intelligence data from technical monitoring of the conversations among EPWs that routinely took place after an encounter with their interrogator. Experience at both the British CSDIC [Combined Services Detailed Interrogation Centre] in London and the MIS-Y program at Fort Hunt demonstrated the value of these listening devices.

"The best results occurred when the 'stool pigeons' were fully briefed on the nature of the information needed. They would then be placed, for example, in a detention room prior to the arrival of a new EPW and live closely with the targeted prisoner over an extended period. Having a stool pigeon in the room of another EPW who had just been interrogated was very effective in obtaining specific information that [the interrogator] was unable to secure in the course of the actual interrogation. A stool pigeon could also be introduced into the exercise yard in an effort to become 'friendly' with obstinate prisoners."[13]

An intelligence interviewing professional may *lessen* a detainee's sense of information power if the detainee comes to believe that the interviewer already knows the information the detainee possesses. For example, a detainee might deny knowing anything about a training camp he attended until the interviewer has him watch video footage that shows him at this camp together with other people being held in the same facility. This information might have even greater impact if the detainee comes to believe that others have been talking about him.

By the same token, an interviewer may plan carefully to surprise the detainee with a critical piece of information. It may be the case that some intelligence interviewers intuitively have an extraordinary sense of timing. Expert interviewers recount many stories where they contrived to present a bolt from the blue in a way that led the detainee to tell a great deal.

Expert intelligence interviewing professionals report that they plan carefully how as well as when to use information. For example, an interviewer may know relatively little about a detainee, or may believe things about the detainee that turn out not to be true. In such cases, sharing *bits* of information to make it appear as if much is known may turn out to be helpful, but this should be done with skill and careful timing to keep the detainee from recognizing a bluff. Simply confronting the detainee with piles of paper that supposedly contain "intelligence" about him is unlikely to convince the detainee that the intelligence interviewing professional already "knows all" and that resistance is useless.

Skill is also needed to avoid altering the detainee's memories (see *Memory*) and under some circumstances to avoid alerting the detainee to answers that the interviewer might expect or desire.

How Can the High-Value Detainee and the Intelligence Interviewing Team Use Relationship Power?

Together with the power of information, relationship power plays an especially important role in intelligence interviewing. On-going behavioral science research reveals more and more about how to build a relationship, and the power that lies within that connection. For example, potentially useful research addresses topics such as the perception of *attractiveness, believability,* and *trustworthiness*. In particular, neuroscientists are learning more about how emotions are communicated between people. These communications may not be *consciously* understood by any of the parties during the interview itself, but nevertheless they occur, and may have an important impact in intelligence interviewing.

Detainee

The detainee, like the intelligence interviewing professional, may use the power of persuasion and"relationship-building." Some high-value detainees may be charismatic, charming, interesting, and attractive. They may come from influential and cosmopolitan families, have confidence in their personal presence and abilities, and be unusually skilled in manipulating others. They may be very intelligent, well educated, and adept at engaging people in conversation about topics of their choosing. Thus, just as the intelligence interviewing professional may draw on his attractive qualities in seeking to disarm a resistant source, these same qualities may serve a detainee in somewhat disarming an interviewer.

A detainee who believes in the justice of his cause might evoke moral authority. For instance, he might try to induce guilt, shame, or defensiveness in the intelligence interviewing professional by discussing the alleged misbehavior of the U.S. Government toward his homeland or by recounting vividly the loss of a family member as a result of American military operations. A female detainee, or a detainee who is unusually young or very old, might strategically use the beliefs of the intelligence interviewing team about gender or age.

Humans are by nature susceptible to persuasion, even when they do not want to be (see *Persuasion*). A highly persuasive detainee may cause an intelligence interviewing professional to lose objectivity, whether or not he recognizes the detainee's behavior as manipulative. The intelligence interviewing team and a systematic vetting process may play essential roles in such situations by helping an individual interviewer to retain a balanced perspective.

Intelligence Interviewing Team

Just as a persuasive detainee may exert some influence over an interviewer, the intelligence interviewing professional can also use persuasiveness with an unwilling detainee. Consider a detainee who is determined to remain silent indefinitely, but becomes intrigued by an interviewer who frequently visits his holding area, bringing the detainee his favorite foods. The interviewer also seems familiar with literature that is important to the detainee, and asks the detainee to explain some famous passages. In addition, the interviewer appears to appreciate the detainee's broader culture and seems eager to learn more. Over days, and perhaps weeks, the detainee might find himself wishing to engage with that interviewer.

Further assume that the intelligence interviewing professional is adept at persuasion (see *Persuasion* and also *Resistances*) and works to meet the detainee's most important "core concerns" (see *Persuasion*). For example, if "status" is important to the detainee the interviewer might ask the detainee to talk about his successes. This seemingly small gesture may mean a great deal to the detainee, and quite possibly draw him into a conversation. By the same token, an interviewer might adopt a high rank for himself, thus "affirming" the importance of the detainee, and also possibly accruing some power of legitimate authority for the interviewer.

Hanns Scharff represents perhaps the best-known example of successful expertise with building and using relationship power by meeting POWs' "core concerns." A man of enormous social intelligence, he was able to put prisoners at ease by treating them with dignity and respect, and to draw them into apparently casual conversations from which he drew a great deal of information. Those who provided information included many Allied officers who had been taught not to "talk."

How Can the High-Value Detainee and the Intelligence Interviewing Team Use Fallback Power?
Detainee

Believing that he has a fallback position can greatly strengthen a detainee's will and ability to resist. A detainee may believe that he can avoid engaging with the interviewer if he is prepared not to talk at all and is willing to remain in custody indefinitely. He may explicitly recognize this as a source of power.

In the most extreme situation, a detainee who is prepared to die, or is willing to provoke others to kill him, has extraordinary power in intelligence interviewing. A detainee's beliefs might even make death appear an attractive or desirable option. Such a detainee might believe that by committing suicide, or refusing medical treatment and food and water until the point of death, he would not only achieve martyrdom but also mobilize comrades or potential recruits and influence public opinion against his captors. These "alternatives" might appear irrational to the captor *and* make complete sense to the detainee.

In another situation, a newly captured detainee may believe he need only withhold information or maintain a deceptive cover story for several days, until a planned attack is carried out. His strategy is to keep silent for a few days and then talk a little if he must. However, if the detainee comes to believe that the intelligence interviewing team already knows of the attack plan, this fallback position may become less attractive, thus lessening this source of power.

Intelligence Interviewing Team

An awareness of having alternatives when going into an interview may increase the intelligence interviewing professional's self-confidence and effectiveness. In contrast to the "imminent catastrophe scenario" sometimes portrayed in movies and on television (see box below), an intelligence interviewing team often does have alternative sources if a particular detainee refuses to provide information. These sources might include other detainees and different kinds of intelligence, such as SIGINT. This kind of power can also provide leverage for the interviewing team even if the detainee only *believes* the intelligence interviewing professional has alternatives. In some cases the intelligence interviewing professional may therefore decide to bluff. (As discussed above, an intelligence interviewing professional might well use this tactic only if he has sufficient information to withstand at least a superficial test from the detainee.)

The Imminent Catastrophe Scenario:"What About the Ticking ......?"

For many people, the mention of"interrogation" immediately calls up scenarios in which the United States apparently faces imminent danger of a major attack, and has captured a terrorist who knows the details of the plot. If the detainee does not "give up" his vital information in short order, must the interrogator use force? This dilemma has captured the public imagination, particularly since September 11, 2001. It has also completely taken over many discussions about interrogation.

Although the imminent catastrophe scenario itself might possibly occur, it need not dictate the future of intelligence interviewing practice, for several reasons. There usually will be alternatives, and an exceptional case can be considered by itself as outlined below. Moral and legal considerations – and short- and longterm consequences of coercion – need not be set aside.

The U.S. Government Case Study of Human Manipulation

In the imminent disaster scenario on television, the U.S. Government somehow has been informed of many different facts:

a) an attack is *imminent*, and
b) the attack will be *catastrophic*, and
c) this *particular* detainee knows all about the attack, and
d) there is *no other source* of information about this attack, and
e) threats of pain or use of unbearable pain will actually get the information – in time to avert the attack.

In this situation, the detainee seems to have all the information power; the interrogator has only physical power. Moreover, in the television script, the interrogator apparently has no time to build a relationship with the detainee or to offer incentives. In some television scenarios, the interrogator then threatens the detainee with unbearable pain, or actually inflicts unbearable pain, while at the same time trying to verify and use any information obtained.

This television script typically sets aside questions of legality and morality, and may ignore some of the long-term and short-term consequences for the country. These include the reputation of the United States at home and abroad, the credibility of the United States when its leaders express moral outrage about violence and atrocities abroad, the safety of U.S. troops when they are captured– and the effects on the interrogator, the detainee, and those who support the detainee's cause. The script may also ignore some related questions, such as "If we use torture with terrorists, what about a drug lord, a Timothy McVeigh, or a kidnapper?"

Both moral and pragmatic arguments have convinced many Americans that torture and near torture are wrong in any circumstances, but others may ask if there are situations that justify the use of torture. In real life the United States would probably *not* have: convincing proof that an attack is imminent, that it will be catastrophic, that this detainee actually knows the details and can be forced to talk, and that the information can be verified and used in time to prevent violence.

In particular, interrogators cannot be certain that pain will persuade a detainee to provide truthful, accurate, and *timely* details. If interrogators use force when they believe an attack is imminent, a detainee could simply tell his captors whatever he needs to say at any given moment to stop the pain. (There is at least one well-known example.) In this situation, a detainee might realize that he must remain silent only for a brief time, until the attack actually occurs. In short, the United States could give up the moral high ground and gain no useful information.

There also are no guarantees that *non-coercive* intelligence interviewing will obtain the necessary information. However, the United States has important recent examples of effective, non-coercive intelligence interviewing with high value detainees. In a real situation, authorities might wish to consider the following questions:

Q. *Does the detainee have only* one *valuable piece of information?*

By inflicting severe pain the interrogator may undermine the chance of learning all the detainee may know. In the case of a high-value detainee the"what else"might be extraordinarily significant; for example, have other attacks been planned? Moreover, high levels of pain could render a detainee unable to remember details even if he wished to do so; recent research on the nature of memory suggests that severe stress can interfere with a person's ability to retrieve information.

Q. *Do decision-making authorities really know that they have no other sources of information, and no other methods of persuasion?*

Might the necessary information be obtained from informants, communications intercepts, or surveillance of the detainee's known confederates? Might there be a skillful intelligence interviewing professional who can rapidly form a useful accord with this detainee? Have the authorities considered every other avenue to discover the information in a timely manner before considering high levels of coercion? If the United States has very credible information about an imminent, catastrophic attack, *and* has captured a person known to be knowledgeable, might the authorities already have substantial intelligence that law enforcement and intelligence agencies could pursue to develop additional information useful for prevention?

Q. *Should an unusual case drive all the discussions of rules, training, research, and future capacity of U.S. Government intelligence* *interviewing/interrogation?*Developing the future of intelligence interviewing around a rare, imminent catastrophe scenario does not make sense.

The United States has another alternative: in a situation where a threat of catastrophe *is* immediate, *and* highly credible, *and* all the questions above have been considered, U.S. law should authorize the President to order personally whatever actions are deemed reasonable and necessary under the circumstances. The legal authority for such discretionary action could include the provision that any such Presidential order should ultimately be made public, perhaps after a specified period of time, to permit judgment by the court of public opinion.

Both long- and short-term interests of the United States suggest shifting focus away from the imminent catastrophe scenario. Far more productive for ensuring national security would be discussions about how the U.S. Government can develop the knowledge and capacity to become a world leader in non-coercive intelligence interviewing. The future might include a vigorous research program about intelligence interviewing, an integrated systems approach involving multiple sources of intelligence, and the development of a professional cadre of intelligence interviewers.

How Can the High-Value Detainee and the Intelligence Interviewing Team Use the Power of Incentives and Disincentives?
Detainee

A detainee can use both incentives and disincentives to some extent. Given the realities of captivity, these are likely to be primarily intangible. At the simplest level, the detainee might explicitly use information as an incentive in a bargain:"I'll tell you about the safe house if you get me a better mattress." Some detainees might offer or agree to a deal that would permit contact with or benefit family members.

More generally, the detainee might use his own behavior as an incentive or disincentive. For example, a skillfully manipulative detainee might use his interpersonal style and his ability to arouse emotion in another person in either a gratifying or a punitive way. He could make it obvious that he will only talk if the intelligence

49

interviewing professional stays away from certain topics, or addresses him respectfully. Alternatively, he might simply act in such an unlikable fashion that no one wants to talk with him. Or he might make believable threats against translators and others, especially if the interview takes place in a context where the detainee is well known and can wield power and cause fear even while detained.

In the well-known case of a high-ranking North Vietnamese captive, Nguyen Tai, interrogators arranged for other detainees to confront Tai and to identify him. Here is what happened: "Tai continued to maintain his cover story, and his attitude toward his confronters was so threatening (when combined with his past reputation) that he thoroughly terrified his accusers, one of whom reportedly committed suicide shortly afterward." Merle L. Pribbenow,"The Man in the Snow White Cell," *Studies in Intelligence*, Vol. 48, No. 1. [Appended to this document as a case study.]

Intelligence Interviewing Team

Intelligence interviewing professionals may have a greater range of options than does the detainee. The thoughtful use of incentives offers several kinds of influence in intelligence interviewing. One use depends on the importance of *reciprocity* in human interaction (see **Persuasion**). In brief, when an individual receives something from another (a gift, a gesture of support), a sense of obligation may arise that leads that individual to want to *give something back*. Recent research suggests that such a response may be "hard wired" into the human nervous system and that it may not be consciously understood. This response therefore can be difficult to resist. A detainee who has been meticulously searched and monitored may own nothing in detention and may value even small offerings or gestures. Since he often has only information to give in exchange, it is easy to understand the potential power of this kind of incentive in intelligence interviewing.

Reciprocity may be important in another way. If a particularly likable intelligence interviewing professional relieves some of the distress caused by capture and detention, a resultant sharp reduction of fear and anxiety might itself prompt some degree of operational accord with a detainee (see *Stress* and *Resistances*).

The intelligence interviewing team might also use incentives to encourage and reward potentially cooperative behavior on the part of the detainee. This may be done intangibly or tangibly. It should, however, be done on an individualized basis, and in a way consistent with the values and interests of a given detainee and of his culture. For example, a detainee who is particularly sensitive to moral authority might be insulted by the suggestion that an "enemy" could buy his cooperation by offering him creature comforts. Even the idea of "making a deal" is likely to vary considerably from culture to culture.

The intelligence interviewing professional may also use a range of disincentives to enhance the apparent negative consequences of resisting. For example, he may withdraw intangible or tangible incentives given for cooperative behaviors, increase the time a detainee must spend in his cell, or limit the detainee's access to others. In addition, the mere ability of the intelligence interviewing team to employ disincentives may remind the detainee that he has little control over his environment, conditions, and activities, and this may decrease his sense of having a fallback position.

An Example of Combining Sources of Power

U.S. interrogators in the Pacific during World War II achieved remarkable success in obtaining not only information, but also some assistance, from Japanese prisoners of war (POWs). The skills used by these interrogators illustrate the sources of power described above, applied in ways that appeared to benefit the prisoners as well as their captors.

Using Many Sources of Power with Japanese Prisoners of War

At the beginning of World War II, Americans considered the Japanese and the Japanese language almost impossible to understand. They viewed Japanese soldiers as skillful, incomprehensible, and ruthless enemies who would fight to the death – Japanese leaders were willing to train and use suicide bombers. Some descriptions at the time characterized the Japanese as almost inhuman.

Japanese military discipline was extraordinarily strict and often abusive. Soldiers and officers knew that their leaders expected them to commit suicide rather than be captured. They were taught that they would bring dishonor on their families and country if they survived captivity; moreover, many believed that Americans would torture and kill prisoners. Many prisoners were malnourished, ill, or injured at the time of capture.

Among the U.S. interrogators were a few Caucasians who had lived in Japan and who cherished Japanese culture, and thousands of Nisei (people of Japanese ancestry who were the first generation to be born outside Japan). These interrogators initially used relationship power and information power: they treated the POWs with respect, providing medical care, food, and friendly conversations about their hometowns and local culture. Most Japanese soldiers had not expected or experienced such treatment.

Interrogators such as Otis Cary and Sherwood Moran also were intuitively able to use the power of a fallback position in an extraordinarily effective way. Captured Japanese soldiers were initially very anxious and fearful about what would happen to them. They believed they could "never go home again" and many assumed they had no "fallback position" except death. Instead, they were offered a very powerful incentive: a "chance to build a new Japan." This new and completely different fallback position served the interests of both the United States and the POWs. The POWs also gained some sense of control over their lives: an increased sense of "autonomy." Fortunately, during the course of the war, interrogators such as Cary, Moran, and their Nisei colleagues trained others to acquire their own sensibility. It is not surprising that a sharp reduction in fear, humane treatment, and respect for their culture, combined with a hope for a new life, would lead to reciprocity and result in cooperation by POWs. Sometimes this unexpected treatment even led Japanese soldiers to encourage others to surrender and leave positions of ambush.

Power Relationships May Change

Power relationships may change during long-term custody of a high-value detainee. Both the intelligence interviewing professional and the detainee have power at the start of the interaction, and both parties may develop – or weaken –their power over time.

- The intelligence interviewing professional and intelligence interviewing team may receive new leads from analysts, or learn how to jog a detainee's memory, or build a very strong operational accord. The team may discover or develop an unexpected, very effective incentive.

- The detainee may make common cause with other detainees and develop common resistance tactics, or may come to understand how to mislead or manipulate his captors. He might gain information during detention, for example, from guards.

- The intelligence interviewing professional may inadvertently strengthen the detainee's sources of power, and thus lose opportunities to obtain information. For example, if the intelligence interviewing professional were to focus harshly on a single issue, the detainee could view the interviewer as abusive, and refuse any operational accord. He could feel more committed to the adversarial identity (see *Interests and Identities*) and hold onto his information whatever the cost.

What About Increasing Anxiety and Fear as a Source of Power?

The idea of using anxiety and fear in intelligence interviewing sometimes leads a discussion back to the imminent catastrophe scenario and the use of force (see box, above). Fear and anxiety may, however, play a somewhat different role.

Some believe that fear and anxiety, especially immediately after capture, are primary factors in motivating a detainee to provide information (see*Stress*). According to this view, the detainee's fear and worry about what may happen to him give the intelligence interviewing team a major source of power. This fear need not be anchored in reality: the intelligence interviewing team may have neither the interest nor the capacity to cause the harm feared by the detainee. What is thought to matter is that detainee believes that such harm is possible. There appears to be little scientific research that speaks directly to this topic. Future studies of intelligence interviewing, and of the effectiveness of different intelligence interviewing strategies, practices, and frameworks (including the physical setting, and the individual plan for working with a particular detainee), should devote attention to the roles of fear and anxiety. Fear and anxiety may both enhance and hinder effective interviewing. In particular, under certain circumstances, a sharp *drop* in fear and anxiety may facilitate building an accord with a detainee, as appears to have happened with many Japanese POWs.

Key Points
Keep Assessing the Sources of Power for Both Parties

As a routine part of preparation for each intelligence interview with a high-value detainee, an intelligence interviewing team might conduct a structured analysis of the sources of power potentially available to that detainee and how they relate to the kinds and depth of information sought. This analysis would be based on seeking to understand the various social *identities and interests* of the detainee. The intelligence interviewing team would then also conduct an analysis of the counterpart sources of power available to themselves, with special attention to sources of power that correspond to each kind of information the detainee may possess. *One size does not fit all.*

To be effective, the intelligence interviewing team might track and analyze how each side uses power throughout the interviewing process. Team members might constantly question their level of certainty regarding their own power and that of a detainee, and whether that level of certainty is justified. They might assess the balance of their sources of power *compared* to those of the detainee, and evaluate whether and how to try to affect the perceptions of the detainee.

The intelligence interviewing team might remember that *no one source of power is necessarily useful to discover and draw out all the kinds of information that a detainee may possess* (see box, "The "detainee's information" is not a simple concept"). A particular intelligence interviewing professional may be well or poorly matched to a given detainee in terms of power. One detainee might offer some information in exchange for certain incentives, while another may respond only to "relationship" (or to one aspect of relationship, such as moral authority), and be insulted by any type of overt bargaining.

Areas of Potential Operational Interest That Merit Further Research

- How might an intelligence interviewing team learn to assess the sources of power available to a particular detainee?

- What affects a detainee's *perception* of his own power and the interviewers' power? How does a detainee's physical, mental, and emotional condition influence these perceptions?

- When and how might overt attempts at "control" enhance or undermine building an effective operational accord?

- How might use of different sources of power affect a particular detainee in a given situation?

- When might relationship-based power be most effective?

- How might an intelligence interviewing team "match" a proposed "interviewing framework" (the plan for working with a particular detainee, in a particular physical setting) to what is known about a detainee?

- How might intelligence interviewing teams assess the relative influence of various sources of power (both the interviewer's and the detainee's) with respect to *different kinds of information*?

- Which sources of power have been most helpful in collecting unexpected, serendipitous, and incidental information?

- Which sources of power may be best for discovering *all* or *a great deal* of the information that a detainee might have ("complete information") as distinguished from just a name, a date, or other discrete facts?

- What can be discovered about using different sources of power in sequence? About the timing of the use of information known to the intelligence interviewing team? About the use of surprise?

The U.S. Government Case Study of Human Manipulation

- How might the review of successful intelligence interviewing cases broaden, extend, and further define the list of sources of power used by intelligence interviewing teams and detainees in various different contexts?

- How might intelligence interviewing teams consider various sources of power – both the interviewer's and the detainee's– in planning to interview a particular female detainee? Or in making a plan to interview a very young, very old, or very sick detainee, or a detainee who had been held by other countries, or a detainee of an unusual, multi-cultural background?

- Which sources of power would be most useful if the intelligence interviewing team wishes to encourage the detainee to return to his country, or to recruit him as an informant?

- How is moral authority understood, and what is known about the power of moral authority in different contexts and in different cultures?

- How might the intelligence interviewing profession and the IC community develop *as many sources of power as possible* – in order to complicate the task of those who might offer resistance training to adversaries?

- Might certain intelligence interviewing professionals be effective with only certain kinds of power and specific detainees?

- Might a particular source of power be available to an intelligence interviewing team only in a certain time frame or context?

- Might that source of power be *developed* only in a certain context, or in a certain time frame, or with certain intelligence interviewing professionals?

Interests and Identities

What Might an Intelligence Interviewing Team Want to Understand About Interests and Identities?

Every person has multiple interests, social identities, and constituencies. Knowledge of a detainee's different interests and social identities may guide a strategy for developing an operational accord,[*] and help persuade the detainee to provide useful information – including useful information that was not anticipated. It may also be helpful for the intelligence interviewing team to analyze their own interests and social identities in order to maintain focus and objectivity, deal with stresses – and to find ways to connect with individual detainees.

Conventional Beliefs

Since the times of Sun Tzu, effective military leaders and political negotiators have considered it essential to "know the enemy," especially in times of war. As Sun Tzu taught, simply pursuing one's own interests, without understanding the interests of the adversary, limits one's ability to anticipate what the adversary will do, and to influence, confound, or convert the adversary. This principle applies in all interactions where the parties may have conflicting goals.

Most interrogators realize that the more they can know about a detainee, the better. In preparing for an interview, these professionals might ask:*"How can I get this person to talk to me? How much does he know and how will I know if he is telling me the truth?"* They seek biographic information: name(s), languages spoken, various kinds of social and political status; details about capture; allegations about what the person may have done; and estimates of knowledgeability. These may be *hard* data from reliable channels, or *soft* data obtained from the screening process. Interrogators recognize that they often begin their task with limited and sometimes questionable information and only a rough idea of the detainee's knowledgeability.

[*] "Operational accord" denotes a special "working" or "professional" relationship between the interviewer and the high-value detainee. It is

characterized by the detainee's willingness to supply accurate information, at least some of the time, in response to the interviewer's questions. The concept also implies that the interviewer has an individualized and effective strategy for interactions with the detainee. Once an operational accord develops, it may allow an intelligence interviewer to engage with, challenge, and debate with the detainee, or agree with him if appropriate, without shutting down the relationship or causing the loss of important information.

Army Field Manual 2-22.3, *Human Intelligence Collector Operations*, currently serves as the primary source of guidance for military interrogators. In addressing"What does the interrogator need to know?" the manual states:

7-3. The key to good HUMINT collection is preparation on the part of the collector....The HUMINT collector must understand the environment and particularly the human component...his source, and the cultural environment.

8-7. HUMINT collectors do not"run" an approach by following a set pattern or routine. Each approach is different, but all approaches have the following in common. They...identify the source's primary emotions, values, traditions, and characteristics and use them to gain the source's willing cooperation.

FM 2-22.3 notes that other kinds of information are also important to develop in the interrogation process. Behavioral science research has provided some ways to identify, gather, and utilize such information.

Behavioral Science Perspectives

Behavioral science findings affirm these points in the Field Manual, as well as the insights of Sun Tzu. One way the intelligence interviewing team can persuade a high-value detainee to provide accurate information is to discover his individual *interests,* as well as his *social identities*. Assessing and tracking a detainee's real interests, and doing so throughout the intelligence interviewing process, allows the intelligence interviewing team to understand what motivates the detainee to provide or withhold information. Moreover, understanding that each detainee has multiple social identities – personal and professional – can give the intelligence interviewing team various paths toward understanding his interests, and thereby help in establishing an operational accord with the detainee.

Although this discussion focuses on the interests and social identities of the detainee, it is also helpful to have a keen understanding of the intelligence interviewers as well. Here are just two examples. A team may help its members to maintain self-discipline and to stay calmly focused on the goal of gaining as much useful information as possible, in the face of manipulation or provocation by a detainee (see **Stress** and **Power**). A team may use the individual interests and social identities of team members to find ways to build an operational accord with the detainee (see box on "Using many sources of power with Japanese prisoners of war" in **Power**).

What Exactly Are "Interests" and Why Are They Important?

In the context of this discussion, "interests" are the *hopes, needs, fears, concerns, wishes*, and *values* of the detainee. They represent the "real reason" why a detainee acts or speaks in a particular way. Without understanding a detainee's interests, intelligence interviewing professionals and teams are likely to make missteps throughout the interviewing process. They may even inadvertently create or bolster the detainee's resistances.

A detainee's interests derive from his *sense of himself,* his *social identities*(discussed in more detail below)*, and his relationships with his constituencies.*

- A sense of self often derives from group membership. Almost all people feel a sense of belonging to one or more groups: their extended family, their gender and age group, their sports team, their religious group, etc. Group membership fills a basic human need to belong, and can play a powerful role in how a person behaves and thinks.

- Social identity is best described as membership in a social group (of any size) that helps define a person's self-concept and self-esteem. Detainees, like all people, have several social identities, personal and professional. For example, a particular detainee might be a member of a certain tribe, clan, or extended family; a fan of a particular soccer team; an expert car mechanic; and a member of an insurgent cell.

- Constituencies are all the people a detainee cares about: the people whose opinions matter to him. They may include his peer networks and comrades, clan and sub-clan, extended family, and political and spiritual leaders.

Learning the detainee's real interests can enable the intelligence interviewing team to:

- Anticipate, understand, and avoid or deal with the resistances of the detainee (see *Resistances*)

- Help build a degree of trust or accord

- Find common interests (including common dislikes) upon which to build a bridge, to establish connections to networks and constituencies, and perhaps to help jog the detainee's memory (see *Memory*)

- Discover what the detainee may value, and provide something of value to the detainee in order to invoke or meet the requirements of *reciprocity (*see *Power and Persuasion)*

- Identify and obtain something with which to trade or to make deals (see *Power*)

- Discover pathways to persuade or influence (see *Persuasion*)

- Gather intelligence of value, whether directly in response to questions or serendipitously and incidentally

Imagine a detainee who repeatedly states he wants to kill all Americans and constantly insults his interviewer. The intelligence interviewer might assume that the detainee's sole interest is to kill his enemies, and therefore might decide that such a detainee is "too radicalized" ever to respond to persuasion. This assumption could cause the interviewer and guards to treat the detainee dismissively, to engage only on the topic of struggle and hate, to ignore the detainee, or to be hostile in return. While this may be a *normal* human reaction when dealing with a highly resistant person, it might only feed the detainee's hatred of Americans and strengthen his views of himself as an adversary and his resistances. Thus, this normal human reaction might well undermine the *intelligence interviewing professional's primary interest*: to obtain accurate information.

In such a situation an intelligence interviewing professional might step back and ask, "What *other* interests might this detainee have?" For example, the detainee may have been revered and feared by many followers prior to detention. Perhaps the detainee's hostile statements reflect an underlying core interest: his desire that others recognize him as powerful and important and treat him accordingly. After discovering this, the intelligence interviewing professional may choose to treat the detainee, at times, as a very important person in order to respond to a"core concern" (see **Persuasion**). This might well meet one of the detainee's interests, perhaps lower his resistances – and help the interviewer to meet his own primary interest.

How Might an Intelligence Interviewing Team Learn the High-Value Detainee's "Real" Interests?

The intelligence interviewing team can discover at least some of the detainee's interests by thorough preparation prior to an interview, including meticulous review of all-source intelligence about a detainee. However, third-party information may or may not be adequate, as sources may be aware of only a small range of another person's true interests and connections. Therefore, the intelligence interviewing team must use skillful listening and observation techniques, as well as broad lines of questioning and discussion. By attending to a detainee's past and present words and behavior, the team can begin to develop hypotheses about a detainee's interests and then continue to reassess and evaluate these over time.

Detainees have an array of interests, some of which are easily identified and are useful in building an operational accord. One way to identify interests is to lower barriers through "small talk." Topics such as food, health, parenthood and children, sports and sport teams bring people together everywhere. In fact, research suggests that many societies, cultures, and tribes have a deeply respected custom of talking about serious topics only after considerable time spent in casual conversation and perhaps eating meals or drinking tea together.

What might the intelligence interviewing team observe once the detainee begins to engage in a dialogue? To learn the detainee's true interests the team must pay close attention to:

- What the detainee says he wants, and the "positions" he takes. Of course, he may not acknowledge his "real interests;" his stated"positions" might be different from his real interests.

- How he acts with respect to what he wants or does not want, and how he seeks and interprets information.

- Whether he is helpful or reticent about various topics and people.

Intelligence interviewing teams can usually discover several dimensions of a detainee's interests to explore. These may include things he wants and things he enjoys. As one example, all detainees have some physical interests. They include medical care for self and family; overcoming illness, injury, or disabilities; physical fitness and sports (and in some cultures, dance); food; and sleep. A detainee may enjoy discussing different parts of a given city or area, the important characteristics of different clans, his tastes and dislikes in food, and activities and skills important to him while he was growing up (for example, different kinds of musical instruments or kites, or playing or not playing on a certain sports team).

The historical record shows that conversations of this kind helped U.S. interrogators to make a connection with German and Japanese POWs during World War II and with North Vietnamese agents and soldiers in the Vietnam conflict.

How Might the High-Value Detainee's Likes and Dislikes Reveal His True Interests?

Identifying a detainee's real interests can be a complex and fluid task. Some detainees may sometimes speak openly and truthfully about what they want. Others may attempt to conceal their true interests in order to influence how they are viewed by the intelligence interviewing team, by their fellow detainees, or by constituencies back home. For example, to gain respect from his peers or his captors, or to maintain his reputation among his comrades after repatriation or death, a detainee might state that he is prepared to die in detention when he *also* would like to be able to give up the fight and go home.

Discovering the detainee's real interests poses a challenge to the interviewing team, because many detainees may take *positions* that are different from their underlying *interests*. For example, a detainee might take the position that he wishes to deal only with a particular intelligence interviewing professional, when his real interest is to be treated respectfully or to talk to someone in his own age group. A detainee might take the position that he will not discuss a particular geographic region, when his underlying interest is not to expose a family member who resides in that area.

In addition, a detainee may or may not *consciously understand or acknowledge* all of his own interests, yet these interests may still significantly influence his actions. This is especially true for interests that have emotional importance. For example, a detainee may not realize how much he would like to be "recognized" as an honorable man or as an expert in some area. Yet if he receives such recognition he might be far more willing to engage in conversation and share some or all of the information the intelligence interviewing professional seeks.

Further complicating the task of ascertaining real interests is that the detainee's interests *may or may not remain stable over time*. Interests can change (although often slowly) with the introduction of new information, or as the detainee gains experience in detention. Such changes may benefit the intelligence interviewing professional. For example, skilled interviewers have described the importance of offering a telephone call back to family, talking at length about the medical problems of the detainee or his children, or bringing the detainee a favorite food from his home region. An expert interviewer has also noted the importance of having the necessary knowledge to engage in serious discussions of the detainee's technical achievements. This helped to turn the detainee's attention back toward a more desirable social identity and interests.

Similarly, a detainee's interests may *vary with context*. A detainee may act differently (perhaps dramatically so) when encountering different intelligence interviewing professionals, when interacting with different sets of peers, or when living in a different environment among different people. This may happen in part because of the detainee's various "social identities"(see below).

A detainee's interests may or may not be *consistent* with each other, and may conflict. For example, prior to detention a detainee might have wanted both to stay at home with his family *and* to fight on behalf of his group and his leaders. As a parent, a detainee may want medical care for his child, but at the same time, as a member of an insurgent cell, he may want to conceal the child's existence or whereabouts.

These conflicting interests provide various opportunities for the intelligence interviewing professional to explore. For instance, even though a detainee may still have interests related to his role in an insurgent group and his relationship with the group's leadership, the intelligence interviewing professional may decide to work with the detainee's wish to return home in an effort to deal with resistance to sharing information.

What Is the Function of "Social Identities"?

Psychologists have identified social identity as one of the fundamental building blocks of human nature. Social *identities* (as noted, everyone has several) describe how a given person sees himself privately and in various roles, how he believes others see him, and his connections to multiple social groups and larger social, political, economic, and religious entities. Thus, the intelligence interviewing professional might first seek to discover *all* the social identities of the detainee, such as his family roles, languages, professional affiliations, and personal interests (including what he likes and dislikes, skills, sports, artistic pursuits, hobbies, etc.). Through discussions with the detainee and with other members of the intelligence interviewing team, the interviewer might explore:

- What functions does each group serve for the detainee?

- How, why, and when did he join a group or groups? (For

example, was he born into the group? Did he join as an adolescent?)

- Does he aspire to join any groups (for example, to affiliate with a particular terrorist group, or to become a martyr)?

- How might these particular group affiliations or membership(s) help the interviewer to jog the detainee's memory? How might they illuminate possible future behavior?

Social identities not only fulfill a basic need for belonging, but also provide a set of mental and emotional guidelines that inform people how to think and behave. Psychologists consider a person "highly identified" with a group when that person believes he or she embodies defining attributes of the group and derives selfesteem from group membership. That group can be as large as a major religion or as small as an extended family or sub-clan. A devout follower of a religious sect, for example, may not know many of his fellow sect members, but his social identity is defined at least in part by the attitudes, beliefs, and behaviors shared by that group. If he is uncertain about what to eat, with whom to speak, or whether he "did the right thing," he might first look for answers in well-defined, easily understood guidelines recognized within that group.

To derive self-esteem from group membership, people constantly compare their group to other groups and seek evidence that their group is "better" in some way. Social psychological research has found that stigmatized minorities (e.g., members of minority religions or races) often have higher levels of self-esteem than their non-stigmatized counterparts. Like stigmatized minorities, religious extremists may have developed an ability to use their collective (group-based) self-esteem to counter the effects of verbal or physical persecution. Many extremist Muslims, for instance, believe that the West threatens the holy sites of Islam and Islamic culture itself. Efforts to undermine resistance through pressure or direct attacks on a detainee's fundamentalist identity may actually strengthen this identity and bolster the detainee's determination to resist.

The U.S. Government Case Study of Human Manipulation

How Can the Team Take Advantage of Cross-Cutting Identities?

Everyone has multiple social identities that stem from family, gender, ethnic and tribal roles, religious and professional affiliations, national and linguistic heritage, and personal interests (likes and dislikes, skills, sports, artistic pursuits, hobbies, etc.). In psychological terms, these "alternate social identities" are called *crosscutting identities.*

Because each of these cross-cutting identities involves different groups of people, they present considerable potential to reduce *inter-group bias.* For example, if a Shiite detainee identifies himself primarily as a Shiite, he may view all non-Shiites (including the intelligence interviewing professional) as members of his religious "out-group." If that same detainee also identifies himself as an engineer, then he may see other engineers – even if they are Sunni, or American, or secular – whom he initially placed in his"out-group" as members of his engineer "in-group."

When two people who belong to two different groups begin to find commonalities or shared experiences, likes, and dislikes, the effects of the initial group distinction may recede over time, potentially dampening the detainee's reasons for reticence or withholding information. To find an avenue that might lead to an accord with the detainee, the intelligence interviewing professional may then seek to identify various social identities of his own (or of a team member) that might align with those of the detainee. Continuing the earlier example, if an intelligence interviewing professional can believably present himself as an engineer, this "engineer-to-engineer" relationship will present greater potential for communication than the"Muslim-to-infidel" or "Arab-to-Westerner"relationship that may have existed before the discovery of an alternate, shared, cross-cutting identity.

As noted earlier, direct attempts to weaken the beliefs that grow out of a detainee's most important social identities may actually strengthen such identities and increase resistance. Instead, one strategy might be for the intelligence interviewing professional to respect (in other words, not seek to attack) the boundaries of the detainee's *salient identity* – for example, as a fighter, or a follower of a particular leader. At the same time he would seek to *strengthen different identities* in order to enhance communication. For instance, talking about children with a man known to be a devoted father may at first seem "off track" but ultimately can decrease resistances, lead to an accord, and yield better intelligence.

Communicating on the basis of a cross-cutting identity may not prove effective immediately. A cherished group-based identity serves as protection and guidance, and the intelligence interviewing team can expect a detainee to seek refuge in it. Eventually, though, strengthening the salience of one or more different social identities and extensive discussion of common shared interests may facilitate accord and decrease resistances. This process, technically called *decategorization*, may lead the detainee to see the intelligence interviewing professional as an individual who shares his likes and dislikes, rather than primarily as a member of an adversary group.

In short, knowledge of a detainee's social identities, and the associated constituencies, gives the intelligence interviewing team key insights into a detainee's possible interests, his loyalties, and what lies behind his resistances. Cross-cutting identities provide a possible path toward less adversarial communication (see *Persuasion*).

What Is the Relevance of Understanding Interests and Social Identities to Meeting "Intelligence Requirements"?

Intelligence requirements (IRs) are important, since they provide guidance on what the larger intelligence community and policy makers wish to know from a particular detainee or group of detainees. However, focusing too soon or too narrowly on IRs may be a poor tactic for working with a detainee. Clearly, a resistant detainee is not likely to be instantly forthcoming with specific answers to specific IR questions asked by an interviewer he does not know, especially if the detainee comes from a culture that values small talk and discussions of common interests. For this reason alone, the team might plan wider conversations that take account of the detainee's interests and social identities.

IRs also may narrow the scope of what an intelligence interviewing professional discusses with a detainee, and much vital information may become lost in a sea of "unknown unknowns." This notion makes sense to most people, but in times of urgency those who manage intelligence interviewing operations –and consumers of the intelligence collected – may press interviewers to think one dimensionally about detainees and "just answer the IR" (see box on "The "detainee's information" is not a simple concept" in *Power*).

Key Points
Understand the Interests and Social Identities of Members of the Team

Intelligence interviewing professionals might continually keep an eye on their own interests and social identities to help in maintaining a calm and objective focus, to help in dealing with their own stresses, and to help in finding ways to build an operational accord with the detainee.

Look Underneath What the Detainee Says He Wants

Intelligence interviewing professionals and teams might continually assess each detainee's interests over time, in different settings, and with different people; search all-source intelligence for clues about his interests prior to detention; and not allow what a detainee *says* to solidify assumptions about what he truly *wants*. It is important to consider that a detainee may not consciously recognize all the interests that drive him. A statement such as "All I want is to get out of here" might actually include the idea that "I want to talk to people who treat me with the respect that I deserve." Recognizing and responding to an underlying interest may increase the detainee's willingness to talk more frankly with the interviewer.

Seek to Understand All the Detainee's Interests and Identities

Even if the intelligence interviewing team knows little about the detainee as an individual, awareness of the various social groups with which he identifies may be a source of operationally relevant information and may present a starting point for conversation.

Simply discussing a detainee's interests and social groups is not likely to create a sufficient basis for an operational accord. An intelligence interviewing professional and team need to identify as many of the detainee's interests as possible in order to recognize cross-cutting identities that potentially align with the team's own knowledge and skills. If the interviewer can plausibly present himself as a "colleague," the detainee may begin to acknowledge some commonalities with the interviewer, which in turn can help to decrease resistances and enhance the interviewer's ability to persuade (*see Resistances and Persuasion*).

Explore Topics Beyond the Intelligence Requirements

A detainee may possess information of great value that falls outside the scope of stated IRs. Understanding the range of the detainee's interests and identities can indicate additional fruitful areas for questioning. For example, knowing that an avid sports fan attended a particular match could provide an opportunity to find out about who was on the team in that place at that time, about road conditions or water shortages in the area, or about the mood of the residents. Thoughtful efforts to explore interests and identities can result in discovery of serendipitous and incidental information of great value, and can provide valuable information on how to persuade the detainee in future interviews (see *Persuasion*).

Areas of Potential Operational Interest That Merit Further Research

- How might link and social analysis methodologies be used to help an intelligence interviewing team understand a detainee's social identities and constituencies on the basis of his interests, and vice versa?

- What sort of backstopping (e.g., documentation, photographs, terminology, professional memberships and affiliations) might an intelligence interviewing professional find useful to present a *fabricated cross-cutting identity* as a real one?

- How does ignoring an undesirable social identity (e.g., "a warrior") affect resistances?

- What more can be learned about the relationship between interests and"resistance points" (see *Resistances*)? That is, what can the interviewing team learn by observing points where the detainee is reticent or silent?

- How can an analysis of "interests" enhance different sources of power in interviewing, and perhaps foster an operational accord with the detainee (see **Power**)?

- How might analysis of social identities be used to plan ways of helping a detainee remember events (see **Memory**)?

- How can explicit understanding of the interests and social identities of members of the intelligence interviewing team help in maintaining objectivity, in building an operational accord, and in learning the various kinds of information a detainee may have?

Stress

What Is the Role of Stress in an Intelligence Interview?

Behavioral science research suggests that the concept of stress is much more complicated than many people assume. Certain conventional beliefs about stress in interrogation, such as "stress leads to breaking," might be reconsidered for two reasons: "stress" is a complex phenomenon, and research results have begun to indicate that the notion of "breaking" may be simplistic, misleading, and illusory.

Conventional Beliefs

Many believe that they understand the meaning of *stress* and the effect it has on the interrogation process. Many consider it an essential component of interrogation – perhaps even as the defining characteristic that distinguishes interrogation from a debriefing or other voluntary interview. This school of thought suggests that the ability to put a detainee under stress is the interrogator's primary source of control and leverage; conversely, an interrogator who does not have the option of stressing a detainee would be viewed as operating at a major disadvantage.

Army Field Manual 2-22.3, *Human Intelligence Collector Operations*, currently serves as the principal source of guidance for military interrogators and others. FM 2-22.3 discusses stress primarily as it relates to"capture shock" and how to take advantage of this time of uncertainty for the detainee. The manual seems to present stress as a condition that will always serve as a motivating factor for the detainee to talk.

8-79. EPWs [enemy prisoners of war] are normally vulnerable to basic incentive and emotional approach techniques. Most EPWs are traumatized to various degrees by the events preceding or surrounding their capture. They tend to be disoriented and exhibit high degrees of fear and anxiety. This vulnerable state fades over time, and it is vital for HUMINT collectors to interrogate EPWs as soon as [sic] and as close to the point of capture as possible. The earlier that an EPW is questioned the more likely he is to cooperate. And the earlier that he begins to cooperate, the more likely he is to continue to cooperate. It is also vital that the HUMINT collector be the first person that the EPW has a chance to talk to. This means that proper silencing and segregation of the sources by whoever is transporting them is an important part of a successful approach.

Additional statements in the Army Field Manual reflect the assumption that interrogators can make productive use of a detainee's feelings of hopelessness and helplessness. The manual also appears to place emphasis on assessing the detainee's areas of weakness, rather than assessing both a detainee's strengths and weaknesses in an effort to learn how best to persuade:

8-49. ...In the emotional-futility approach, the HUMINT collector convinces the source that resistance to questioning is futile. This engenders a feeling of hopelessness and helplessness on the part of the source.

8.73 ....By using nonpertinent questions, the HUMINT collector can move the conversation in the desired direction and, as previously stated, sometimes can obtain leads and hints about the source's stresses or weaknesses or other approach strategies that may be more successful.

M-1. As part of the Army's efforts to gain actionable intelligence in the war on terrorism, HUMINT collectors may be authorized, in accordance with this appendix, to employ the separation interrogation technique, by exception, to meet unique and critical operational requirements. The purpose of separation is to deny the detainee the opportunity to communicate with other detainees in order to keep him from learning counter-resistance techniques or gathering new information to support a cover story; decreasing the detainee's resistance to interrogation....

Beyond those reflected in FM 2-22.3, additional widely held beliefs include:

- Inducing moderate or severe stress in the detainee is the primary, even essential, way to conduct interrogations. Those who hold this view suggest that a detainee will only comply with the interrogator's agenda and begin to answer questions when the detainee reaches a certain level of *discomfort* (a product of stress).

- The interrogator should establish a position of dominance over the detainee. At no time should the detainee be able to question who is in control. In addition, the detainee must *always* be kept aware that he no longer controls his environment and cannot predict anything about his future.

- Stress will undermine the detainee's physical, emotional, and mental resourcefulness. While the detainee may possibly be able to resist at the outset, stress will systematically erode his ability to wage an ongoing battle of wits with the interrogator. As continuous stress reduces the detainee's physical stamina and sense of well-being, he will begin to lose the contest of wills and will provide the information the interrogator seeks. •High levels of stress may cause the detainee to *break*: to escape from unbearable stress into a posture of compliance and complete or near complete "cooperation." In the extreme view, the relentless pressure exerted by the interrogator's pointed, rapid-fire questioning, combined with fatigue from long interrogations, varying degrees of *sleep deprivation, stress positions*, and the inherently stressful nature of detention and of uncertainty about the future, ultimately causes the detainee to cooperate unconditionally.

Behavioral Science Perspectives

Research findings about the effects of stress raise doubts about the accuracy, and utility, of these conventional beliefs. No systematic studies of stress in interrogations with terrorism detainees have been found. However, several ideas from behavioral science might guide intelligence interviewing teams of the future in how they consider, and choose to use, stress in the course of their interactions with detainees.

What Exactly *Is* Stress?

Although behavioral scientists have extensively studied the nature and effects of stress, a universally accepted definition remains elusive. At a fundamental level, stress involves some manner of disruption in homeostasis: the process by which humans regulate their internal environment (e.g., thoughts, emotions, physiological arousal) to maintain a stable and constant state.

Stress itself is not inherently negative. In fact, people experience certain stressors as generally positive and motivating. Consider the examples of moving to a different city to start a desirable job, or feeling productively busy on an interesting task. Psychologists refer to this type of stress as *eustress*. However, when most people discuss "stress" in a day-to-day context they mean *distress:*stress that is perceived as negative and uncomfortable. Even eustress, despite its positive and even motivating effects, can be taxing to a person's system.

What Does Research Tell Us About Stress in Interrogations?

Although some view stress as an important source of leverage in interrogation, no research has been found on the relationships between different kinds of stressors and interrogation outcomes. Available research on the effects of stress on a person in detention has focused primarily on developing counter-strategies (e.g., resistance training).

In the 1950s and 1960s U.S. scientists studied the role of stress in the so-called *communist model of interrogation*: a hostile form of interrogation that sought to debilitate the detainees through physical and psychological pressure and sleep deprivation. The researchers concluded that the purpose of applying these stressors was to gain compliance and produce confessions. *Compliance* in this context refers to the detainee's willingness to defer to, or agree with, an interrogator, *but not necessarily to provide accurate or useful information*. This research also led to the design of the SERE program, discussed below.

By contrast, no scientific studies could be found that systematically examined the uses of stress in an *intelligence interview*, where the goal is to gather accurate and useful information. Therefore, little is known scientifically about the potentially constructive roles that different types of stress may play in generating accurate intelligence, *as distinguished from producing compliance.*

How Might a High-Value Detainee Experience Stress During Capture and Interviews?

Individuals vary in what they perceive as stressful or as uncomfortable. How a particular detainee perceives his situation, and the previous experiences and beliefs he brings to that situation, may determine what he finds motivating, demotivating, energizing, or debilitating.

That being said, being confined is inherently stressful and can be frightening to most people. Meeting with an intelligence interviewer, even one who approaches the interaction in a conversational tone, is potentially stressful for some detainees (although not others) and can provoke anxiety. Simply being asked to provide information, even rudimentary information about identity and current well-being, may be stressful for some detainees. Levels of stress in an interrogation or interview can therefore range from mild to extreme.

Does "Capture Shock" Cause High-Value Detainees to Reveal Information?

Most people initially experience heightened distress when detained. This is a reasonable response to encountering the unexpected and uncertain nature of capture, the discomfort of being held against one's will, and the loss of the ability to forecast, and control, events. The nature and intensity of that initial stress —often referred to as *capture shock* – may vary considerably among detainees depending on their perceptions of the experience, their coping skills, and their general preparation for such an experience.

Some anecdotal evidence suggests that certain detainees do provide intelligence information during the "capture shock" phase or in the immediate relief from the shock of capture. In a military setting, tactical intelligence may result when interviewers collect pieces of information from several different individuals shortly after they are captured. However, the rate at which this "capture shock" occurs, which detainees experience it under what conditions, and how to use this potentially important time are unknown. In particular, research is needed as to the relevance of capture shock to intelligence interviews of high-value detainees.

U.S. Army Captain John A. Burden, a Japanese language officer who led the first combat intelligence team on Guadalcanal and in other South Pacific battles during World War II, provided a firsthand account of POW operations in the South Pacific area. In the after-action report detailing his experiences on Guadalcanal, he described the attitude of Japanese POWs as falling into three distinct phases. During the first, immediately after capture, Japanese soldiers were terrified of being tortured or killed. Burden indicated that this fear did not result from Japanese military propaganda, but from personal experience: most Japanese soldiers on Guadalcanal had served two or more years in China, and may have believed that Chinese guerillas never took prisoners or that they tortured captives or put them to death. Burden concluded, "After spending two or more years training under these conditions it is only natural the Japanese troops should assume that such a fate was to be expected, regardless of who the opponent was."

After 24 to 48 hours of detention, the second phase set in. The Japanese soldiers realized they would not be tortured or killed, and were surprised by the good treatment and food they received. As a result, their "fear changed into gratitude" and they were "filled with a desire to reciprocate." Burden noted the Japanese soldiers "talked freely" and their information was "usually reliable." He described this as the most effective phase for interrogation.

The third phase began after 10 days to two weeks of detention. During this stage, detainees grew accustomed to the food and good treatment and became "mentally lazy." As a result, information was harder to get and proved less reliable.[14]

Detainees who have received training in what to do if captured (resistance training), who have been previously detained under similar circumstances, have themselves detained people, or have given a great deal of thought to how they could manage detention may feel less stress upon capture than those without such training, experience, or forethought. Their sense of familiarity with the detention environment and their ideas about how to act may lower the initial level of stress. In addition, some detainees may have become accustomed to hardship as a result of difficult living conditions, physical injury, or serious, protracted deprivation, while others have known greater comfort. These previous experiences are likely to influence how detention is experienced.

Thus, while there may indeed be overall patterns of stress reactions related to detention, these patterns and how they affect cooperation could vary depending upon the types of people being detained, their lives prior to detention, their expectations about what they will face in captivity, and their real interests (see *Interests* and *Identities*). Without knowing a given individual's history or training or interests, an intelligence interviewing team may find it difficult to anticipate how that person will respond to an induced or incidental stressor or to a series of stressful events.

How Can an Intelligence Interviewing Professional Use Various Sources of Stress?

Some social science theorists have suggested that a moderate level of stress is *necessary for optimal performance*. This might be called a theory of "productive" stress. However, this research has primarily focused on topics such as performance in physical activity or test taking. These studies also suggest that the "optimal" state of arousal produced by stress would depend on both the task and the individual.

It is not clear that recent research on productive stress applies to intelligence interviewing. For example, how would one define "optimal functioning" in the context of an intelligence interview? From the *interviewer's* perspective, optimal functioning for a relatively cooperative detainee who is willing to share information might mean that the detainee is motivated, and recalls and provides detailed and useful information (see *Memory*). From the perspective of a *resistant detainee*, however, optimal functioning might work against the interviewer's goal; an "optimal" amount of stress may actually bolster the detainee's resistances and enable him to withhold information (see"*The Man in the Snow White Cell*" *case study*).

Even if the concept of productive stress were well understood, efforts to manage stresses may still encounter major difficulties. As described above, a detainee's emotional experience will depend upon how he appraises and interprets his situation, what he wants, and how he copes with the experience. These individualized *perceptions* make predicting and managing a detainee's overall stress levels quite challenging. Moreover, in a sequence of interviews, sources and levels of stress may vary greatly for many reasons.

How Does Stress Affect a High-Value Detainee's Ability to Answer Questions?

While uncertainties about the effects of moderate stress levels still call for further research, social science findings are clear in one area: too much stress is likely to be *counterproductive*, as it produces a wide range of psychological and physical difficulties. For example, high levels of stress can have a substantial and negative impact on an individual's abilities to think, reason, recall, and provide detailed information. Since the intelligence interviewing professional's questions require the detainee both to think and recall, the potential for stress to undermine a detainee's abilities in these areas might be of acute interest to anyone involved in intelligence interviewing (see *Memory*).

Fear

Some believe in using fear to increase the stress on a detainee and motivate the detainee to divulge information. Indeed, fear can be a powerful motivator of human behavior, although no studies of the effects of fear that speak directly to intelligence interviews have been found.

As with *any* tactic, fear may sometimes cause a person to reveal information. But this does not mean that fear in general would be an effective strategy to employ with every detainee. Some psychological studies suggest that fear could present a complicated and potentially risky factor in intelligence interviewing.[15]Inducing intense emotions, such as fear, in any person can have unintended consequences. As noted above, high levels of stress could actually damage both a detainee's motivation and ability to share intelligence information.

Fear also may be a time-limited motivator. With repeated exposure, a detainee is likely to habituate; that is, he may become accustomed to fear and build immunity to its effects.

Ongoing fear is likely to contribute to a detainee's intense negative feelings toward the intelligence interviewing professional and further strengthen him in an enemy "social identity" (see ***Interests and Identities***). This may make it difficult for the interviewer to assume an alternative attitude when such a change is indicated, or to try to build an operational accord.*The interviewer (and potentially later interviewers) may be trapped in the role of hated tormentor.

In essence, though fear in some situations may produce short-term *compliance*, heightening and sustaining fear may severely disrupt development of an operational accord and actually compromise long-term success (see ***Power***).

Sleep Deprivation

Contrary to some common assumptions, the research literature includes strong documentation that sleep deprivation can interfere with mental functioning and physiological processes in a way that could significantly diminish a person's capacity (let alone willingness) to provide accurate, useful information. This is particularly true if the subject matter is technical. Sleep deprivation may also undermine a detainee's ability to distinguish facts or"truth" from other thoughts or suggestions, possibly making the information provided by a sleep-deprived detainee less reliable.

*"Operational accord" denotes a special"working" or "professional" relationship between the interviewer and the high-value detainee. It is characterized by the detainee's willingness to supply accurate information, at least some of the time, in response to the interviewer's questions. The concept also implies that the interviewer has an individualized and effective strategy for interactions with the detainee.

The U.S. Government Case Study of Human Manipulation

"Breaking"

The concept of breaking a detainee– which some imagine as a culminating point when the detainee "surrenders" and permanently ceases all efforts to resist –appears to be a false premise that profoundly misrepresents the nature of human interactions and decision making. It also indicates a serious lack of understanding of how memory works (see *Memory*). Those who operate on the basis of this concept risk missing valuable information the detainee may possess, let alone the possibility of persuading the detainee to provide"complete" information (see *Persuasion*).

More useful concepts may be those of *steps forward*, also known as *moments of progress,* or specific *breakthroughs*. A step forward occurs when the intelligence interviewing professional can elicit useful, accurate information from the detainee through carefully designed questions and persuasion, and by creating a social and environmental context that makes deliberate – and accidental– disclosures more likely.

"Learned Helplessness"

In the past several years, some have suggested that inducing a state of "learned helplessness" in a detainee will cause him to become more"cooperative." There appear to be several problems with this idea. First, no studies of learned helplessness could be identified that speak directly or indirectly to the context of intelligence interviewing. Second, it is difficult to understand how intelligence interviewing professionals could intentionally create a state of learned helplessness in all detainees and, even if they could, why they would want to do so.[16]

It is hard to believe that detainees who experience learned helplessness would or could provide accurate and complete intelligence information. In fact, inducing learned helplessness may – by definition – be worse than useless. If a detainee does not believe his statements and actions will affect his situation or cause his treatment to improve or worsen, what motivates him to tell the truth? He may simply fabricate an answer to satisfy the intelligence interviewing professional, or he may withdraw and become unresponsive. In addition, a learned belief that his actions or inaction are meaningless may override the detainee's previous expectation that his behavior will matter. This might make it more difficult to use the skills of intelligence interviewing (see *Persuasion* and *Power*).

What Happens When Stress Is Decreased for a High-Value Detainee?

Experienced interviewing professionals often provide anecdotes suggesting they can effectively lessen as well as deepen sources of stress in an intelligence interview. They may do this deliberately, in ways consistent with their goals and the detainee's current situation. For example, many interviewing professionals speak of the effectiveness of using the "good cop/bad cop" approach with a detainee. (The theory suggests that reduction in stress associated with the "good cop" may motivate a detainee to talk.) Social science research suggests that reducing stress levels can have several possible effects:

1. A detainee who is committed to not divulging information may feel bolstered in his resistance to the intelligence interviewing professional once the stress level is reduced. He may believe that he has less to worry about and therefore can focus on not responding to, or on deceiving, the interviewer.

2. As stressing stimuli decrease, a detainee may feel less need to devote energy to self-monitoring and "defending." He may also feel somewhat grateful (as when the "good cop" takes over the questioning from the "bad cop"). When he has less stress to cope with, the detainee may relax his defenses somewhat and be more receptive to other sources of influence. The relief may cause him to convey information – knowingly or unknowingly.

3. Repeatedly increasing and decreasing distressing stimuli may cause a detainee to build some tolerance or immunity to his distress reaction. As a person's coping resources are alternately taxed and then relaxed, the overall reserve of coping power may build or strengthen over time. This has been likened to the way our muscles get stronger: by progressive overload, followed by recovery. Increasing, then decreasing, the stress on a resistant detainee may therefore have the effect of increasing his power to resist.

The U.S. Government Case Study of Human Manipulation

Because stress is often a matter of perception, the intelligence interviewing professional must consider how the detainee may *interpret* (or think about) the changed stress. What one person experiences as causing or decreasing distress may be seen differently by another. For example, Army colonel Larry Guarino described the efforts of his North Vietnamese captors to increase POWs' stress levels by making one of them empty all the toilet cans: "Ron Storz inherited the chore from me, and it did have one thing on the plus side – it gave him an excellent opportunity to talk to some prisoners who were hard to reach. Storz did a great job, pretending he was talking to the guards, while passing information..."[17]

Furthermore, a detainee may have certain beliefs and perceptions about the extent to which the intelligence interviewing professional can control a stressful situation. For example, an experienced intelligence interviewing professional interviewed a senior Iraqi engineer who had knowledge of high-level planning documents. In the course of their conversations, the interviewer showed concern for the detainee's worry about his family, and was able to arrange for the detainee to make telephone calls to check on his family's health and welfare. This helped convince the detainee that the interviewer was an important person, and also decreased some of the stress (in this case, anxiety) that the detainee was experiencing. The interviewer also allowed the engineer to retain a photograph of his family that he had always carried with him. The interviewer's actions contributed to building an accord with the detainee, who ultimately provided valuable information.

Conversely, a detainee who believes the intelligence interviewing professional is the source of some stress may develop negative feelings and attributions. An initially cooperative detainee was concerned about his cleanliness and personal hygiene. He came to believe that his interrogator was responsible for his limited opportunities to shower in detention. (In fact, the interrogator had tried to get permission for the detainee to shower more often, but had failed.) Over a several-week period, the accord that the interrogator had developed with the detainee vanished and the detainee retreated into sullen silence.

These observations suggest the importance of the environment and context within which intelligence interviewing professionals and teams operate. To the extent possible, an intelligence interviewing environment might be designed so that the intelligence interviewing team can systematically deal with stressors that may affect a given detainee (see *Persuasion*).

How Does Stress Affect Intelligence Interviewing Professionals and Teams?

Consideration of stress in custodial intelligence interviewing might not center only on the detainee, but might also encompass the situation, experiences, and working conditions of the intelligence interviewing team itself. No behavioral science research has been found that examines the effects of stress on intelligence interviewing professionals, yet these professionals experience serious stresses from many sources. These sources may include unreasonable expectations from senior leaders, time pressure, dangerous and uncomfortable living and working conditions, illness, limited knowledge about the background and behaviors of detainees, protracted hostility from detainees and host populations, the loss of comrades, and conflicts with peers and persons from other organizations interested in a detainee, to name just a few.

Under such circumstances, some custodians, including interrogators, have treated detainees in ways that violate the norms of acceptable behavior. While such behaviors have had obvious and well-publicized effects on detainees, their long-term effects on custodians and interrogators are less well understood. There are anecdotal reports of long-term deleterious psychological effects on interrogators who followed direction to engage in behaviors that they believed"crossed the line" in interrogations. Some have experienced crises of faith and conscience.

While stress, in and of itself, will not usually cause skillful intelligence interviewing professionals to behave inappropriately, they might wish to pay attention to their own need for relief from stress and seek guidance from team members or other sources of support when pressures grow intense. Further, the environment and overall intelligence interviewing structure and system might be designed in such a way to recognize, address, and limit the amount of stress imposed on the intelligence interviewing team.

Key Points

"Stress" Has Many Dimensions

Stress is a complicated and poorly understood aspect of interrogation. There are many sources of stress, and people experience sources of stress very differently. While no direct studies of stress in intelligence interrogations were found, some existing research data might guide consideration of how an intelligence interviewing team views the management of stresses in its interactions with detainees.

Re-examine Assumptions

Certain conventional beliefs about stress in interrogation, such as "stress leads to breaking" are simplistic, poorly founded, and might be reconsidered and rethought. Instead, intelligence interviewing professionals might try to create *steps forward, moments of progress,* or specific *breakthroughs*– which may not result from stress.

Contrary to the popular view of a complete, final "surrender," these steps forward are often momentary or discrete, temporary events. While the cause and effect of one forward step may inform the effort to generate another, intelligence interviewing professionals cannot routinely rely on one single process or set of activities to achieve steady progress with a given detainee. As one experienced intelligence interviewer said about his interactions with a high-value detainee who was providing information: "I had to re-sell him on being cooperative every time we met."

Consider and Plan for Stress-Related Issues Prior to an Interview

An intelligence interviewing professional or intelligence interviewing team might review the following questions before beginning an intelligence interview:

- What might this particular detainee experience or be experiencing as stressful?

- How might certain stressors (both eustress and distress) help to build an operational accord, or conversely, increase this detainee's resistance?oMight certain kinds of stress actually *fuel* the detainee's motivation, and capacity, to resist?

- What stressors might overwhelm a detainee, or his memory, and therefore restrict or compromise the information he might provide?

- How might an interviewer identify ways to decrease stress on a detainee that might lead to his providing information?

- How might the individual interviewer, or the team, respond to signs of stress in the detainee?

- How might permitting or using certain kinds of stress limit or enhance the options of an intelligence interviewing professional or team to adopt other tactics with the detainee in the future

- What are the sources of stress for the intelligence interviewing professional, or the team as a whole?

- How might this stress affect the interviewer's or the team's interests, skills, and performance?

- How might a particular source of stress be alleviated or otherwise managed?

Understand the Stress That Affects the Intelligence Interviewing Team

The organizations employing intelligence interviewers might lay plans to recognize and address the multiple stressors that affect intelligence interviewing professionals. Ideally, as intelligence interviewing increasingly becomes a professional activity, new studies will lead to greater understanding of the stress on members of an intelligence interviewing team, and the teams will receive better support.

Areas of Potential Operational Interest That Merit Further Research

- What sources or levels of stress – if any – might enhance the intelligence interviewing professional's efforts to obtain useful information from a detainee?

- How might particular sources of stress or stress levels bolster certain resistances in some detainees?

- How does/might an intelligence interviewing team deal with the stressors inherent to the detention and interviewing context in ways that will help elicit useful intelligence from a detainee?

- How often does "capture shock" occur in detainees, and how might it be managed?

- •How might intelligence interviewing professionals and teams identify and respond to symptoms of increasing stress in a detainee?

- How might stress affect intelligence interviewing professionals and teams, and how might this stress be alleviated or otherwise managed?

- What might be done to increase the effectiveness of interviewers and teams who are working under serious stress?

Resistances

What Might an Intelligence Interviewing Team Wish to Know About Resistances[2]*?

In custodial intelligence interviews, a high-value detainee may, at least initially, be unwilling to provide information. While preparing to interview a detainee, an intelligence interviewing team may benefit from constructing plans to understand and manage resistances. Behavioral science research on resistances suggests promising ways to analyze reticence and to respond to detainees who hesitate to engage in any dialogue, or who appear unwilling to share information at particular times or on certain issues.

Conventional Beliefs

The over-arching term"resistance" has sometimes been applied to any apparent motivation or action to withhold information in an interrogation. Some interrogators have viewed "resistance" as if it were a single barrier – one that they needed to "break" (see *Stress*). Language in the revised Army Field Manual 2-22.3, *Human Intelligence Collector Operations*, acknowledges that this is not always the case, but seems to offer little guidance as to how an interrogator might seek to approach a detainee who is sophisticated in withholding pockets of information:

8.75. ...The HUMINT collector must also be aware of the fact that a source can begin to cooperate in certain areas while continuing to resist strongly in other areas. The HUMINT collector should recognize the reason for refusal, overcome the objection, and stress the benefit of cooperating (reinforce the approach)....

Some interrogators believe that the capacity to resist cooperating with an interrogator comes from the detainee's "willpower."According to this belief, the interrogator must therefore overcome that willpower before the detainee will comply with the interrogator's demands and requests. Other interrogators see resistance as a set of responses, techniques, and skills that detainees have been trained to exhibit. The revised Army Field Manual provides this guidance:

* The term"resistance" suggests that resistance is a single barrier, and one that needs to be overcome or "broken." This teaching paper uses the term "resistances" to reflect the many types and multi-layered complexions of resistances that are sometimes used by detainees.

8-77 ...most interrogation sources (90 percent or more) cooperate in response to the direct approach. Unfortunately, those sources who have the placement and access to make them high priority sources are also the ones with the highest degree of security awareness. A source who uses counterinterrogation techniques such as delaying, trying to control the conversation, or interrogating the HUMINT collector himself may

---

- Be an intelligence trained soldier.

- Be survival, evasion, resistance, and escape (SERE) trained.

- Be a terrorist.

- Have been a detainee or previously incarcerated.

While the Army Field Manual advises interrogators to be aware of potential resistance, it seems to offer few suggestions on how to identify and work with the many types of resistances they are likely to encounter, or to consider that some behavior that looks like resistance may in fact not be resistance at all (see *Memory*).

8-19. ...The HUMINT collector will continue to use direct questions as long as the source is answering the questions in a truthful manner. When the source refuses to answer, avoids answering, or falsely answers a pertinent question, the HUMINT collector will begin an alternate approach strategy.

8.76. If a cooperative source balks at answering a specific line of questions, the HUMINT collector must assess the reason for the refusal. The HUMINT collector may have arrived at a topic that the source finds particularly sensitive. Other reasons that might cause a source to stop answering questions are fatigue or unfamiliarity with the new topic. If this topic is critical, the HUMINT collector may have to reinforce the previously successful approach or may have to use a different approach.

Finally, the manual suggests an assumption that dealing with resistance is a relatively easy task, and that all sources will eventually cooperate. 8-74. Each source has a point where he will begin to cooperate and answer questions.

4-46. A commander normally must prioritize HUMINT collections and DOCEX.... If documents and human sources are determined to be equally likely of [sic] containing priority information, human sources are normally exploited first due to—

- ...The fact that an individual's resistance is easier to bypass immediately after undergoing a significant traumatic experience (capture). Capture thrusts them into an unfamiliar environment over which they have no control and are [sic] vulnerable to various approach techniques.

Behavioral Science Perspectives

The U.S. Government Case Study of Human Manipulation

There appear to be no scientific studies of resistances in intelligence interviews. However, both law enforcement literature and studies of persuasion and influence include findings about resistances:

Resistance hounds persuasion the way friction frustrates motion. To accomplish the latter, you have to expect and, preferably, manage the former. It makes sense that those who desire to understand persuasion should also seek to understand the nature and operation of resistance to persuasion.[18]

How Can an Intelligence Interviewing Team View the Multiple Dimensions of "Resistances"?

Psychologists have identified different types of resistance and ways to resist. Social psychologist Eric Knowles defines three kinds of resistance:[19]

Reactance

The resistance is directed against the persuasion process and/or the persuader. The resistor – in this case, the detainee –conveys the message "You might as well give up" by saying something like "You can't make me talk." The intelligence interviewing professional may feel that the detainee is hostile, stubborn, or defiant.

Skepticism

The resistance is directed against the specific offer or proposal. The detainee conveys the message "I'm not sure this is the best alternative for me" and perhaps offers several reasons why the proposal will fail. The intelligence interviewing professional may feel that the detainee is suspicious or simply looking for excuses.

Inertia

The resistance is directed against any change from the status quo. The detainee conveys the message "I've done all I'm going to do." The detainee may appear completely uninterested and ignore the intelligence interviewing professional or may simply repeat short, incomplete statements or slogans. The intelligence interviewing professional may feel that the detainee is unresponsive, disengaged, and forgetful or scatterbrained.

How Might an Intelligence Interviewing Team Analyze a High-Value Detainee's Resistances?

An intelligence interviewing professional can find ways to avoid or deal with detainee's resistances without fully recognizing the reasons or motivations behind them. But if some of the detainee's motivations and real interests are discernible, understanding them can assist the intelligence interviewing professional and the team in dealing with the resistances. After each round of analysis, an intelligence interviewing team can form hypotheses about the detainee's resistances. For example, if the detainee answers a question with "I don't know," or if he is reticent, the team may consider various explanations in order to plan ahead. The team might ask itself such questions as:

- What information do we have about the detainee's level of intelligence and sophistication?

- What do we think this detainee knows? Is it possible that he simply does not know the answer?

- Might a particular point of reticence actually *convey*information? For example, if the detainee is willing to talk about some topics but not others, might that provide clues about the importance of certain information he is protecting? (See *Interests and Identities* and *Power.*)

- What do we know about past and current factors that might influence the detainee's ability to remember? (See *Memory* for a discussion of the reasons why memory failure might appear as resistance.)

- Do we have specific data that suggest the detainee has been formally trained to resist questions generally or to resist providing certain kinds of information? If so, what kind of training may the detainee have received? How might we verify or invalidate the assumption that the detainee has been trained to resist? If the detainee received training, what would be the implications for planning the next interviews?

- Is it possible that the detainee has not been trained but has resistance plans of his own? If so, what would be the implications for planning the next interviews?

Such situations are worthy of careful study. For example, if the issue is memory, the intelligence interviewing team might plan ways to help the detainee remember. If the issue is conscious resistance, the team might analyze it as above to aid in planning interviews to avoid or otherwise deal with resistances.

In addressing all these questions, the team might constantly reexamine the validity of its assumptions. For example, is an estimate of a detainee's knowledgeability based on a single human or technical source, such as an intercept, or is it confirmed by multiple, independent sources? Some situations may involve determined, long-term, conscious resistance by a detainee (see box below); it is important for the team to try to identify these by asking questions such as those above.

"The Man in the Snow White Cell" (the second case study in this booklet) tells the very unusual story of long-term resistance by a high-level North Vietnamese detainee, Nguyen Tai. A 2001 article in the *Saigon Times Magazine* added a vignette to the story of Tai's detention, "Tai spent several days thinking of a word to reply to enquirers automatically so that he could not be 'trapped.' Finally, he chose the word 'forget' for his answers. He was asked about the list of his leaders, the espionage base, the communications network, and his father's name, but he always said, 'Forget.'"

It appears that Tai planned carefully to use the word *forget,* rejecting other possible words. *Forget* was very simple; he would not have to think under duress. And the word would not easily be used against him if he or the questions were misquoted or quoted out of context.

What Strategies Might Help an Intelligence Interviewing Team to Deal with Resistances?

Research in social psychology has revealed strategies that may diminish a person's resistances. Psychologists, behavioral economists, and others have documented the powers of using relationship, persuasion, and incentives to move people toward a position or behavior (see *Interests and Identities*, *Persuasion* and *Power*). Research also indicates that an intelligence interviewing professional could craft influence strategies and tactics that avoid, reduce, or eliminate a person's resistances. They include:

"Sidestepping" resistance – The intelligence interviewing professional can redefine the transaction from one in which he explicitly tries to push the detainee to "cooperate," to one in which he tries to influence the detainee to *collaborate* with him in pursuing a common goal. This was part of what happened with the Japanese POWs in WWII when they were interrogated by men who appreciated and cared about the Japanese people and Japanese culture (see *Power*).

A master intelligence interviewing professional who knew a great deal about the detainee's religion assumed the role of a student/recent convert to Islam who wanted to join with the "teacher" (the detainee) to understand more about Islam. The interviewer asked, "Would you help me understand what religious doctrine you have followed that allows for attacks against others?" He later followed up by asking about any doctrine in Islam that permits attacks against fellow Muslims. This "sidestepping" decreased the detainee's resistances to discussing his religion and other beliefs, and allowed the interviewer to ask questions that led the detainee to explore broader interpretations of his religion that he had not previously considered.

Addressing resistance directly – In an intelligence interviewing context, resistance can be like the proverbial elephant in the room. Sometimes it is useful for an intelligence interviewing professional to acknowledge it, openly express understanding of it, and talk about it directly. For example, the interviewer might preface a statement or an offer by saying:"You're not going to like this," or "You're going to find the next thing I tell you hard to believe."

Addressing resistance indirectly – An intelligence interviewing professional can sometimes avoid a detainee's resistance in a more indirect way by removing a detainee's "need" to resist. The interviewer might accomplish this by bolstering a detainee's sense of competence and self-esteem[20] or by casting the detainee in a different (nonadversarial) social role, such as that of a professional or expert. For example, an intelligence interviewing professional might say to an engineer: "I've learned more from you than from other people who are considered experts. Could you please explain to me...."

Distracting or disrupting resistance – Because resistance works best when the detainee is fully focused on resisting, the intelligence interviewing professional might use distraction to get the detainee off balance, divert his attention, and then ask a question. In one instance, an intelligence interviewing professional formally concluded a session but then, as the detainee was leaving the room, asked him in his native language (which the detainee did not know the interviewer spoke) for the name of a senior operative. The detainee, startled by hearing his own language and somewhat off guard because the session officially was "over," blurted out the answer.

Consuming resistance – Resistance requires mental and emotional energy. Most people have only limited reserves of energy to resist the interviewer as well as regulate and control themselves. If the intelligence interviewing team can find ways to consume these reserves while preserving the detainee's ability to think clearly and recall important information (see *Stress*), the detainee may have less energy remaining for resistance. For example, a detained senior military officer resisted any real discussion by rattling off a long series of questions in rapid-fire succession. The intelligence interviewing professional slowly and deliberately answered each one in turn, until the detainee essentially ran out of questions.

Using the resistance – Just as some forms of martial arts use an attacker's momentum against him, an intelligence interviewing professional might use the force of a detainee's resistance to introduce a proposed discussion. For example, an intelligence interviewing professional might introduce a proposal by saying: "I might have something that could help you, but I'm not sure you're ready to hear it."

What Strategies Might Move the High-Value Detainee Toward Providing Information?

In pondering how to foster discussion that leads to useful information, an intelligence interviewing professional might consider some of the"tried and true" tactics of persuasion and influence that derive from extensive social science research (although this research was not done in the context of interrogation). At least six basic principles underlie potentially successful tactics (see more detailed discussions in **Persuasion** and **Power**).

Liking – People tend to be more easily and strongly influenced by people they like, including those whom they view as attractive, similar to them, friendly, and appreciative.

Authority – People are more likely to be influenced by the arguments of a person whom they perceive as an authority or an expert, especially on the topic under discussion.

Reciprocity – People are predisposed to give something to those from whom they have already received or expect to receive something, whether tangible or intangible.

Commitment and *Consistency* – People like to think that their beliefs, statements, and actions are mutually consistent. Persuasive overtures may have greater effect when presented as harmonizing with a detainee's beliefs (especially beliefs that the detainee has stated aloud).

Social Validation or Social Proof – People are more likely to be influenced to take a particular action if they know that other people (especially a large number of people or people who are very much like them) have also chosen to take that action.

Scarcity – People tend to view something that is plentiful or easily attainable as less desirable than something scarce or rare. Incentives may appear more attractive if only a few are offered or if they are available for only a short time.

Key Points

Interviews with highly skilled intelligence interviewing professionals, and reviews of detainee cases, suggest that *countering* a detainee's resistances can be quite challenging. Avoiding and dealing with a detainee's resistances requires constant assessment. Many detainees do not cooperate initially, despite possible"capture shock." Almost all experienced intelligence interviewers emphasize the importance of completing a careful review of the documents found on or with a detainee, as well as information available about a detainee from a range of intelligence sources, prior to talking with the detainee. They note that this review potentially affords some leverage to the interviewer in terms of "information power" (see **Power**), and can help in planning a way to address, avoid, or deal with resistances.

"Not Answering" May or May Not Be Resistance

A detainee who does not answer a question may not be resisting (at least not in a "trained" manner). Sometimes a detainee who says that he does not know the answer to a question may actually not know. Intelligence interviewers may choose to be cautious, and not jump to the conclusion that a detainee is "resisting" and that "counter-resistance techniques" are needed. Effective resisting is possible (see box above.) However, there is little evidence that effective *training* about how to resist questioning over time even exists, let alone whether terrorist adversaries have undergone sophisticated resistance training.

"Resistance" Is Not a Unitary Concept

Many detainees display points of resistance over the course of intelligence interviews. These may derive from different interests that the detainee has, and may be expressed in different ways. Even "cooperative" detainees may have topics they would prefer to avoid discussing. This may also be helpful; reticence may itself be a source of information. ("Why did he stop talking just at that point?")

"Working with resistances" may be viewed as a *process*, since points of resistance tend to change over time. Intelligence interviewing professionals and teams will need constant analysis, and different strategies at different times, over the course of one or more interviews.

Seek Ways to Avoid or Deal with Resistances Rather Than "Eliminate" Them

Most detainees will maintain some types and levels of resistance throughout a long-term series of interviews. An intelligence interviewing professional can often find ways to avoid, deal with, or counter a detainee's resistances and obtain useful information. While it may not always be necessary to understand all the reasons behind a detainee's resistances in order to deal with them, such understanding is likely to increase the amount and utility of the information provided. Ideally, intelligence interviewing teams might seek to understand the detainee's motivations (see *Interests and Identities* and *Power),* consider how to plan a strategy that has the greatest promise of succeeding (see *Persuasion*), and then be prepared to adapt, depending on the detainee's responses.

Areas of Potential Operational Interest That Merit Further Research

- How can an intelligence interviewing team learn to recognize and analyze reticence and resistances?

- How can an intelligence interviewing team discern if a detainee has received formal resistance training – or is practicing his own resistance plans? Are these two forms of resistance plans different in practice, and if so, how are they different?

- How might an intelligence interviewing team keep track of a detainee's resistances?

- What are more effective and less effective ways to avoid and deal with a detainee's resistances?

Memory

What Is the Role of Memory in the Intelligence Interviewing Process?

Behavioral science research suggests that memory may be a more complicated phenomenon than most interrogators have assumed in the past. A fuller understanding of the cognitive processes involved in memory may enable the intelligence interviewing team to assess more accurately whether a detainee genuinely "does not remember" or is withholding information. Such an understanding may also enable the team to help detainees recall information more accurately and completely.

The U.S. Government Case Study of Human Manipulation

Conventional Beliefs

Many interrogators and analysts assume that detainees, under most conditions, can accurately recall information related to dates, places, actions, and people in reasonably robust detail. When a detainee reports inaccurately –or claims to have an incomplete memory about a given topic – interrogators may interpret this as evidence of unreadiness or unwillingness to provide information. In other words, they identify resistance, rather than capacity to remember, as the central problem (see *Resistances*). As a result, they may concentrate their efforts on dealing with resistance, and miss opportunities to work with a detainee to help him remember important information.

Army Field Manual 2-22.3, *Human Intelligence Collector Operations*, which the U.S. military has adopted as its primary guidance on detainee interviewing, makes no reference to memory in relation to the detainee's ability to recall information of potential intelligence value. Current interrogation training simply emphasizes proper questioning techniques to ensure that the interrogator can collect actionable intelligence. According to the Field Manual,"good questioning techniques enable the HUMINT collector to obtain accurate and pertinent information and to extract the maximum amount of information in the minimum amount of time." This statement implies that most detainees have a strong ability for accurate recall and that expert questioning by the interrogator can effectively elicit remembered information.

The Field Manual does, however, recognize that poorly designed questions can lead to erroneous answers by undermining the detainee's ability to think, recall, and respond clearly. For example, it cautions against the use of:

- Leading Questions (questions that require a "yes" or"no" answer rather than a narrative response; e.g.,"Did you meet the leader?"). Leading questions encourage a detainee, particularly one who is frightened or trying to curry favor, to give the answer that he thinks the HUMINT collector wants to hear.

Compound Questions (two questions asked at the same time; e.g.,"When you met the leader, was he carrying a gun or a knife?")

Compound questions are easy to misunderstand and may confuse the detainee. They also allow the detainee to provide incomplete answers.

- Vague Questions (questions that do not include sufficient detail for the detainee to understand exactly what the HUMINT collector is asking; e.g., "What do you know about the leader?") This type of question may also confuse and/or mislead the detainee.

Behavioral Science Perspectives

Cognitive science research illuminates both the powers of memory and its fragilities. Topics of particular relevance to intelligence interviewing include (1) strategies to enhance memory, which depend on an understanding of how and why people forget, (2) framing questions in order to reduce suggestibility, and (3) the potential impact of stress on memory (see also *Stress*).

How Does Memory Work?

Human memory has both impressive capacities and delicate vulnerabilities. Cognitive researchers describe memory as having "fragile power." In other words, human memory for *gist* (i.e., general concepts) can be quite good, whereas memory for details is often fallible and vulnerable to suggestion, alteration, or forgetting. For example, an individual may remember the quality, character, and overall content of a conversation at a meeting, but at the same time make several errors with regard to who said what.

Another error can occur in what is known as *source monitoring.** Errors in source monitoring mean that a person may retain a memory, but forget or misattribute the source of that memory – and, therefore, the information. For example, a memory may have originated in a daydream, a story that the person had told or had heard, a movie, photo, or book – or a real event.

Memories are real in that humans create images and retain representations in their "mind's-eye," *but a "real"memory is not necessarily accurate.* Moreover, humans are often poor judges of the accuracy of their own memory. Considerable research has shown no relationship between confidence and

* This should not be confused with the detainee or *source* being questioned.
accuracy: a person may be quite confident that a memory is accurate when in fact it is not.

People process information in stages, on a dynamic continuum: *perception and attention encoding consolidation and association storage retrieval*. These stages are interdependent. *Attention*, for example, affects *retrieval*, and vice-versa. Consequently, what we *attend* to (what we pay attention to) in our environment has an influence on what and how we *encode*(store), and ultimately what we *remember*.

Important to the concept of the information processing continuum is that there is significant variability in how individuals function at each of these stages. For example, individuals suffering from anxiety or defensiveness actually *attend* to information in their environment differently than those who are less anxious. In short, personality and context affect what information is *attended* to in the first place, how it is *associated* with other information, and thus how it is *remembered*.

In addition, imagine two detainees who received the same training in making explosives: one has little background in chemistry, while the other has an undergraduate degree in the subject. The detainee with a scientific background is likely to associate and consolidate many more details of the chemical processes involved and to remember them later. Therefore, an intelligence interviewing team might expect vast differences in the amount of detail these two detainees could provide about the same training.

Forgetting: How Does the Passage of Time Affect Memory? Do Some Memories Last Longer Than Others? If So, Why?

Memory decays over time without use, but not all memories decay at the same rate. Furthermore, there are multiple memory systems (sensory, motor, declarative, episodic). Once retrieved, information apparently becomes easier to retrieve again, thus slowing decay.

The mere act of retrieving a memory is a memory *modifier*, and in this way memory is dynamic. Facts and episodes, once remembered, assist the retrieval of some information while hindering the retrieval of other information. Thus, while many believe that changes in details when repeating a particular story may signal an effort to deceive, the intelligence interviewing team can in fact expect that an individual's story will change slightly with each telling, as new details become activated for retrieval. Small changes in a detainee's story *might* indicate that the detainee is recalling information with increasing accuracy rather than attempting to deceive.

Many believe that memory is directly related to an individual's general intelligence level and/or how hard the person tries to remember specific information. Actually, the availability of a memory is largely independent of the effort to retrieve it, and poor retrieval may result from *ineffective consolidation of information*. In other words, assuming that an individual is trying to remember, successful retrieval of a memory depends largely upon how and whether it was stored into memory, also known as the *storage strength* of the memory. The factors that can affect this include:

- Personal importance (the importance an individual places on it)
- Retrieval practice
- Depth of processing
- Retrieval strength

While research has revealed differences in the way people think (e.g.,"associative" versus "linear" cognitive styles), no evidence suggests a similar distinction in memory. Memory is predominantly associative. Researchers believe that even when a person recalls sequences, the different components of a sequence are activated by association to other components. The more meaningful and personally relevant those associations are, the more easily the person will retrieve that information. Providing cues or prompting with partial detail can help the person to recall information that is less easily retrieved.

How Might Interviewing Tactics Enhance Accurate Recall? What Skills Are Effective? How Might One Know When to Use Them, and with Whom?

Research shows that "mnemonics" (e.g., "Thirty days hath September...") can enhance a person's ability to recall information. While exploring all mnemonics goes beyond the scope of this paper, one of the most effective mnemonics employed at the retrieval stage of memory involves *cueing* or *prompting*. An example of cueing would be providing partial information designed to facilitate full retrieval. For example, if a detainee experiences difficulty recalling the name of a town an interviewer could ask "Is the name of the town long or short?" or "Did you ever see the name of the town written down? If so, can you picture it now?"

Another retrieval stage mnemonic is based on the concepts of *encoding specificity* and *state-dependent learning*, which have important implications for intelligence interviewing. Research on encoding specificity indicates that information is not learned by itself, but rather is encoded and learned along with its *context*. State-dependent learning suggests that information is retrieved more easily within the same context in which it was encoded. For example, people are more likely to remember information encoded and learned in the desert if they can recall or re-create the environmental context as they try to retrieve that information.

Framing and Suggestibility

How Can the Intelligence Interviewer's Plans for the Interview and the Way He Asks Questions Influence a Detainee's Ability to Recall Information Accurately?

Except in its listing of questions to avoid (discussed above), the Army Field Manual apparently does not consider that the manner in which questions are posed can influence the detainee's ability to recall information accurately. The scientific literature on memory suggests that intelligence interviewing professionals might benefit from remaining acutely aware that the form of their questions – as well as their overall approach to a detainee – may make the detainee vulnerable to suggestion and, therefore, to false recollections (see **Persuasion**).

The U.S. Government Case Study of Human Manipulation

The strength of human memory lies in its plasticity (i.e., the ability to change) and in its vast storage capacity. This strength, however, comes at the cost of a fallible retrieval process, including a process vulnerable to being fed false and misleading detail. Scientific literature on *post-event suggestibility* highlights that memory is quite malleable, even when an individual tries to present information accurately. Furthermore, once an individual has recalled information falsely, it may be difficult for that person to distinguish a false memory of the information from a real one.

People recognize and recall information more quickly if that information has been discussed beforehand. Priming memory with hints and cues may facilitate the flow of information, but it may also corrupt the accuracy of that information, even for a cooperative detainee. Think of priming a water pump: putting a little water into the pump speeds up the flow of water, but the output then contains both well water and the water used to prime the pump. Similarly, the data used to improve recall may become mixed in with the information stored in the person's memory.

This occurs because memory is *associative*. Thinking about a list of related objects (e.g., *haystack, thread, thimble, eye,* and *sewing*) activates associated semantic (mental information) networks, causing one to think of an object related to the list (e.g., *needle*). When asked to recall the original list of items, most people incorrectly claim that *needle* was included, *even when they have been alerted that there may have been an attempt to suggest a false memory.* Once the concept of "needle" is activated via the information provided, it becomes a"real" memory regardless of accuracy.

A particular mood-state might occasionally serve as a kind of "context" that could facilitate retrieval of memories. For example, making a detainee anxious might possibly cause him to remember events that he experienced at other times in his life when he experienced anxiety. However, *while in a state of anxiety, he may be less able to remember events that he experienced when he was in different mood-states, such as being excited or calm.* Thus, although internal mood-state can become a cue to information associated with that mood, retrieval of information may be impaired when the mood is incongruent with the memory.

How Might Stress Affect a High-Value Detainee's Ability to Recall Information?

In the past, many interrogators mistakenly believed that increased levels of stress (i.e., distress) have minor or no negative consequences for memory and, further, that high levels of stress can actually facilitate the retrieval process (see *Stress*). In fact, stress is a complex concept and is not well understood empirically as it applies to the intelligence interviewing environment. However, research in cognitive science does show quite clearly that high levels of stress do affect memory, and generally do not enhance it.

Behavioral research also suggests that memory suffers when a person is "multitasking" and that any type of stressor – physical, mental, or emotional – may add to a person's "cognitive load." Under stress, mental resources that a person could use for accurate and detailed retrieval may be diverted to processing information about the stressor. For example, the more stress students experience before and during a difficult exam, the more poorly they usually perform. Distractions introduced during the exam may further detract from optimal performance. Similarly, a detainee will probably have more difficulty accurately and fully recalling the details of a conversation he had overheard between fellow terrorists if he cannot take his mind off his belief that his family is in danger.

The Effects of Highly Stressful Situations on Memory

According to a report published in the *International Journal of Law and Psychiatry*, "Contrary to the popular conception that most people would never forget the face of a clearly seen individual who had physically confronted them and threatened them for more than 30 minutes, a large number of subjects in this study were unable to correctly identify their perpetrator."

Five hundred and nine recruited participants took part in the project, which involved four separate but similar studies. Participants were active duty military personnel enrolled in SERE (survival, evasion, resistance, and escape) training, where the nature of the stressful conditions is patterned after those reported by military personnel who had been prisoners of war (POWs). The SERE training includes food and sleep deprivation for 48 hours followed by simulated, yet very realistic, interrogations. The interrogations were either "high stress" (including physical confrontation) or "low stress" (during which the interrogator attempted to trick the subject into revealing information). Twenty-four hours after release from the mock POW camp, the participants were asked to identify their interrogator and/or guard from either a live"line up" or from photographs. Over half of participants in low-stress interrogations were better able to identify their captors than participants in high-stress interrogations. Highlighting the complicated nature of stress and memory, however, many individuals from the high- and low-stress interrogations were equally able to recognize their captors, and a minority of participants in high-stress interrogations were better able to remember their captors compared to participants in low-stress interrogations.[21]

Key Points

Changes in Detail Do Not Necessarily Imply Deception

Research on memory suggests that intelligence interviewing professionals should not automatically interpret alterations in memory content as attempts to deceive. Changes in the details of a detainee's story might be a byproduct of the elaborative nature of memory retrieval.

High-Value Detainees' Stories and Level of Detail Will Vary

People often remember the same situation very differently. These differences are due to many factors, to include individuals' level of interest in and familiarity with a specific topic, their skill in recalling information, and how they are asked to recall the information. Therefore, intelligence interviewing professionals might expect that two sources who attended the same meeting would report some similar but also some different memories. While general themes are likely to be consistent, detailed information will probably vary.

Questions Might Minimize Leading Information

Research suggests that an intelligence interviewing professional might seek to include as little leading information as possible in his initial questions. Each bit of information presented to the detainee activates networks of information potentially available for retrieval. But when parts of given memories become activated, the detainee may misinterpret his sense of familiarity with that information as evidence that he has an accurate memory of a first-hand experience. The interviewer's efforts to "fill in"information gaps might well contaminate details of information and possibly subsequent retrieval.

Insights into the nature of *primed information* and *suggestibility* indicate that intelligence interviewing professionals might also try to be judicious in how they employ such questioning techniques as *repeated questions*(designed to check the detainee's veracity) and *rapid fire questions*. Under certain conditions, each technique has the potential to undermine accurate recall. To protect against alterations of memory content, intelligence interviewers might cast a"wide net" (e.g., "Tell me how you got here")before narrowing in on specific topics ("Identify every person you saw at the safe house you ran").

Cognitive Interviews Can Improve Recall

The Cognitive Interview has empirical support as a method for enhancing recall and has been widely used for enhancing the accuracy of eyewitness memory. This style of interview helps by utilizing many of the techniques mentioned above, such as *cueing, prompting,* and helping the detainee recall the *context* of the event.

The Cognitive Interview asks four specific questions, some about linear sequences, others about contextual associations:

> 1.   Tell me everything you can remember about the event, including what you saw, heard, touched, smelled, and tasted. (Context Reinstatement)

> 2.   If I were an observer of the event, tell me what I would have seen (smelled, etc.). (Change of Perspective).

> 3. Tell me everything that happened, only this time go in reverse order. (Alteration of Sequence).

4. Try hard to tell me everything you can remember about the event, and don't leave anything out. (Increased Effort and Reiteration).

Areas of Potential Operational Interest That Merit Further Research

- How can the Cognitive Interview be adapted for a detainee population? What other questioning protocols might be employed to foster accurate and detailed recall?

- How might environmental conditions (the conditions of confinement and of intelligence interviewing) be designed to promote accurate and detailed recall?

- What visual, auditory, or kinesthetic cues might be introduced to foster memory but not induce false memories? For example, do music, tastes, or smells have an effect on memory?

- If so, what kinds of music, food, tastes, and smells, for which persons, in what situations, under what conditions, might enhance memory?

- How might the circumstances and emotional context in which the detainee acquired the information that is being sought be estimated and assessed?

- How does language affect recall? For example, might a detainee's recall improve, or change, if he were questioned in his native language rather than in what is for him a second language?

- Under what circumstances and conditions might a detainee be vulnerable to developing false memories that he believes to be true?

- For example, how may a desire to please the intelligence interviewing professional predispose the detainee to fabricate information that he believes to be true?

- What are the potential impacts of captivity-related stresses on a detainee's memories (see *Stress*)?

105

- What may be the effects of a strong operational accord on a detainee's memories?

Endnotes

[1] Robert B. Cialdini, *Influence: the Psychology of Persuasion*, Revised Edition (New York: Quill, 1993)

[2] Dan Ariely, *Predictably Irrational: The Hidden Forces That Shape Our Decisions* (New York: Harper, 2008)

[3] Ulrich Straus, *The Anguish of Surrender: Japanese POW's of World War II* (Seattle, WA: University of Washington Press, 2003)

[4] Cialdini, op.cit.

[5] Cialdini, op.cit. [6] Roger Fisher and Daniel Shapiro, *Beyond Reason: Using Emotions as You Negotiate*(New York: Viking, 2005)

[7] Howard Gardner, *Changing Minds: The Art and Science of Changing Our Own And Other People's Minds* (Boston, MA: Harvard Business School Press, 2006)

[8] Joshua Kurlantzick, "Fighting Terrorism with Terrorists," *The Los Angeles Times*, Jan. 6, 2008.

[9] International Crisis Group; "Deradicalisation"and Indonesian Prisons," *Asia Report* N° 142, 19 November 2007

[10] Gardner, op.cit.

[11] William A. Donohue and Paul J. Taylor, Role Effects In Negotiation: The One-Down Effect, Negotiation Journal, Vol 23, No. 3 (July 2007), p. 322

[12] Merle L. Pribbenow, "The Man in the Snow White Cell," Studies in Intelligence, Vol. 48, No. 1. [Appended to this document.]

[13] S. Kleinman, "MIS-Y: A Case Study in Strategic Interrogation," unpublished paper, 2008

[14] John A. Burden, Captain, U.S. Army. "Interrogation of Japanese Prisoners in the Southwest Pacific: Intelligence Memo No. 4." 22 July 1943. Enemy Prisoner of War Interrogation Files (MIS-Y), 1943–1945.

Records of the War Department General and Special Staffs, Record Group 165. NARA, College Park, MD

[15] Rosen, J.B., Schulkin, J. (1998) From normal fear to pathological anxiety. Psychological Review 105(2), 325-350.

[16] The theory of learned helplessness was first developed in the 1960s as a result of experiments with animals. It emerged from studies showing that many dogs who were exposed to inescapable shock eventually stopped trying to escape, even when placed in situations where they had the opportunity to do so. (Seligman & Maier, 1967; Overmier & Seligman, 1967) The theory of learned helplessness has evolved over the years as it applies to humans. Today, a good deal of research suggests that people with a certain attributional style are more prone to experience feelings of learned helplessness and ultimately depression. These feelings are often associated with the feeling of uncontrollability, a lack of motivation, and poor cognition.

[17] Larry Guarino, *A P.O.W.'s Story: 2801 Days in Hanoi* (New York: Ballantine Books, 1990)

[18] Knowles, E. S. & Linn, J. A. (Eds.), *Resistance and Persuasion.* (Mahwah, NJ: Lawrence Erlbaum Associates, 2004)

[19] Knowles, E. S., & Riner, D. D. "Omega approaches to persuasion: overcoming resistance". In A. R. Pratkanis (Ed.), *Science of Social Influence.* (New York: Psychology Press, 2006)

[20] Jacks, J. Z., & O'Brien, M. E. "Decreasing resistance by affirming the self," In Knowles, E. S. & Linn, J. A. (Eds.), Resistance and Persuasion. (Mahwah, NJ: Lawrence Erlbaum Associates, 2004), pp. 235-257

[21] *International Journal of Psychiatry and the Law,* Vol. 27/3: 265–279, May/Ju

Section II - Case Studies and Teaching Notes

Introduction

Case Studies and Teaching Notes

This section contains two case studies and associated teaching notes. The first study describes early intelligence interviews of Mohammed Rasheed Daoud al'Owhali, a key figure in the bombing of the U.S. embassy in Nairobi, Kenya, in 1998. The second examines the interrogation of Nguyen Tai, the most senior North Vietnamese officer captured during the Vietnam War.

These two case studies, together with their teaching notes, offer practical illustrations of the concepts discussed in the six teaching papers in this booklet. The cases are intended for use in conjunction with the papers. Like the teaching papers, the case studies are necessarily brief. The ideas raised provide a basis for discussion, analysis, and research about intelligence interviewing.

Each case is presented in two versions: the case by itself, and the same case augmented with teaching notes. (For the sake of brevity, footnotes, endnotes, and references appear only in the first version.) In the teaching notes, behavioral science concepts from the six papers are highlighted in bold italic print.

Each of the behavioral science concepts represents a kind of shorthand. For example, readers should interpret the term *information power* as encompassing both the information itself and a person's expertise in analysis and in using the information. Similarly, the term *relationship power* spans concepts such as liking, the impulse toward reciprocity, and the effectiveness of legitimate authority, moral authority, charisma, perceived trustworthiness, leadership, emotional and social intelligence, and empathy. In this booklet, a *fallback position* means an alternative plan or action – for the detainee or intelligence interviewing professional – that a person perceives as available. (Some readers may know this concept as a BATNA.)

Incentive power and the *power of disincentives* both include *"tangible things of value"* and *"intangibles."* The idea of *disincentives* is discussed in the six papers and al-'Owhali primarily in terms of intangibles. *Disincentives* as used in discussions of *Tai* include extended periods of solitary confinement, temperature extremes, gross physical discomfort, and torture.

The teaching notes also use a kind of shorthand to refer to various *principles of persuasion* and the *core emotional concerns*, as well as ideas about understanding and dealing with *interests, social identities and constituencies*; *resistances*; *stress* and issues of *memory*. If a term seems unfamiliar, readers may find it helpful to refer to the relevant discussion in the six concept papers. Case studies may help to improve and extend our understanding of intelligence interviewing and contribute ideas for research. While military, law enforcement, and intelligence organizations have produced various kinds of after-action reports on interrogations, "thick" cases for teaching are rare to non-existent. By the same token, the two cases in this booklet are lean: al-'Owhali draws on one FBI agent's memories and various records while *Tai* incorporates interrogator memories and some of the recollections of Nguyen Tai as culled from Tai's own memoirs. These form the base case, written by a highly skilled (retired) CIA professional. (There are also a few excerpts from articles about Tai.) Each of these sources is clearly very important.

Ideally, future teaching case studies could reflect the viewpoints of more actors, and include more records and many more details about the context. For example:

•In the case of *Tai*, the Pribbenow case study draws on Tai's own memoir. It would be valuable to have a similar account from al-'Owhali as well, so the case could reflect al-'Owhali's report of his thinking.

•The case of *Tai* includes some recollections from American interrogators about the intelligence interviews with Tai. It would have been valuable to have access to any recollections from South Vietnamese interrogators and South Vietnamese guards about interactions with Tai.

The case of *al-'Owhali* includes an overview of the intelligence information received from the detainee. *Tai* might be a stronger case if some of the intelligence reports from the South Vietnamese and American interrogators had been available.

The notes on the two case studies are intended to raise ideas, not to prescribe a "right way" to conduct intelligence interviews. Despite their limited scope, these two case studies of high-value detainees do offer a number of ideas for consideration and discussion:

Intelligence interviewing professionals may find that understanding and carefully utilizing the multiple, non-coercive *sources of power* can help them craft effective interview strategies.

Intelligence interviewing professionals may find that understanding and carefully utilizing the multiple, non-coercive *sources of persuasion* can help them craft effective interview strategies.

Information, relationship, and a *fallback* position (BATNA) are important sources of power for both interviewers and detainees. They also help to enhance the power of *incentives and disincentives*.

An *operational accord* built on non-coercive persuasion may enable intelligence interviewing professionals to obtain both *useful* and "*complete*" information.

Effective intelligence interviewers are able to identify, avoid, and work with many types of *resistances*.

Understanding – and also finding commonalities with – a detainee's *interests and social identities* may enhance persuasion.

Understanding and working with a detainee's *core emotional concerns* may enhance persuasion.

The interviewing *context* and the whole environment for the team appear to be very important. As examples, guards may have played significant roles in both *Tai* and *al-'Owhali*. Time pressure was important in each case.

A team approach may greatly enhance the effectiveness of HVD interviewing, especially with respect to seeking, analyzing, and using *information*.

Stress may either enhance or hinder the effectiveness of intelligence interviewing, and may affect *memory*.

Fourteen Days in Nairobi: The Interrogation of Mohammed Rasheed Daoud al-'Owhali

April 2009
The Nairobi Embassy Bombing

FBI Special Agent Stephen Gaudin[1] had just wrapped up an assignment and was heading out on vacation. He had been supporting the 1998 Goodwill Games, an international sporting event held that year in the New York (NY) metropolitan area. With five years in the Bureau, he had recently transferred to the NY office in Manhattan from his previous Kingston, NY, post. In upstate New York, he had gained criminal law enforcement experience by pursuing drug dealers, bank robbers, fugitives, and kidnappers. He had never been involved in a terrorism investigation.

On August 7, 1998, at around 10:30 AM local time, two near-simultaneous bomb attacks hit the US embassies in Nairobi, Kenya, and Dar es Salaam, Tanzania. The Nairobi attack killed 218 people, including 12 Americans, and injured thousands of others, many of them blinded by flying glass.[2] The Joint Terrorism Task Force (JTTF) based at the FBI NY office suspected al Qa'ida,[3] a group completely unknown to most of the law enforcement community at the time. The NY office pressed hard to lead the investigation. In the end, the FBI deployed over 300 agents from both the Washington and NY field offices to investigate the embassy bombings: the largest number of agents working on any overseas investigation in the history of the FBI.

The FBI chose Gaudin for the investigative team in part to provide security. He had been an officer in the Army's 82nd Airborne Division and had seen six years of active service. In addition to his military experience, thirty-five-year-old Gaudin was a member of the NY Office's SWAT team and was assigned a collapsible MP-5 submachine gun. His initial assignment on the trip was as bodyguard to Pat D'Amuro, the Assistant Special Agent in Charge of the NY Field Office's National Security Division, who was going to Nairobi. It would be Gaudin's first trip to Africa.

[1] A team comprising psychologists, intelligence interviewers, and information specialists interviewed Gaudin for this report in 2008–2009. In addition, team members reviewed court records from the trial of Mohammed Rasheed Daoud al-'Owhali: *United States of America v. Usama bin Laden, et al.* U.S. District Court, Southern District of New York, S (7) 98 Cr. 1023, February 5–July 10, 2001. The study chair thanks senior FBI leadership for permitting SSA Gaudin to share his recollections of this case.

[2] See the Appendix to this case study for a brief summary of the Nairobi Embassy bombing. The embassy's Emergency Action Plan did not include provisions for vehicular bombs. Embassy employees were not trained to seek cover or stay clear of windowbrs in such circumstances. See U.S. Department of State, "Report of the Accountability Review Boards, Bombings of the US Embassies in Nairobi, Kenya and Dar es Salaam, Tanzania, on August 7, 1998," January 1999;

http://www.state.gov/www/regions/africa/board_overview.html

[3] Alec Station, a CIA unit dedicated to tracking bin Laden, was set up in January 1996. They uncovered an al Qaeda presence in Kenya that same year.

With a police escort, the NY team traveled by city transit bus to Washington, D.C. Gaudin lay down in the aisle of the bus to catch what sleep he could before the mission began. The team boarded a C-5 military cargo plane. Gaudin, familiar with flying on military aircraft, was able to sleep more easily than most others on the transatlantic flight. The team was on the ground in Kenya on August 9, oneand-one-half days after the blasts. They were met at the Nairobi airport by Kenyans with little knowledge of English. Luckily, they had a female agent on board who could speak Swahili.

The U.S. Government Case Study of Human Manipulation

The Man Who Didn't Fit In

When the FBI team arrived at the blast site, search and rescue teams were still pulling people out of the rubble. US officials, including the FBI, set up a command post, as well as a tip line, at another country's embassy building. The tip line received hundreds of calls of many different kinds. For example, zealous callers provided leads pointing to a "suspicious man with a pizza oven," a Somali "ninja team" allegedly dropped by helicopter, and "a Lebanese man at the train station."

Among these calls was one fielded by Special Agent Debbie Doran. It reported "a man at the Ramadah Hotel who didn't fit in." The man apparently had been injured in the attack and was refusing help. Doran kept the reluctant caller on the line, even persuading him to agree to call back.

On August 11, D'Amuro realized the futility of having a bodyguard amidst the chaos of downtown Nairobi. He reassigned Gaudin to follow up on "the man who didn't fit in." Nobody knew if this man had played any role in the Nairobi attack. "If you don't like that lead," D'Amuro told Gaudin, "I've got plenty of other ones."

On the morning of August 12, FBI Special Agent Steven Bongardt and New York City Police Detective Wayne Parola joined Gaudin for the ride to follow up on "the man who did not fit in." All three men served on the JTTF, but they had no prior experience working together. They were accompanied by two Kenyan Criminal Investigation Division (CID) officers and a Kenyan driver. They traveled in an enclosed truck with the CID men in the cab and the Americans in the back.

As it turned out, the Ramadah Hotel was in Eastleigh, a 30-minute drive from the capital city. As they neared the hotel, they drove through an open-air market and refugee slum where men walked the streets armed with AK-47s. Gaudin banged on the window separating the cab from the bed of the truck. "Where are we going?" he demanded. The CID men stopped the truck and walked to the back to speak to the Americans. They explained that Eastleigh was inhabited mainly by Somalis. In fact, Eastleigh was also known by the nickname Somalitown. The Kenyans warned their colleagues, "Keep down. They don't like Americans here."

Gaudin tried to contact D'Amuro to inform him of the apparent threat in their surroundings. D'Amuro, Gaudin believed, would have wanted to make the call on whether the group should proceed. But phone service was out and D'Amuro could not be reached. They continued on their mission.

The truck pulled to a stop in Somalitown. Many people were in the streets, and they quickly became interested in the truck. A man on the street approached their vehicle, leaned his back against the truck and, without trying to draw attention, stated, "I told you not to come here. What are you doing here? You are going to get me killed!"

Realizing he may have been the tip line caller, Gaudin asked him his name. When he refused to answer the agents asked, "What about calling you Bill?"

"No, I don't like this name," he replied.
"How about Michael? Everyone likes Michael Jordan."

"Okay, I like this name." He informed them, "The man you are looking for is no longer at the Ramadah Hotel. He is at the IFTIN Lodge." The IFTIN Lodge was also located in Eastleigh, near the Ramadah.

Their arrival at IFTIN Lodge attracted a lot of attention. A crowd started to form. The Americans in the truck recalled that the 1993 Battle of Mogadishu ended with 18 American soldiers and at least 3000 Somali militia and civilians killed. It seemed safer for the Americans to stay in the truck than to go into the hotel.

The CID detectives confirmed that there was a man in the hotel who had recently checked in. They did not immediately go to the room and pick him up because they were unarmed. They told the Americans that, as sergeants, they had not yet been issued guns. Gaudin lent them a pistol and holster. He held onto his MP-5.

The Kenyans returned with the suspect. The man had visible stitches on his forehead and bandages on his hands. In his pockets he had 1900 Ksh (Kenyan Shillings), equivalent to $32, and also eight $100 banknotes. These bills featured the oversized Benjamin Franklin, and had first been issued in 1996 as part of the U.S. currency redesign. (These new $100 bills were not fully in circulation back home; Gaudin had never seen one before.) The suspect also had a casualty card, in the name of Khalid Salim, from MP Shah Hospital in Nairobi, stamped August 7, 1998.

Interview and Investigation
August 12

The "man who didn't fit in" claimed to be Khalid Salim Saleh bin Rasheed from Yemen. He spoke Arabic, but said he spoke only minimal English and no Swahili. He claimed to have lost all his belongings in the blast, although he wore clean clothes. Kenyan law stipulates that a person may be detained for 48 hours if he or she cannot produce identification. Since the suspect had no official ID or passport, the Kenyans took him into custody for further investigation. Bin Rasheed was put in the back of the truck, without handcuffs.

What with the presence of guns, an unrestrained person of interest, the tight quarters, and the crowds outside, the mood in the back of the truck was understandably tense. Gaudin spoke to the suspect in English to inform him of their destination and assure him of his safety. "Everything will be okay," Gaudin said, gently touching the man's knee.

When Gaudin was a boy, his grandmother had given him butterscotch as a way to comfort him, and he had brought butterscotch with him to Africa. Wanting to reduce the tension, Gaudin reached into his pocket and handed out butterscotch candy to everyone in the truck, including the detainee. Bin Rasheed accepted the candy, smiled graciously, and remained calm. He indicated that he understood he would be safe. The Americans did not question bin Rasheed in the truck.

For the first two nights, the suspect was kept in a general holding cell at the Jomo Kenyatta Airport Police Station in Nairobi. He shared his cell with one other individual who, as it turned out, was not involved in the attacks. The suspect was then transferred to Kenyan CID Headquarters.

Back at the Command Post, Parola read the suspect his Advice of Rights (AOR) in English. (In Kenya, the right to a lawyer does not attach immediately, and refusing to answer questions *may* be used against you.) Department of Justice attorneys had counseled the FBI to use the overseas AOR form, which read as follows:

We are representatives of the United States Government. Under our laws, you have certain rights. Before we ask you any questions, we want to be sure that you understand those rights. You do not have to speak to us or answer any questions. Even if you have already spoken to the Kenyan authorities, you do not have to speak to us now.

If you do speak with us, anything that you say may be used against you in a court in the United States or elsewhere.

In the United States, you would have the right to talk to a lawyer to get advice before we ask you any questions and you could have a lawyer with you during questioning. In the United States, if you could not afford a lawyer, one would be appointed for you, if you wish, before any questioning.

Because we are not in the United States, we cannot ensure that you will have a lawyer appointed for you before any questioning. If you decide to speak with us now, without a lawyer present, you will still have the right to stop answering questions at any time.

You should also understand that if you decide not to speak with us, that fact cannot be used as evidence against you in a court in the United States.

I have read this statement of my rights and I understand what my rights are. I am willing to make a statement and answer questions. I do not want a lawyer at this time. I understand and know what I am doing. No promises or threats have been made to me and no pressure or coercion of any kind has been used against me.

Parola and Gaudin questioned the suspect in a small room at the Kenyan CID Headquarters while Bongardt went out to verify bin Rasheed's story. With experience working Hezbollah cases for JTTF, Parola initially did almost all the questioning.

The first interview lasted one hour and was conducted in broken English. Bin Rasheed stated that he was a khat[4] salesman. He claimed to have flown to Nairobi from Yemen to visit Harun, a 28-year-old man whom he had met a year before. When Harun failed to pick him up at the airport, bin Rasheed took a taxi to the Ramadah Hotel, a 30-minute drive from the airport. He further stated that the taxi driver chose the hotel because Arabic was spoken there. Later, Harun picked him up at the hotel and took him to his house in Nairobi. Bin Rasheed claimed he was standing in a bank near the embassy at the time of the explosion. He said that he had lost his briefcase, which contained his passport, in the chaos following the "accident" in the capital. He also lost sight of his friend Harun, and assumed that he had died in the explosion. Bin Rasheed reported that he visited a walk-in clinic and was transferred to a hospital where he received stitches to his forehead, his wrists, and the center of his back. Unable to find his way back to Harun's house, he returned to the Ramadah Hotel. Having lost all his possessions, he negotiated with the hotel to stay without payment. He claimed to be wearing the clothes he wore on the day of the blast.

Bin Rasheed's story just did not sound right to the Americans. They did not suspect that bin Rasheed had played a role in the attack, but they thought his story warranted further investigation. They made arrangements to secure an Arabic translator for the second interview in order to capture the story more clearly.

[4] Khat is an amphetamine-like stimulant common in East Africa and the Arabian Peninsula. It is an important crop in Yemen, but is banned in Saudi Arabia.

A native Arabic speaker, a woman, served as their first translator. Both bin Rasheed and the translator were uncomfortable being in the same room. Gaudin hung his poncho liner in a doorway as a makeshift curtain and positioned the suspect on one side and the translator on the other. Gaudin read the overseas AOR aloud and the interpreter orally translated it into Arabic. After the suspect spoke just one sentence, the translator called a time out and beckoned the Americans to her side of the curtain. She reported that bin Rasheed spoke *fusha*, a classical rather than a colloquial form of Arabic. According to her, this indicated that he was well educated and certainly not a "poor or working class person."

Over the course of the three-hour interview, bin Rasheed claimed to have flown in from Yemen and to have received money from his

Yemeni uncle Mohammed bin Rasheed.

At one point, the team photographed bin Rasheed, documenting his wounds. They discovered more lacerations in addition to those on his forehead and hands: his clean shirt had hidden the big bandages covering stitches on his back.

Understanding the Context of the Interviews

When logistically possible, Gaudin went to bin Rasheed's holding cell, then walked with him to the interview room. Gaudin arranged for bin Rasheed to be without handcuffs. While they walked Gaudin would often ask bin Rasheed, "You okay?" Outside the interview room, bin Rasheed would converse in broken English with Gaudin about current events, even asking about the Monica Lewinsky scandal. Bin Rasheed asked, "What's with your president?" while shaking his finger, implying "shame, shame, shame."

Whenever bin Rasheed asked for permission, he was allowed to pray. Gaudin accompanied bin Rasheed to the bathroom so he could wash in preparation for prayer. Having never seen this ritual before, Gaudin asked him to explain what he was doing. Bin Rasheed showed Gaudin his washing ritual and explained its significance.

Gaudin spontaneously shared several meals with bin Rasheed during the interviews. Gaudin would often miss breakfast due to his interviewing schedule, so he would bring MREs [Meals Ready to Eat] to the interview room. Gaudin noticed bin Rasheed's interest while he made "Ranger cookies," a famous concoction of cocoa powder, crackers, non-dairy creamer, and coffee. He asked bin Rasheed if he would like some, and in fact these"cookies" became a favorite snack for the prisoner.
August 13

On day two, the JTTF team started checking out parts of bin Rasheed's story. They looked at hundreds of paper arrival and departure cards at the Nairobi airport. Bin Rasheed had taken Gulf Air Flight 0713 from the United Arab Emirates (UAE) – not Yemen. His arrival card listed the Ramadah Hotel as his intended destination – the very hotel he earlier had claimed "the taxi driver had chosen" for him.

The U.S. Government Case Study of Human Manipulation

During the third interview, Parola's tone became livelier and louder. According to Gaudin, Parola sensed that bin Rasheed did not like him and built on that dislike, setting up Gaudin as the good guy. Parola confronted the suspect about the inconsistencies in his story and asked him accusingly, "What else are you lying about?" Bin Rasheed denied lying about anything.

Gaudin then took the lead and told the suspect that his story was not believable. He accused bin Rasheed of having the same counter-interrogation training that Gaudin had received in the military. "If you remember your training, you are supposed to tell a story that would be believable and easy to remember. But, most important, your story is supposed to be *logical*."This got the suspect's attention. Bin Rasheed pulled his chair closer to Gaudin and asked, "Where was I illogical?"

Gaudin offered a few examples."Why does your airport arrival card list the Ramadah Hotel as your intended destination when you claim the taxi driver chose it? Why did you ask the Ramadah for time to pay for your room? Why not use the money that you have? Why didn't you go to the Yemeni embassy?"

To the last question, bin Rasheed replied, "I didn't want them to think I was involved"in what he referred to as "the accident."

Bin Rasheed had large cuts and other injuries, yet no blood on his pants or shirt. Gaudin tried to get bin Rasheed to admit that his clothes were too new and clean to have been worn on the day he was injured in the "accident." Gaudin talked about the neatness of his appearance. "I've been in the country a shorter time than you and my clothes are dirty."

Bin Rasheed replied in a fairly flippant, almost smug way, "Arab men are cleaner."

Gaudin challenged in a firm, fairly unemotional tone, "You have a solution for getting rid of blood? Okay, that is logical. And it is logical that God made a piece of glass slip down your shirt and make a right turn and cause a big injury to your back. And all this happened without putting a hole in your shirt or a scar anywhere else on your back." "Anything can happen with God's grace," bin Rasheed responded.

Gaudin also noticed that bin Rasheed's belt appeared brand-new – yet another indicator that a part of the detainee's story could not possibly be true. Gaudin intended to compare their two belts for signs of wear. He hoped to prove the belt was new and catch the suspect in a lie about the clothes. So......... Gaudin began his gambit slowly, by leaning over and intently studying bin Rasheed's shoes. He wanted bin Rasheed to be thinking about anything other than his belt.

Conscious of Gaudin's staring at his shoes, bin Rasheed defensively said that one couldn't expect one's shoes to stay clean in such a dusty environment. Catching bin Rasheed off guard, Gaudin replied, "I don't care about your shoes. I care about your belt." Gaudin got up, and in a swift movement unbuckled his own belt, showing the suspect how stretch and sweat marks develop in a worn belt. He then slammed his hand against the table and shouted at bin Rasheed to stand up and take off his belt. Bin Rasheed snapped to attention like a new recruit at basic training. When bin Rasheed unbuckled his belt, not only was it unworn, but, to everyone's surprise, a price tag in Kenyan shillings was clearly visible on the inside surface. The suspect sat back down deflated and said to Gaudin, "You're good." He then asked to pray.

The team declared a time out for prayer. When they resumed the interview, bin Rasheed sat back down in the chair with, it seemed, renewed energy. At the same moment, Bongardt knocked on the door, eager to question the suspect on the basis of information he had gathered at the hotel where bin Rasheed had been staying. Because the team members had not conferred among themselves prior to Bongardt's entrance, Bongardt was unaware of the progress that had been made. Gaudin later chided himself for neglecting to coordinate thoroughly with Bongardt.

Bongardt accused bin Rasheed of wearing new clothes, explaining that he knew someone had brought new clothes to bin Rasheed at the hotel and that the old clothes were put into a brown bag. Bin Rasheed remained silent, laughing.

The team then called in John Anticev, an experienced FBI agent – they wanted his professional opinion given his legendary successes interviewing terrorists in the past. Anticev had worked the 1993 World Trade Center attack as well as the case against Omar Abdel-Rahman, the Blind Sheik. (As it happened, Anticev was leading an investigation of another suspect, Mohamed Odeh. Odeh had been picked up using a fake passport when he arrived in Pakistan on a flight from Kenya. He eventually confessed his role in the plot.) Based on his prior experiences, Anticev knew that a great deal could be learned from examining telephone records. He recommended to his colleagues, "Let's find out whom he has called."

In the presence of Gaudin and Parola, Anticev then began his discussion with bin Rasheed by asking him if he had had a chance to pray. With a calm demeanor Anticev had the suspect repeat his story, and asked bin Rasheed about persons he believed bin Rasheed knew. Bin Rasheed acknowledged that he knew them and seemed to enjoy lecturing a Westerner about the importance of these particular men. They chatted until late in the evening. "There's one other person we haven't talked about," Anticev observed. "Usama bin Laden." Bin Rasheed's eyes narrowed and he stopped talking. A small smile appeared on his face. Anticev, who had been listening like a captivated student, suddenly thrust a pen and paper into bin Rasheed's hand. "Write down the first telephone number you called after the bombing!" Bin Rasheed reported that he called Sameer al-Hada and relayed a phone number that translated from Arabic as 967-1-200578. After giving up the number, bin Rasheed stopped cooperating.[5]

The team then took custody of the clothes bin Rasheed was wearing, replacing them with a new button-down shirt and slacks. They also obtained a flight manifest indicating that bin Rasheed's flight to Nairobi had originated in Lahore, Pakistan, with connections in Karachi, Pakistan; Muscat, Oman; and Abu Dhabi, UAE. They learned that a return ticket had been issued for travel on August 10.

Gaudin, Parola, and the CID men also visited the hospital where bin Rasheed said he had been treated. Although no one remembered seeing the suspect, a janitor mopping the floor at the hospital approached the team. The janitor asked if they had come "for the keys and bullets." He said he had found keys and bullets in the hospital – on a window sill of the men's bathroom – and had called the police. The team retrieved these items from the Kenyan police, not knowing they would have any significance for the investigation.

The team then brought the phone number supplied by bin Rasheed to the telephone company. They asked for a list of all calls made to the Yemeni number from anywhere in Kenya during the first two weeks of August.

The Kenyans upgraded the charge against bin Rasheed from inability to provide identification to suspicion of murder. Bin Rasheed could now be held for fourteen days before being formally charged with murder.

August 14

In the fourth interview, Parola told bin Rasheed, "Stop calling the explosions an 'accident.'" He showed him morgue photographs and asked, "Why did so many people have to die? If the real target was the embassy, why did so many innocent Kenyans have to die?"

[5] Details of the Anticev/bin Rasheed interchange are drawn from Wright, L. (2006). *The looming tower: Al-Qaeda and the road to 9/11, pg. 277.* New York: Knopf. As Wright points out, this Yemeni telephone number would prove to be one of the most important pieces of information the FBI would ever discover, allowing investigators to map the links of the al-Qaeda network all across the globe.

Provoked, bin Rasheed lectured on the injustices in Palestine and refugee camps in Southern Lebanon. He fumed, "Your embassy was attacked because of your foreign policy!"

For logistical purposes, on his third night of detention, bin Rasheed was moved to a private holding cell in the basement of Kenyan CID headquarters. where the interviews were taking place.

August 15

On day four, bin Rasheed asked,"Are we going to clear up my file today?" The team decided to leave the suspect alone in his cell. They did not want him to think he was especially important. They also needed time to run down leads, write reports, and digest what they had learned so far.

August 16

Gaudin discreetly observed bin Rasheed reading an English-language magazine in his cell. When he inquired, the Swahili-speaking guards reported that they had been able to communicate with the detainee in English without difficulty. The guards confiscated the magazine without revealing that an interrogator had seen it.

Gaudin entered the cell and asked bin Rasheed if he needed anything. Bin Rasheed requested some milk, which Gaudin delivered. Bin Rasheed thanked Gaudin for the milk.

There was no interview on August 16.
August 17

The FBI brought in their own Lebanese-American interpreter, an older man named Mike Feghali whom Gaudin described as looking and acting like"your favorite uncle."[6] Parola took the lead in the next interview. The interviewers brought in the morgue photos once again, since this had seemed to draw an emotional response from bin Rasheed in past interviews. They showed bin Rasheed a picture of a baby and mother fused together. Parola relentlessly repeated statements like, "This wasn't necessary." "Someone screwed up." "Why was the bomb put there?" "Why did so many innocent people have to die?" Bin Rasheed finally responded, "You're saying this is *my* fault? This is *your* fault. This is *America's* fault!"

[6] The interpreter was Christian, not Muslim, a fact none of the investigators was aware of during the interrogations.

Parola challenged bin Rasheed about some of the inconsistencies in his story, and bin Rasheed admitted to getting his cash via wire transfer from his friend Sameer al-Hada, whom he had called at the Yemeni number. The money was transferred to a shop in Eastleigh called Sheer Gold. Parola continued to confront bin Rasheed emotionally and relentlessly, and finally got him to admit that the U.S. embassy was the target of the attack. With emotions high, bin Rasheed launched into a tirade, shouting "If you put me on trial for this my tribe is going to kill you," and pushed Parola. He turned to Gaudin and threatened him and his family as well.

August 18, 19, and 20
On August 18, bin Rasheed received medical attention from an FBI

paramedic. His stitches were removed.

The U.S. team did not have access to the suspect on August 18 and 19. The Kenyan CID were preparing for an identification parade, a procedure similar to a police lineup in the United States. Previously hospitalized eyewitnesses were now ready to view the suspect. Kenyan law stipulates that a lineup be administered by police officers not affiliated with the investigation at hand. The identification parade was held at another police station miles outside the city on the morning of August 20. Eight stand-ins appeared in the lineup together with bin Rasheed. In Kenya, the witness must face the lineup without the protection of a one-way mirror and the witness must touch the shoulder of the accused to single him out. Out of six witnesses who claimed to have seen the persons involved in the attack, one identified bin Rasheed as the man who got out of the truck that had exploded. The rest of the witnesses failed to make any identification.

It had taken a little time to learn about calls made to the phone number, but on August 20 the team received the Kenyan reports on the phone number provided by bin Rasheed. Gaudin and Bongardt pored over the reports. The phone number was, in fact, a Yemeni number. Only two within-Kenya phone numbers had placed calls to that number: a call center situated near the Ramadah and IFTIN hotels, and a house in Nairobi.

In Kenya, the telephone company keeps a written record of the caller's name when collect calls are placed. The collect call log listed the caller as Khalid Salim. The call center fit with bin Rasheed's story, but the house clearly required further investigation. A series of other calls had also been made from the house before the bombing, the last of which had been initiated less than one hour before the attack.

The house was located at 43 Runda Estates. It was a nice villa with a two-car garage in a part of town where many embassy officials from various countries resided. The landlord described the tenant as "a local guy living with a bunch of Arabs." The tenant had a six-month lease and had paid the lease term and security deposit in cash[7] in May. On the day of the bombing, it was reported, the tenant returned to pick up his security deposit and return the keys.

Bongardt took photos of the house. The FBI team was not able to get an Evidence Response Team (ERT) to the house right away. When they finally checked the villa, the ERT reported no evidence of explosive residue. Incredulous, Gaudin found out that the team had skipped the garage. D'Amuro sent the ERT back. This time they got a positive test. "The garage lit up like a Christmas tree," they said.

At this point in the investigation, the team noticed a heightened interest in their case. Supervisors now asked regularly for status updates and reports.8

On the night of August 20, the United States launched Tomahawk missile strikes against locations in Sudan and Afghanistan in retaliation for the embassy bombings. The al-Shifa pharmaceutical plant in Khartoum, alleged to be producing chemical weapons for al Qa'ida, was destroyed.[9] In Afghanistan, terrorist training camps near Khost were targeted; however, bin Laden and his men had already fled in anticipation of U.S. retaliation.[10]

Officials in Washington, considering the situation on the ground in Kenya to be too dangerous, started pulling the FBI out of Nairobi. D'Amuro recalled Parola first. Gaudin and Bongardt then focused on getting as much information as possible out of the suspect before they too would be pulled out.

August 21

On August 21, the Kenyan newspaper *The Nation* ran a short front-page article with the headline, "Face of the Grenade Thrower." Bin Rasheed, the paper reported, was accused of riding in the bomb truck and throwing a grenade at guards before the embassy blast. The story was complete with a picture of a smiling bin Rasheed with hands clasped together in a triumphant pose. Although the article included no statement by the suspect, it seemed clear that bin Rasheed must have cooperated with the photographer. It appeared that the photographer had paid someone off to get access to the detainee. Interestingly, the reported accusations had not come from the interrogation team. In fact, the team had yet to establish bin Rasheed's role in the blast –if any.

7 It is common in Kenya to pay for such transactions in cash.8 U.S. intelligence

uncovered phone call records listing calls to the Yemeni number from UBL's satellite phone. This information was not shared at the time with the team interrogating al-'Owhali.

[9] The factory produced anti-malaria and veterinary drugs. There was ultimately no proof that the plant had been storing or manufacturing chemical weapons.

[10] At least 20 people, including locals and low-level militants, were killed in the Afghanistan strikes.

The Americans were told to wrap up whatever they could. They were to prepare to evacuate. The FBI team therefore had to deal with a likely deadline on their investigation. Gaudin fingerprinted bin Rasheed in his holding cell. Gaudin and Bongardt posed in a photo with the suspect so that they would have a means of documenting his height.[11]

The team by now had accumulated a great deal of evidence that contradicted bin Rasheed's original story. They had the phone call records, the arrival card, the flight manifest, the explosives residue test results from the house, and the deception about clothes.

Gaudin began the next interview by saying, "Today you don't get to talk. You listen." Gaudin and Bongardt told bin Rasheed that they knew he was involved and could prove it, but all they really cared about was why all those innocent people had to die. They proceeded to place much of the evidence in front of him– the phone records, arrival card, and flight manifest. Gaudin said, "We found the house. Let me describe it to you. It's a big house with a terracotta roof and a number 43 on it." When shown the photo of the villa, bin Rasheed acknowledged that the intelligence interviewers seemed to know everything.

Bin Rasheed said, "If you promise I'll be tried in the United States, I'll tell you everything. America is my enemy, not Kenya. I will tell you all about my involvement with the bombings, bin Laden, and al Qa'ida." His reasoning was that he wanted the United States to know why the bombing took place. He asked, "Will I be able to tell my story?" He wanted a guarantee from President Clinton.

Gaudin had never heard of al Qa'ida before.

The team immediately relayed the request to Patrick Fitzgerald, the

Assistant U.S. Attorney for the Southern District of New York (SDNY), who was in Kenya supporting the investigation. Bin Rasheed asked for time to pray the Istikhara, an Islamic prayer for guidance. He planned to sleep and wake up the next morning with his decision as to whether or not to cooperate with the Americans.

August 22

With bin Rasheed's significance unfolding, Gaudin suggested to Fitzgerald and D'Amuro that they "bring in the A-team" to talk with the suspect. Gaudin had hoped that Doran and Anticev would take over.

They replied, "No, you got him to the table. You need to bring him the rest of the way." Fitzgerald then explained to bin Rasheed his full AOR, not the modified overseas version. The suspect was presented a Document of Understanding (DOU) stating the suspect's rights and his desire to be tried in the United States. The DOU further stated that law enforcement would make their best efforts to bring the suspect to the United States to stand trial. The interpreter orally translated both documents into Arabic. Gaudin said to bin Rasheed, "I've been with you for ten days. You know me now. I wouldn't go over this with you if I didn't think it could really happen." After two hours of discussion, the suspect agreed to sign the form without a full guarantee that his demands would be met. He trusted the Americans would do their best.

[11] Al-'Owhali was 5'7" tall and weighed 140 lb. FBI Executive Summary (status and findings of the FBI investigation into the embassy bombings as of November 18, 1998) http://www.pbs.org/wgbh/pages/frontline/shows/binladen/bombings/summary.html

However, the suspect stated,"I cannot sign this form. This is not my name. My name is Mohammed Rasheed Daoud al-'Owhali." A new form was typed up with the correct name and al-'Owhali signed it. The DOU text read as follows:

I ... have been fully advised of my rights, including my right to remain silent and my right not to answer questions without a lawyer present. As I have been previously told, I understand that anything I say or have said can be used against me in court in the United States. I also understand that if I choose not to answer questions my refusal to answer questions cannot be held against me in court. I further understand that if I choose to answer questions, I can always change my mind and decide not to answer any further questions. I understand that both Kenyan and American authorities are investigating the murder of the various American and Kenyan victims in and around the United States embassy in Nairobi.

I have a strong preference to have my case tried in an United States Court because America is my enemy and Kenya is not. I would like my past and present statements about what I have done and why I have done it to be aired in public in an American courtroom. I understand that the American authorities who are interviewing me want to know who committed the bombing of the embassy and how it was carried out.

I am willing to waive my rights and answer the questions of American authorities upon the condition that the undersigned law enforcement authorities make all best efforts to see that I am brought to the United States to stand trial. I understand that the undersigned prosecutor is only empowered to make recommendations to the Attorney General of the United States and other executive officials of the United States Government and I further understand that the United States Government only intends to act with the mutual agreement of the Kenyan government.

No other agreements or promises have been made other than as set forth in this document.

Al-'Owhali then explained, "I was willing to die in the execution of the plot, but not as a bystander." His mission was twofold: to force the embassy guards to lift the steel drop bar at the entrance to the underground parking garage,[12] and to unlock the truck padlock should the detonator switch fail and throw a grenade into the truck to ignite the explosives. After he had jumped out of the truck, al-'Owhali realized he had left his pistol on the front seat. He threw a stun grenade at the guards who ran away in terror without lifting the drop bar.[13] Al-'Owhali ran too because his mission was complete. To stay and be killed would be suicide, not martyrdom, he maintained. Martyrdom was acceptable, but suicide was against the teachings of Islam.

Al-ʻOwhali wanted to tell his whole story from beginning to end. When he was done, the investigators could go back and ask questions. He warned that it was a very emotional story.

At this point, the tone of the discussion became similar to that of an after-action review. Like two soldiers comparing notes after a battle, Gaudin and al-'Owhali reviewed what went well and what went wrong in the operation.

August 23, 24, and 25

Once he had signed the DOU, al-'Owhali talked for three days about his role in al Qa'ida and the bombings. He provided the names, descriptions, and roles of his fellow cell members. At first he only supplied kunyas or nicknames, but if shown a photograph he relayed a great deal of information about the person pictured. He also provided details of the Dar es Salaam attack, unwittingly filling in gaps in U.S. knowledge.

Al-ʻOwhali's Story: From Radicalization to Action

Mohammed Rasheed Daoud al-ʻOwhali was born in Liverpool on January 18, 1977, to devout and wealthy Saudi parents. His father had been studying for a master's degree in England. A year after his birth, al-ʻOwhali returned with his family to Saudi Arabia. Religion played a central role in his life. As a teenager, he read conservative religious magazines such as *al Jihad* and *al Mujahedeen*. He read books such as *Love and Hour of the Martyrs*, which glorified men who sacrificed their lives in jihad. He listened to cassette tapes of speeches by Sheik Omar Abdel Rahman, the blind Egyptian cleric later convicted for conspiring to blow up the Lincoln and Holland tunnels and other NY City landmarks.

[12] The drop bar was closer to the road than the gate to the garage. Since the gate was controlled from within the embassy, the bombers never intended to breach the gate. If they could get past the drop bar, however, they would be able to position the truck closer to the embassy building.[13] Unbeknownst to al-'Owhali, the drop bar was manually

129

activated, controlled by a counterweight. Without the guards, he could have simply lifted the drop bar himself by pushing a switch. The grenade drew many people in the Ufundi/Cooperative House buildings to the windows. As a result, there were a high number of casualties from flying glass when the bomb was detonated.

Al-'Owhali was deeply troubled by Kissinger's Promise,[14] which many in the Arab world considered a grand U.S. Government plan to occupy the Arabian Peninsula in order to control oil resources. The U.S. military had maintained a presence in Saudi Arabia since the 1990 Gulf War; this was seen as a threat to the holy cities of Mecca and Medina. In addition, the United States supported the Saudi government, viewed by many Arabs as corrupt and not true to the tenets of Islam).

While al-'Owhali was studying at Mohamed bin Saud religious university in Riyadh he met with a friend who had just returned from fighting on behalf of Muslims in Bosnia. Together they discussed joining the jihad in Bosnia, Chechnya, or Tajikistan. Al-'Owhali dropped out of the university after only his second year to join the fight.

Because he was underage al-'Owhali asked his father for permission to travel. Originally setting out for Tajikistan, al-'Owhali landed in Peshawar, a Pakistani town on the border of Afghanistan known for recruiting jihadists. In 1996 a recruiter sent him to the Khaldan training camp. The man in charge of hospitality at the camp gave al-'Owhali his first alias in what would be a series of aliases. He was told never to use his true name from then on, or to reveal his country of origin. He received basic military training and periods of instruction in religious ideology.

Based on his performance, al-'Owhali was chosen by the emir of the camp to have an audience with UBL. He asked UBL for a mission right away. UBL said that his time would come and encouraged him to get more training. Al-'Owhali then received advanced training at other camps, including al-Siddiq, al-Farouq, and a camp near Khost known as the Jihad Wal camp. He was trained in security and intelligence, how to kidnap, how to seize buildings, and how to hijack buses and planes. He also received intensive training in the management and operation of a cell.

Later al-'Owhali claimed not to have taken *bayat*, an oath of loyalty, to UBL. He explained that he had wanted a mission that would result in the death of Americans. If he pledged *bayat*, he explained, he risked having to accept a noncombatant or logistical assignment.

Al-'Owhali became friends with Azzam,15 a young Saudi whom he met at the camps. Azzam nursed al-'Owhali back to health after a bout with tuberculosis.

[14] Henry Kissinger, National Security Advisor and Secretary of State under the Nixon administration, negotiated a cease-fire between Arab states and Israel after the Yom Kippur War of 1973. [15] Azzam was an alias for 24-year-old Jihad Mohammed Ali from Saudi Arabia.

Al-'Owhali asked UBL for permission to fight alongside the Taliban. He distinguished himself in what he called the "C Formation" battle in Kabul. Despite being outnumbered, he and five other men were able to repel enemy forces and hold their ground. For his loyalty and service, al-'Owhali was trusted to carry his rifle in the camps, even in the presence of UBL.

Al-'Owhali's Timeline of the Nairobi Attacks

During his time in Afghanistan, Azzam recruited al-'Owhali for a suicide mission in East Africa.

With a clean shave, al-'Owhali traveled to Yemen on an Iraqi passport in the name of Abdul Jabbar Ali Abdul Latif. In Yemen he stayed with Sameer alHada,[16] a fellow veteran of al-'Owhali's alleged victorious battle with the Taliban.

Al-'Owhali met with Azzam's cousin Bilal,[17] who helped al-'Owhali secure a Yemeni passport in the name of Khalid Salim Saleh bin Rasheed. While in Yemen, al-'Owhali telephoned his parents in Saudi Arabia. His father visited him in Yemen.

When al-'Owhali returned to Pakistan, Khallad[18] explained the upcoming mission as a suicide attack against a U.S. target in East Africa. He did not name the specific country. Al-'Owhali and Azzam were both instructed to make martyrdom videos. Khallad filmed al-'Owhali's video and even instructed him what to say in it. He told him to claim affiliation with the Third Martyr Barracks, First Squad of the El Bara bin Malik Division of the Liberation Army of the Islamic Holy Lands, a fictitious group. The video required five or six takes because al-'Owhali kept breaking into fits of laughter at his alleged group's name.

Al-'Owhali and Azzam were present in the background while John Miller of ABC News interviewed Osama bin Laden in Khost, Afghanistan, on May 28, 1998. UBL is positioned in front of a map of Africa. UBL warned of attacks against American targets.

On July 31, al-'Owhali left Lahore for Nairobi with stops in Karachi, Muscat, and Abu Dhabi.

On August 2, al-'Owhali arrived in Nairobi. He was one day late because he had missed a connecting flight. The delay caused al-'Owhali to miss the pre-arranged pickup at the airport. He had called Khallad to explain, and Khallad had

[16] Sameer al-Hada was the son of Ahmed al-Hada. Sameer al-Hada blew himself up by hand grenade in 2002 when facing arrest by Yemeni police.

[17] Bilal is an alias for Abdul Rahim al Nashiri. He was captured in November 2002. As of 2009, he is being held at Guantanamo Bay.

[18] Khallad is an alias for Tawfiq bin Attash, a senior al Qaeda operative who was the mastermind behind the USS *Cole* attack. He was captured in Karachi, Pakistan, in 2003. In September 2006, he was transferred from a secret CIA detention site to Guantanamo.

immediately informed the cell in Kenya. Khallad had then called al-'Owhali back, and gave him detailed instructions to continue on to Nairobi, check into the Ramadah Hotel in Eastleigh, and wait to be picked up there. Harun[19] arrived at the hotel later on that same day and paid the bill. Harun took al-'Owhali back to the rented villa in Nairobi where he resided with the other operatives.

Azzam arrived at the villa on August 3 from Mombasa. He was accompanied by the cell leader, Saleh.[20] Saleh described the mission in more detail and revealed that there would be two bombings, one in Nairobi and one in Dar es Salaam.

A Toyota truck was loaded with twenty crates containing a mixture of TNT, aluminum nitrate, and aluminum powder. Al-Owhali went into the garage of the house at 43 Runda Estates to see the truck. He and Azzam were instructed how to ignite the bomb.

On August 4, Saleh took al-'Owhali on a walk-through of the embassy grounds to show where he wanted the bomb placed. Al-'Owhali tried to persuade Saleh to change the plan and relocate the truck from the back of the embassy to the front or to the underground parking garage. He wanted to minimize Kenyan casualties and maximize American deaths. Saleh told him the plan was already set. This was the location chosen and the plan would not be changed.

On August 5, Abdel Rahman[21] wired the explosives to batteries in the back of the truck and an ignition switch on the dashboard. The mission was scheduled for August 7.[22] Friday morning was chosen because devout Muslims would be praying at their mosques.

On the day of the attack, al-'Owhali dressed in black shoes, baggy denim jeans, a short-sleeved collared shirt, and a blue cotton jacket. He placed a collect call to al-Hada in Yemen. He tucked four grenades into his belt and placed a pistol in his jacket pocket. He left the house with Azzam at 9:45 AM for the embassy.

Harun led the way to the target in a separate vehicle and waved the bomb truck on as they got close to the embassy.

Azzam instructed al-'Owhali to remove his jacket so he could better access the grenades. Al-'Owhali and Azzam listened to Islamic chants from the truck tape deck on the way to the target. "Will these two friends meet again in paradise?" the chanter asked.

[19] Harun is an alias for Fazul Abdallah Mohammed, an ethnic Kenyan from the Comoros Islands. As of 2009, he is still at large.

20 Saleh is an alias for the Egyptian Abdullah Ahmed Abdullah. As of 2009, he is still at

large.21 Abdel Rahman is an alias for the Egyptian Muhsin Musa Matwalli Atwah. In 2006, he was killed by Pakistani forces during an airstrike on a village near the Afghan border. [22] It was later noted that the day of the bombing coincided with the eight-year anniversary of the announcement that U.S. troops would be sent to Saudi Arabia in advance of the First Gulf War. Al-'Owhali did not reveal that this date had any special significance; however, he may not have known. Some believe that this is an American interpretation of the importance of this date.

The truck entered the rear embassy parking area and stopped at the drop bar. Another vehicle was exiting the parking garage. Al-'Owhali jumped out of the passenger seat, forgetting his gun. He yelled at the guards in English to lift the drop bar, and threw a stun grenade when the guards hesitated. The guards ran away. There was a great deal of confusion, but the drop bar remained down. Azzam began repositioning the truck so that it was parallel to the embassy building. He also fired a pistol out the window of the truck at the embassy.

It was unclear to al-'Owhali what Azzam intended to do next. He felt he could serve no purpose by staying. He ran toward the Ufundi/Cooperative House. Azzam detonated the bomb.

Al-'Owhali was thrown to the ground by the force of the explosion, suffering several injuries. He lost two grenades. He walked to a local clinic for treatment. He disposed of the remaining grenade in a trash can at this location.

He was transferred by ambulance to MP Shah Hospital. After getting stitches, he reached into his pocket to see if he had any money. He found the extra bullets and the keys to the truck padlock. He washed these items in the men's bathroom sink to get rid of any fingerprints. After unsuccessfully trying to flush them down the toilet, he placed them on the bathroom window ledge and left the hospital.

He was unable to find his way back to the villa and instead took a taxi to the Ramadah Hotel. He convinced a sympathetic desk clerk to loan him the money to pay for the cab. He negotiated staying at the hotel without payment until he could contact his people in Yemen. The desk clerk secured some clean clothes for al-'Owhali from a Yemeni acquaintance.

On August 8, with no extraction plan, al-'Owhali made collect calls to al-Hada in Yemen asking for money and travel documents. He instructed al-Hada to tell Khallad that he "did not travel," a code phrase that Khallad would understand to mean that al-'Owhali was still alive.

Within a few days, al-'Owhali picked up the money transfer at a jewelry store near his hotel. He paid his bill at the Ramadah and checked out. He then checked into the nearby IFTIN Lodge.

The "Tone" of the Intelligence Interviews

With his interrogators, al-'Owhali talked about religion as much as he did about the bombing. Al-'Owhali explained that the Bible and the Qu'ran share a narrative history. The Qu'ran includes both a book devoted to Mary and the story of Noah's Ark. They discussed similarities among people of "The Book": Christians, Jews, and Muslims.

Al-'Owhali explained that Muslims were allowed to marry people of the Book. He told Gaudin, "I could marry your sister. She could convert to Islam, but she wouldn't have to."

The discussions at times were deep and serious, and could invoke serious anger as well as more friendly discussion. For example, when Gaudin countered, "Then I could marry *your* sister," al-'Owhali became filled with rage. He stood up and said, "If you marry my sister, I have the right and duty to kill you. If she married you, then any children would be raised with your religion, not hers."

When asked what it would take to stop attacks against the United States, al'Owhali related a series of conditions. There should be no U.S. presence in Saudi Arabia; the United States would have to stop providing support to enemies of the Muslims – specifically Israel and the Serbs; and the United States should stop using its influence to support leaders in the Arab world who opposed implementation of sharia law.

On August 24 or 25, the team got photographs of Azzam and Bilal from the Saudis. Al-'Owhali identified both pictures. He kissed Azzam's photo and wept. Then he lapsed into a poetic chant, singing of someday joining Azzam in paradise.

When shown the morgue photos once again, al-Owhali explained, "This isn't the way it was supposed to be. I told them we should have attacked from the front." He claimed, however, that innocent people died because of U.S. foreign policy. The attack was necessary to broadcast the story of the injustice wrought on Muslims globally.

The Revelation of Actionable Intelligence

Al-'Owhali at a certain point claimed to have information on a matter of public safety. After receiving a written guarantee that the information would not be used against him, he warned the agents of future attacks. He told them that plans were in place to attack the United States inside its borders but that they weren't ready yet. Requesting that the Kenyan police not be present, he also told the Americans about a future attack in Yemen.[23] He provided details, including that al Qa'ida would conduct the attack on a U.S. Navy ship while it was refueling in the port of Aden.

[23] A document filed by the defense with the SDNY court states that al-'Owhali had discussed "a possible attack in Yemen" with the FBI. On October 12, 2000, the USS *Cole*, a U.S. Navy destroyer, was bombed in Aden. Seventeen sailors were killed and thirty-nine others were injured in the blast.

The Government of Kenya (GoK) considered their country to be a victim rather than a source of transnational terrorism.[24] Because the U.S. embassy had been the intended target, GoK quickly agreed to hand over the prosecution to U.S. authorities, even though twenty times as many Kenyans as Americans had died in the attacks. The two countries worked well together on the joint investigation. Kenyan CID investigators were present at all interviews of al-'Owhali while he was in Kenya. The Americans and Kenyans also conferred as a team between interviews, and GoK supported the American investigation even after the United States withdrew its investigators.

Although the Pakistani authorities caught Odeh, several other operatives remain at large.

Prosecution and Aftermath

Al-'Owhali told Gaudin he expected to be released through a prisoner swap. He believed that his group would take hostages, including ambassadors, to exchange for him.

This case would mark the first time the FBI was sent abroad to investigate a bombing committed overseas, found the persons responsible, and brought them back to the United States to face trial. On August 26, just fourteen days after al'Owhali was picked up as "the man who didn't fit in," al-'Owhali was flown from Nairobi to New York, arriving early in the morning of August 27. He was accompanied by FBI personnel, primarily members of the Hostage Rescue Team, an elite group that provides force protection. He did not want to discuss the attacks during the flight. He was booked in New York and charged with murder. He listed "Mr. Steve" as his next of kin.

At the December 2000 hearing to suppress his confession, al-'Owhali and Gaudin were not permitted to speak. But Gaudin recalls that al-'Owhali looked pleased to see Gaudin, openly smiling in his direction. At subsequent legal proceedings, al-'Owhali made frequent eye contact with Gaudin.

The trial of al-'Owhali and his three co-defendants began on January 2, 2001.[25]The court ruled that only the statements al-'Owhali had made after August 22, when he received his full AOR, would be admissible in court. On May 29, 2001, after a six-month trial, the jury returned its verdicts. All four defendants were convicted of all 302 counts in the indictment.

Fortuitously, on September 11, 2001, as it happened, al-'Owhali was in the Metropolitan Correctional Center, just six blocks away from the WTC. On October 18, 2001, all four men received the sentence of life in prison without the possibility of parole.

[24] The Nairobi cell included locals. As noted, Fazul Abdallah Mohammed, AKA Harun, is an ethnic Kenyan from the Comoros Islands.

[25] His co-defendants included Mohamed Sadeek Odeh, Khalfan Khamis Mohamed, and Wadih El-Hage.

The United States built a new $68 million embassy building in Nairobi outside the downtown area. The Nairobi bombing site has become a memorial park.

In 2001, Stephen Gaudin was sent to language school in Vermont to learn Arabic. He was posted for two years in Yemen as a legal attaché at the U.S. embassy in Sana'a and still works for the FBI.

Mohamed Rasheed Daoud al-'Owhali is now serving his sentence at the federal Administrative Maximum Facility (ADX) (also known as the Supermax) in Florence, Colorado. He is currently appealing his conviction.

References

Anatomy of a terrorist attack: An in-depth investigation into the 1998 bombings of the U.S. embassies in Kenya and Tanzania. (2005). Matthew B. Ridgway Center for International Security Studies at the University of Pittsburgh.

http://www.ridgway.pitt.edu/docs/working_papers/Anatomy%20v6-FINAL%20DOCUMENT.pdf

Berens, M. J. (2001, September 23). Peering into Bin Laden's network: Recruits taught how to sow fear. *Chicago Tribune.*

Bergen, P. L. (2001). Investigation and retaliation: The embassy bombings. In*Holy war Inc.: Inside the secret world of Osama Bin Laden* (pp. 105-126). New York: The Free Press.

Face of the grenade thrower. (1998, August 21). *The Nation (Kenya).*

Gaudin, S., & Bongardt, S. (1998). *Memorandum summarizing interrogation of Mohammad Rasheed Daoud al-'Owhali conducted between 22 to 25 August 1998 at the CID Headquarters in Nairobi, Kenya*: FBI.

http://intelfiles.egoplex.com/embassy-owhali-interrogation.pdf

Gaudin, S (2008, May 6). Reacting to Nairobi bomb suspect's confession, nonbroadcast segment from War on the west [Television

series episode]. In*Age of terror*. London: BBC Two.
http://news.bbc.co.uk/2/hi/programmes/age_of_terror/7380687.stm

Hamm, M. S. (2005). *Crimes committed by terrorist groups: Theory, research and prevention*. Terre Haute: Indiana State University.
http://www.ncjrs.gov/pdffiles1/nij/grants/211203.pdf

Leader, S., & Danis, A. (2001). Tactical insights from the trial.*Jane's Intelligence Review*.

Nairobi bombing map. (1998). *Washington Post*.
http://www.washingtonpost.com/wp
srv/inatl/longterm/eafricabombing/maps/nairobimap.htm

Report of the Accountability Review Boards on the Embassy Bombings in Nairobi and Dar es Salaam on August 7, 1998. (1999, January).
http://www.state.gov/www/regions/africa/accountability_report.html

United States of America v. Usama Bin Laden et al., S (7)98 Cr. 1023, Opinion on Miranda warning outside the United States. (2001, February 16). New York: Southern District of New York.
http://cryptome.info/usa-v-ubl-mwo.htm

United States of America v. Usama Bin Laden et al., S (7)98 Cr. 1023, Transcript of day 14 of trial. (2001, March 7). New York: Southern District of New York.
http://cryptome.info/usa-v-ubl-14.htm

United States of America v. Usama Bin Laden et al., S (7)98 Cr. 1023, Transcript of day 15 of trial. (2001, March 8). New York: Southern District of New York.
http://cryptome.info/usa-v-ubl-15.htm

War on the west [Television series episode]. (2008, May 6). In *Age of terror*. London: BBC Two.
http://news.bbc.co.uk/2/hi/programmes/age_of_terror/7306413.stm

Wright, L. (2006). *The looming tower: Al-Qaeda and the road to 9/11*. New York: Knopf.

Appendix: The Nairobi Embassy Bombing

The U.S. Government Case Study of Human Manipulation

The U.S. Embassy, a seven-story concrete structure built to withstand earthquakes, was located in busy downtown Nairobi. It lacked sufficient set-back from the street and shared tight quarters with the two-building Ufundi/Cooperative House complex. This complex included a four-story office building housing a secretarial college, and a 22-story building housing offices and a bank. Embassy security was provided by unarmed host-nation guards. Ambassador Prudence Bushnell had repeatedly warned Washington of the embassy's vulnerabilities, but her recent letter to Secretary of State Madeleine Albright had gone unanswered.

The impact of the blast ripped off the rear of the embassy and leveled the smaller Ufundi building. Ambassador Bushnell was attending a meeting with the Kenyan Minister of Commerce in the larger Ufundi building. She was briefly knocked unconscious and was cut by flying glass, but was otherwise unharmed.

Investigations would later show that planning for the embassy attacks started as early as 1994. Kenya, with its porous borders, corruption, weak governance and marginalized Muslim population, was a terrorist safe haven. Usama bin Laden (UBL) sent Ali Mohammed, a naturalized U.S. citizen and former member of both the Egyptian and U.S. armies, to scout targets in Nairobi. The U.S. embassy, with its many security vulnerabilities, topped the list. Looking at the surveillance photos, UBL had apparently marked the area to the rear of the building as the best location for a truck bomb. When Bushnell was appointed ambassador in 1996, the target became even more attractive: the death of a female U.S. ambassador would draw extra publicity.

The United States received three warnings of planned attacks on the Nairobi embassy in the year leading up to the bombing. In August 1997, Wadih El-Hage was questioned by the FBI and his computer was examined by the CIA. However, documents from a search of his house were not translated due to resource constraints. It was later learned that El-Hage had established the Kenyan al Qa'ida cell.

In the summer of 1997, an informant told the CIA that al Haramein, a charity working with Somali refugees, was planning an attack on the embassy. According to the CIA, there has never been any evidence linking the charity to the bombing. In November 1997, Mustafa Mahmoud Saud Ahmed approached the embassy to report a truck bomb plot. He was discredited as a fabricator, although he was later implicated in the Dar es Salaam attack.

Mohammed Rasheed Daoud al-'Owhali: Case Study with Teaching Notes

The case study of Mohammed Rasheed Daoud al-'Owhali tells the story of an intelligence interviewing team that was able to deconstruct a high-value detainee's cover story remarkably quickly. The team was then able to gain very important intelligence. The case offers an exceptional example of skilled intelligence interviewing and investigative work.

Mohammed al-'Owhali had had no intention of providing truthful information to the Americans. In ten days the intelligence interviewing professionals were able to persuade al-'Owhali to provide a detailed account of the terrorist attack in which he participated. He also provided vital, previously unknown information on al Qa'ida. Following the interviews, al-'Owhali was prosecuted in the United States court system; he remains incarcerated today.

The *al-'Owhali* case study is based primarily on interviews with FBI SSA Stephen Gaudin,[*] one of the intelligence interviewing professionals involved in the al'Owhali case. The story of al-'Owhali has attracted some attention over the years, and has been featured in various news broadcasts and books. These sources were also used, together with court records and trial transcripts.

As with the case of *Nguyen Tai* in this booklet, one cannot know with certainty that every element in the present case study of *al-'Owhali* is accurate. The details have been reconstructed based on intelligence interviewers' recollections (see *Memory*) of events in August of 1998. An advantage of this case, however, was the direct access to Stephen Gaudin, who had kept extensive notes on the al'Owhali interview.

The case illustrates:

The U.S. Government Case Study of Human Manipulation

- The apparent benefits of building an *operational accord* at the first moment a detainee comes into contact with Americans\

- The benefits of building strong *relationships* with many Kenyan colleagues – from the moment of contact

- The importance of both environmental and interviewing *context*–including the actions of many who came in contact with the detainee, for example, an unidentified observer, a hospital worker, and guards

- The benefits of a team approach among the Americans
  * The study chair thanks senior FBI leadership for permitting SSA Gaudin to share his recollections of this case.

- The critical importance of constantly validating or disaffirming the details of a detainee's *information* throughout the intelligence interviewing process

- The *information* power to be gained from simultaneous interviewing and investigative work, drawing on a highly skilled team and helpful host country colleagues

- Many examples of working effectively, and in various ways, with a detainee's *resistances*

- The importance of *information* and *relationship power*, and how to leverage these sources of power together in order to *persuade*

- Effective *persuasion* by several intelligence interviewing professionals who appear to have addressed the real *interests* of the detainee

- Ways in which to understand and build upon common *social identities* between interviewer and detainee

- The importance of addressing a detainee's *core emotional concerns*

- The ebb and flow of *stress* throughout the interview process, with skillful management of frustration and anger by the intelligence interviewing professional

- An intriguing example of a detainee changing his *fallback* position into another *fallback*, which became the basis for a deal

- A successful deal that resulted in much useful information because of skill in meeting the detainee's *interests*

This case, with its teaching notes, was assembled to accompany and help to illustrate some ideas presented in the six teaching papers in this booklet. Like the papers, the notes here are not intended to present either doctrine or a "correct view" of intelligence interviewing. Instead, the goal is to raise ideas for discussion, for teaching, and for research. Readers will likely want to read the teaching papers first.

The al-'Owhali story itself is printed in black text. Teaching notes appear in red text. Potential questions for the reader, and for use in teaching this case, are presented in blue text. Key ideas from the teaching papers are shown in bold italic print.

Fourteen Days in Nairobi: The Interrogation of Mohammed Rasheed Daoud al-'Owhali

April 2009
The Nairobi Embassy Bombing

FBI Special Agent Stephen Gaudin had just wrapped up an assignment and was heading out on vacation. He had been supporting the 1998 Goodwill Games, an international sporting event held that year in the New York (NY) metropolitan area. With five years in the Bureau, he had recently transferred to the NY office in Manhattan from his previous Kingston, NY, post. In upstate New York, he had gained criminal law enforcement experience by pursuing drug dealers, bank robbers, fugitives, and kidnappers. He had never been involved in a terrorism investigation.

Teaching Notes: Gaudin had conducted hundreds of interviews as an FBI agent, primarily during the course of criminal investigations of drug deals, organized crime, and bank robberies. While these interviews were not terrorism related, the experience would prove very valuable, as it gave Gaudin a good understanding of how to gather evidence and garner information from less-than-cooperative suspects and of how a "typical criminal" might respond during an interview. This served as a useful point of comparison when he worked with persons who had received training on how to evade questioning.

On August 7, 1998, at around 10:30 AM local time, two near-simultaneous bomb attacks hit the US embassies in Nairobi, Kenya, and Dar es Salaam, Tanzania. The Nairobi attack killed 218 people, including 12 Americans, and injured thousands of others, many of them blinded by flying glass. The Joint Terrorism Task Force (JTTF) based at the FBI NY office suspected al Qa'ida, a group completely unknown to most of the law enforcement community at the time. The NY office pressed hard to lead the investigation. In the end, the FBI deployed over 300 agents from both the Washington and NY field offices to investigate the embassy bombings: the largest number of agents working on any overseas investigation in the history of the FBI.

The FBI chose Gaudin for the investigative team in part to provide security. He had been an officer in the Army's 82nd Airborne Division and had seen six years of active service. In addition to his military experience, thirty-five-year-old Gaudin was a member of the NY Office's SWAT team and was assigned a collapsible MP-5 submachine gun. His initial assignment on the trip was as bodyguard to Pat D'Amuro, the Assistant Special Agent in Charge of the NY Field Office's National Security Division, who was going to Nairobi. It would be Gaudin's first trip to Africa.

*Teaching Notes: Some of Gaudin's potentially useful **social identities** are clear: he is a law enforcement officer and a former soldier. These **identities** could become useful when he comes into contact with other individuals who, while fighting for an entirely different cause, may also view themselves as protectors of their group and soldiers in a cause. At the very least, they might help Gaudin to recognize the **interests** and background of a suspect with similar experience, and they might form a basis for building an **operational accord** with such a suspect.*

With a police escort, the NY team traveled by city transit bus to

The U.S. Government Case Study of Human Manipulation

Washington, D.C. Gaudin lay down in the aisle of the bus to catch what sleep he could before the mission began. The team boarded a C-5 military cargo plane. Gaudin, familiar with flying on military aircraft, was able to sleep more easily than most others on the transatlantic flight. The team was on the ground in Kenya on August 9, one and-one-half days after the blasts. They were met at the Nairobi airport by Kenyans with little knowledge of English. Luckily, they had a female agent on board who could speak Swahili.

The Man Who Didn't Fit In

When the FBI team arrived at the blast site, search and rescue teams were still pulling people out of the rubble. US officials, including the FBI, set up a command post, as well as a tip line, at another country's embassy building. The tip line received hundreds of calls of many different kinds. For example, zealous callers provided leads pointing to a "suspicious man with a pizza oven," a Somali "ninja team" allegedly dropped by helicopter, and "a Lebanese man at the train station."

Among these calls was one fielded by Special Agent Debbie Doran. It reported "a man at the Ramadah Hotel who didn't fit in." The man apparently had been injured in the attack and was refusing help. Doran kept the reluctant caller on the line, even persuading him to agree to call back.

On August 11, D'Amuro realized the futility of having a bodyguard amidst the chaos of downtown Nairobi. He reassigned Gaudin to follow up on "the man who didn't fit in." Nobody knew if this man had played any role in the Nairobi attack. "If you don't like that lead," D'Amuro told Gaudin, "I've got plenty of other ones."

Teaching Notes: Gaudin described this time in Nairobi as very chaotic. The FBI had little experience working internationally; swarms of people continued to gather at the site of the bombing; and the number of potential leads appeared endless, ranging from the possibly useful to the absurd. Despite the chaos the agents on the ground remained flexible in their roles, and sought to discover possible leads in every way they could.

On the morning of August 12, FBI Special Agent Steven Bongardt and

The U.S. Government Case Study of Human Manipulation

New York City Police Detective Wayne Parola joined Gaudin for the ride to follow up on "the man who did not fit in." All three men served on the JTTF, but they had no prior experience working together. They were accompanied by two Kenyan Criminal Investigation Division (CID) officers and a Kenyan driver. They traveled in an enclosed truck with the CID men in the cab and the Americans in the back.

As it turned out, the Ramadah Hotel was in Eastleigh, a 30-minute drive from the capital city. As they neared the hotel, they drove through an open-air market and refugee slum where men walked the streets armed with AK-47s. Gaudin banged on the window separating the cab from the bed of the truck. "Where are we going?" he demanded.

The CID men stopped the truck and walked to the back to speak to the Americans. They explained that Eastleigh was inhabited mainly by Somalis. In fact, Eastleigh was also known by the nickname Somalitown. The Kenyans warned their colleagues, "Keep down. They don't like Americans here."

Gaudin tried to contact D'Amuro to inform him of the apparent threat in their surroundings. D'Amuro, Gaudin believed, would have wanted to make the call on whether the group should proceed. But phone service was out and D'Amuro could not be reached. They continued on their mission.

The truck pulled to a stop in Somalitown. Many people were in the streets, and they quickly became interested in the truck. A man on the street approached their vehicle, leaned his back against the truck and, without trying to draw attention, stated, "I told you not to come here. What are you doing here? You are going to get me killed!"

Realizing he may have been the tip line caller, Gaudin asked him his name. When he refused to answer the agents asked, "What about calling you Bill?"

"No, I don't like this name," he replied.
"How about Michael? Everyone likes Michael Jordan."

"Okay, I like this name." He informed them, "The man you are looking for is no longer at the Ramadah Hotel. He is at the IFTIN Lodge." The IFTIN Lodge was also located in Eastleigh, near the Ramadah.

The U.S. Government Case Study of Human Manipulation

*Teaching notes: Despite the tense situation, the agents remained calm and quickly assessed both this man's **interests** and their own. Gaudin recalls that he was thinking, "Just give me what I need and I'll get out of here." If this man was in fact the caller, he obviously wanted to provide **information** without being identified and placed in harm's way – a key aspect of his **role** at that time and one that the agents needed to respect. The agents quickly identified these **interests**, and "indirectly" addressed the man's **resistances**, by providing him with a pseudonym. Using a famous person's name may have caused the caller to feel momentarily important or at least recognized. The caller, with his **interest** in anonymity met and possibly a **core concern** of **status** acknowledged, provided valuable **information**.*

Their arrival at IFTIN Lodge attracted a lot of attention. A crowd started to form. The Americans in the truck recalled that the 1993 Battle of Mogadishu ended with 18 American soldiers and at least 3000 Somali militia and civilians killed. It seemed safer for the Americans to stay in the truck than to go into the hotel.

The CID detectives confirmed that there was a man in the hotel who had recently checked in. They did not immediately go to the room and pick him up because they were unarmed. They told the Americans that, as sergeants, they had not yet been issued guns. Gaudin lent them a pistol and holster. He held onto his MP-5.

*Teaching notes: It seems possible that this interaction strengthened the Americans' **affiliation** with the CID detectives – it affirmed the Kenyans' **status**, and affirmed a measure of **autonomy**; it certainly affirmed their **role** as important members of the team.*

*Query: This teaching case does not center on the power of **relationships** built with Kenyan colleagues, but, as it turned out, the Kenyans and Americans provided a great deal of help to each other. Might this particular interaction have helped?*

The Kenyans returned with the suspect. The man had visible stitches on his forehead and bandages on his hands. In his pockets he had 1900 Ksh (Kenyan Shillings), equivalent to $32, and also eight $100 banknotes. These bills featured the oversized Benjamin Franklin, and had first been issued in 1996 as part of the U.S. currency redesign.

The U.S. Government Case Study of Human Manipulation

(These new $100 bills were not fully in circulation back home; Gaudin had never seen one before.) The suspect also had a casualty card, in the name of Khalid Salim, from MP Shah Hospital in Nairobi, stamped August 7, 1998.

Interview and Investigation
August 12

The "man who didn't fit in" claimed to be Khalid Salim Saleh bin Rasheed from Yemen. He spoke Arabic, but said he spoke only minimal English and no Swahili. He claimed to have lost all his belongings in the blast, although he wore clean clothes. Kenyan law stipulates that a person may be detained for 48 hours if he or she cannot produce identification. Since the suspect had no official ID or passport, the Kenyans took him into custody for further investigation. Bin Rasheed was put in the back of the truck, without handcuffs.

Teaching notes: This somewhat relaxed custody might have implications for future interactions. Gaudin noted that leaving bin Rasheed uncuffed was not the American agents' decision – the Americans were simply assisting the Kenyan CID. He added, however, that at this point "cuffing would have been going in the wrong direction of rapport."

*Gaudin has mentioned that he likes to put himself in other people's shoes and prefers to treat them the way he would want to be treated. He is keenly observant, with strong empathic skills and intuition. The ability to identify another person's **interests** and **core concerns** quickly is a very effective set of skills; it allows Gaudin to connect quickly with people and build some degree of **relationship**.*

Query: As an exercise, the reader may want to try to imagine throughout this case: "If I were the detainee...." and"If I were the U.S. agent....what would I be thinking and feeling?"

What with the presence of guns, an unrestrained person of interest, the tight quarters, and the crowds outside, the mood in the back of the truck was understandably tense. Gaudin spoke to the suspect in English to inform him of their destination and assure him of his safety. "Everything will be okay," Gaudin said, gently touching the man's

148

knee.

When Gaudin was a boy, his grandmother had given him butterscotch as a way to comfort him, and he had brought butterscotch with him to Africa. Wanting to reduce the tension, Gaudin reached into his pocket and handed out butterscotch candy to everyone in the truck, including the detainee. Bin Rasheed accepted the candy, smiled graciously, and remained calm. He indicated that he understood he would be safe. The Americans did not question bin Rasheed in the truck.

*Teaching notes: The agents could have treated bin Rasheed in many ways. Gaudin, perhaps almost automatically, chose from the start to begin building an **operational accord** with bin Rasheed. Rather than concern himself with the barriers of language and culture, Gaudin offered reassuring words and gestures by drawing on his own experiences of what had comforted him in the past. The simple act of sharing an item of food, and of doing so immediately, may illustrate Cialdini's **principles of persuasion**, specifically **liking** and **reciprocity**. Gaudin's action also conveyed the message that bin Rasheed was, at least for this moment, equal to the others in the truck, potentially addressing **core concerns** of **appreciation, affiliation,** and **status**.*

*Gaudin's sharing of food also affirmed, even if very briefly, a shared "human" identity with the detainee. This treatment may have started to create a **crosscutting identity** for bin Rasheed, one that was different from his **role** of detainee. Gaudin's reaching out may have begun to set the stage for reducing **resistances,** and for creating opportunities to **persuade**.*

*At this point Gaudin had almost no **information power** and little power of **incentives** or **disincentives**. But he immediately began to build **relationship** power. Research findings offer some reason to believe that significant **relationship** power may be won or lost at first contact; this appears to have been a skillful first contact.*

Query: Readers might consider some alternative ways bin Rasheed might have been treated at this point in time. What might have been the potential short- and long-term implications of alternative treatment?

For the first two nights, the suspect was kept in a general holding cell at the Jomo Kenyatta Airport Police Station in Nairobi. He shared his cell with one other individual who, as it turned out, was not involved in the attacks. The suspect was then transferred to Kenyan CID Headquarters.

Query: The agents had limited say concerning the detainee's custodial environment. If bin Rasheed had been in U.S. custody, might there have been a better setting (bin Rasheed by himself, with another detainee in a videotaped room, with a confederate or someone he knew)? How, if at all, might other settings have been better or not better?

Back at the Command Post, Parola read the suspect his Advice of Rights (AOR) in English. (In Kenya, the right to a lawyer does not attach immediately, and refusing to answer questions *may* be used against you.) Department of Justice attorneys had counseled the FBI to use the overseas AOR form, which read as follows:

We are representatives of the United States Government. Under our laws, you have certain rights. Before we ask you any questions, we want to be sure that you understand those rights. You do not have to speak to us or answer any questions. Even if you have already spoken to the Kenyan authorities, you do not have to speak to us now.

If you do speak with us, anything that you say may be used against you in a court in the United States or elsewhere.

In the United States, you would have the right to talk to a lawyer to get advice before we ask you any questions and you could have a lawyer with you during questioning. In the United States, if you could not afford a lawyer, one would be appointed for you, if you wish, before any questioning.

Because we are not in the United States, we cannot ensure that you will have a lawyer appointed for you before any questioning.

If you decide to speak with us now, without a lawyer present, you will still have the right to stop answering questions at any time. You should also understand that if you decide not to speak with us, that fact cannot be used as evidence against you in a court in the United States.

I have read this statement of my rights and I understand what my rights are. I am willing to make a statement and answer questions. I do not want a lawyer at this time. I understand and know what I am doing. No promises or threats have been made to me and no pressure or coercion of any kind has been used against me.

Parola and Gaudin questioned the suspect in a small room at the Kenyan CID Headquarters while Bongardt went out to verify bin Rasheed's story. With experience working Hezbollah cases for JTTF, Parola initially did almost all the questioning.

*Teaching Notes: Consider the intelligence interviewers' **sources of power** at this point. They had begun to build **relationship power**, but they had almost no **information power**, making it very difficult to vet any of bin Rasheed's story. Bongardt's investigations provided one way to add to the **information power** of the intelligence interviewing team.*

*Bin Rasheed, on the other hand, possessed a good deal of **information power** at this time. He had all of his own potentially valuable knowledge, he likely hypothesized that his interviewers knew very little about him or his possible role in the attack, and he may have been trained in how to manage being taken into custody. At this point he appears to have been thinking through his **fallback** position: that is, constructing a cover story to deceive the agents and perhaps help to win his release from custody.*

The first interview lasted one hour and was conducted in broken English. Bin Rasheed stated that he was a khat salesman. He claimed to have flown to Nairobi from Yemen to visit Harun, a 28-year-old man whom he had met a year before. When Harun failed to pick him up at the airport, bin Rasheed took a taxi to the Ramadah Hotel, a 30-minute drive from the airport. He further stated that the taxi driver chose the hotel because Arabic was spoken there. Later, Harun picked him up at the hotel and took him to his house in Nairobi. Bin Rasheed claimed he was standing in a bank near the embassy at the time of the explosion. He said that he had lost his briefcase, which contained his passport, in the chaos following the "accident" in the capital. He also lost sight of his friend Harun, and assumed that he had died in the explosion. Bin Rasheed reported that he visited a walk-in clinic and was transferred to a hospital where he received stitches to his forehead, his wrists, and the center of his back. Unable to find his way back to Harun's house, he returned to the Ramadah Hotel. Having lost all his possessions, he negotiated with the hotel to stay without payment. He claimed to be wearing the clothes he wore on the day of the blast.

*Teaching Notes: Here bin Rasheed used **information** to create a **fallback** or cover story. Had his story been accepted, he might well have been released.*

*However, in an environment where he was encouraged to tell his story, bin Rasheed began to convey some minor details about himself. He also began to disclose potential inconsistencies, even though the agents knew little about him. For example, Bin Rasheed's claim that he was wearing the same clothes he had worn when the blast occurred led Gaudin to pause and think, "Something is not quite right." This little bit of **information** was not enough to cause Gaudin to assume that bin Rasheed was involved in the attack, but it did lead the interviewers to conclude that they should keep listening to the suspect and investigating his claims.*

Bin Rasheed's story just did not sound right to the Americans. They did not suspect that bin Rasheed had played a role in the attack, but they thought his story warranted further investigation. They made arrangements to secure an Arabic translator for the second interview in order to capture the story more clearly.

*Teaching Notes: Note the importance of the sense that "something is not quite right," which may have been based in part on an intuitive, perhaps nearly automatic analysis of details, as well as an explicit cognitive analysis of objective **information**. Research has begun to show that intuition of this kind is part of **relationship power**, and that it relies heavily upon emotional reactions during an interchange. Of course it is also critical to keep comparing one's intuition with more objective, all-source **information,** to ensure that perceptions and emotions are subjected to external checks.*

A native Arabic speaker, a woman, served as their first translator. Both bin Rasheed and the translator were uncomfortable being in the same room. Gaudin hung his poncho liner in a doorway as a makeshift curtain and positioned the suspect on one side and the translator on the other. Gaudin read the overseas AOR aloud and the interpreter orally translated it into Arabic. After the suspect spoke just one sentence, the translator called a time out and beckoned the Americans to her side of the curtain. She reported that bin Rasheed spoke *fusha*, a classical rather than a colloquial form of Arabic. According to her, this indicated that he was well educated and certainly not a "poor or working class person."

*Teaching Notes: By hanging the liner in the doorway, the intelligence interviewers demonstrated **appreciation** for bin Rasheed's **interest** of being an observant Muslim. (The interviewers were, of course, also respecting the **interests** of the female interpreter.) This act may have helped to set the stage for bin Rasheed to feel some sense of **liking** (a **persuasion principle**) for the interviewers, possibly without his even being aware of this happening. It also may have encouraged the continued development of an **operational accord**, or at least it did not damage the **accord** that had been established thus far.*

*Bringing in a substantive expert, in this case a native speaker of Arabic, quickly and unobtrusively increased the intelligence interviewing team's **information power** about bin Rasheed – a much-needed gain at this early stage of the interviewing process.*

Over the course of the three-hour interview, bin Rasheed claimed to have flown in from Yemen and to have received money from his Yemeni uncle Mohammed bin Rasheed.

At one point, the team photographed bin Rasheed, documenting his wounds. They discovered more lacerations in addition to those on his forehead and hands: his clean shirt had hidden the big bandages covering stitches on his back.

Understanding the Context of the Interviews

When logistically possible, Gaudin went to bin Rasheed's holding cell, then walked with him to the interview room. Gaudin arranged for bin Rasheed to be without handcuffs. While they walked Gaudin would often ask bin Rasheed, "You okay?" Outside the interview room, bin Rasheed would converse in broken English with Gaudin about current events, even asking about the Monica Lewinsky scandal. Bin Rasheed asked, "What's with your president?" while shaking his finger, implying "shame, shame, shame."

Whenever bin Rasheed asked for permission, he was allowed to pray. Gaudin accompanied bin Rasheed to the bathroom so he could wash in preparation for prayer. Having never seen this ritual before, Gaudin asked him to explain what he was doing. Bin Rasheed showed Gaudin his washing ritual and explained its significance.

*Teaching Notes: Gaudin continued to work to build **relationship power** and an **operational accord** with bin Rasheed. By permitting bin Rasheed to walk without handcuffs Gaudin allowed bin Rasheed some sense of **autonomy**, a **core concern**. Gaudin also respected bin Rasheed's **role** as a Muslim (an important message of **appreciation)** and encouraged bin Rasheed to take on the **role** (and **cross-cutting identity**) of a teacher to Gaudin. Casting bin Rasheed in **roles** other than those of "detainee" and possibly "jihadist" may ultimately have helped to decrease some of bin Rasheed's **resistances** to providing information of value.*

Gaudin spontaneously shared several meals with bin Rasheed during the interviews. Gaudin would often miss breakfast due to his interviewing schedule, so he would bring MREs [Meals Ready to Eat] to the interview room. Gaudin noticed bin Rasheed's interest while he made "Ranger cookies," a famous concoction of cocoa powder, crackers, non-dairy creamer, and coffee. He asked bin Rasheed if he would like some, and in fact these "cookies" became a favorite snack for the prisoner.

*Teaching Notes: Reflecting back, Gaudin recognized that at this early stage he "just knew" that bin Rasheed had a military background. This intuition may have derived from both conscious and instinctive observation of tiny details of the interactions with bin Rasheed. Such details will have been illuminated by Gaudin's own training as a soldier. Sharing "Ranger cookies" helped build a **cross-cutting identity** between Gaudin and bin Rasheed, and may have responded to the detainee's **interest** in attention (**appreciation**).*

*A spontaneous sharing of food tends to evoke feelings of **reciprocity** and **affiliation**, two of Cialdini's **principles of persuasion**. When one person gives a gift to another person, an impulse to **reciprocate** often* *follows, even if the gift was not desired. Why is this potentially important? One possible answer: detainees have little to offer in exchange, other than information.*

August 13

On day two, the JTTF team started checking out parts of bin Rasheed's story. They looked at hundreds of paper arrival and departure cards at the Nairobi airport. Bin Rasheed had taken Gulf Air Flight 0713 from the United Arab Emirates (UAE) – not Yemen. His arrival card listed the Ramadah Hotel as his intended destination – the very hotel he earlier had claimed "the taxi driver had chosen" for him.

*Teaching Notes: The intelligence interviewers' **information power** continued to build. This **source of power** would also prove useful in deconstructing bin Rasheed's **fallback** position, his cover story.*

During the third interview, Parola's tone became livelier and louder. According to Gaudin, Parola sensed that bin Rasheed did not like him and built on that dislike, setting up Gaudin as the good guy. Parola confronted the suspect about the inconsistencies in his story and asked him accusingly, "What else are you lying about?" Bin Rasheed denied lying about anything.

*Teaching Notes: Gaudin recalled that this "Bad Cop/Good Cop" routine was not planned in advance; it simply reflected the difference between his and Parola's interviewing styles. Perhaps because it was unintentional it likely appeared quite authentic. It probably helped to build the **accord** between bin Rasheed and Gaudin. However, at this point, when his **resistance** was **directly** addressed, bin Rasheed continued to maintain his story. Research highlights the importance people attach to being, and being perceived to be, **consistent**. Being exposed as inconsistent can make a person feel suddenly powerless, especially if it takes away an important **fallback** position.*

*Query: Is it possible that another tactic at this juncture would have avoided or decreased (or increased) some of bin Rasheed's **resistances**? How does building an **operational accord** fit in with the interviewing strategy at this point? (See the next interchange for possible answers.)*

The U.S. Government Case Study of Human Manipulation

*Query: While not immediately effective, was it useful to introduce a heightened level of **stress** at this point in the interview? May there be many different ways of building an **operational accord**? Suppose there had been no added **stress**? Or yet more **stress**?*

Gaudin then took the lead and told the suspect that his story was not believable. He accused bin Rasheed of having the same counter-interrogation training that Gaudin had received in the military. "If you remember your training, you are supposed to tell a story that would be believable and easy to remember. But, most important, your story is supposed to be *logical*."This got the suspect's attention. Bin Rasheed pulled his chair closer to Gaudin and asked, "Where was I illogical?"

*Teaching Note: Gaudin added his own contribution to the **stresses** in the room. However, his entrance into the discussion may have seemed"different" to bin Rasheed. First, bin Rasheed already had at least some **relationship** with Gaudin at this point. Second, Gaudin raised his question in a way that could be viewed as **sidestepping** the content of **resistance** and **disrupting** the resistance by catching bin Rasheed off guard. Instead of confronting bin Rasheed directly with a charge of lying, Gaudin asserted that the story was not believable, implying that bin Rasheed had failed in resistance-craft. Thus, the apparent message was not that bin Rasheed lacked honor (that he was a liar), but that he had made an error.*

*It seems that Gaudin, in this way, may have subtly changed tack: he was challenging the method of the **resistance**. Rather than refute Gaudin's harsh judgment of his story, bin Rasheed, perhaps impulsively, asked how he might have failed – and, in this way, he began to show his hand. Gaudin may have succeeded here because he asked a question about process rather than content, and about competence rather than character.*

*How did it happen that Gaudin "knew" enough about bin Rasheed to **sidestep** a central point of **resistance** in this way? One possible answer: Gaudin's military background and years of experience in the FBI gave him a particular kind of **information power**. Gaudin was able to recognize that bin Rasheed's ability to evade questions and to have a seemingly legitimate answer for every question was much like the skill* *conveyed in his own counter-interrogation training. This knowledge, coupled with his familiarity with how a "typical criminal" who had no such training might respond (a criminal might simply say, "Hey, it wasn't me, man; it was this other guy"), led Gaudin to trust his intuition.*

*Fortunately, Gaudin was also able to work within the **operational accord** he had begun to form with bin Rasheed and the **cross-cutting identity** of "soldier." These factors may have caused bin Rasheed to care about what Gaudin thought, although probably not consciously, and as a result he provided an emotionally based response. This strategy permitted a small but significant **step forward**.*

Gaudin offered a few examples. "Why does your airport arrival card list the Ramadah Hotel as your intended destination when you claim the taxi driver chose it? Why did you ask the Ramadah for time to pay for your room? Why not use the money that you have? Why didn't you go to the Yemeni embassy?"

To the last question, bin Rasheed replied, "I didn't want them to think I was involved" in what he referred to as "the accident."

*Teaching Note: Gaudin maintained the momentum of the interview. He **sidestepped** possible **resistances**, and possibly also **distracted** bin Rasheed by asking a litany of questions, all following the same line of thought, which could be interpreted as a critique of bin Rasheed's cover story. Bin Rasheed then responded with what appeared to be one honest answer.*

Bin Rasheed had large cuts and other injuries, yet no blood on his pants or shirt. Gaudin tried to get bin Rasheed to admit that his clothes were too new and clean to have been worn on the day he was injured in the "accident." Gaudin talked about the neatness of his appearance. "I've been in the country a shorter time than you and my clothes are dirty."

Bin Rasheed replied in a fairly flippant, almost smug way, "Arab men are cleaner."

Gaudin challenged in a firm, fairly unemotional tone, "You have a solution for getting rid of blood? Okay, that is logical. And it is logical that God made a piece of glass slip down your shirt and make a right turn and cause a big injury to your back. And all this happened without putting a hole in your shirt or a scar anywhere else on your back."

"Anything can happen with God's grace," bin Rasheed responded.

Teaching Notes: It might be tempting for an interviewer to get caught up in the argument at this point, particularly after a detainee offers what appears to be an insult. Interviewers are often, after all, under a good deal of **stress** *themselves. It is important to note that giving in to the* **stress** *could have turned this exchange into a* **step backward** *– baiting an interviewer can be used as a* **resistance** *technique to pull the interviewer off his path.*
Gaudin reflects that instead he ignored bin Rasheed's insults. "I wanted him to be cocky." Gaudin is not certain now whether he automatically decided, or explicitly realized, that entering into a confrontation off the subject at hand might have **distracted** *him from his goal of getting intelligence* **information**. *In any case, experienced interviewing professionals are able to maintain the self-discipline not to be diverted, and Gaudin was skillful enough – in the moment– to* **deflect** *a direct confrontation, while maintaining some pressure so that bin Rasheed knew Gaudin was not convinced.*

Gaudin also noticed that bin Rasheed's belt appeared brand-new – yet another indicator that a part of the detainee's story could not possibly be true. Gaudin intended to compare their two belts for signs of wear. He hoped to prove the belt was new and catch the suspect in a lie about the clothes. So……… Gaudin began his gambit slowly, by leaning over and intently studying bin Rasheed's shoes. He wanted bin Rasheed to be thinking about anything other than his belt.

Conscious of Gaudin's staring at his shoes, bin Rasheed defensively said that one couldn't expect one's shoes to stay clean in such a dusty environment. Catching bin Rasheed off guard, Gaudin replied, "I don't care about your shoes. I care about your belt." Gaudin got up, and in a swift movement unbuckled his own belt, showing the suspect how stretch and sweat marks develop in a worn belt. He then slammed his hand against the table and shouted at bin Rasheed to stand up and take off his belt. Bin Rasheed snapped to attention like a new recruit at basic training. When bin Rasheed unbuckled his belt, not only was it unworn, but, to everyone's surprise, a price tag in Kenyan shillings was clearly visible on the inside surface. The suspect sat back down deflated and said to Gaudin, "You're good." He then asked to pray.

*Teaching Note: Gaudin **distracted, disrupted,** and **avoided** bin Rasheed's **resistances** by first focusing on his shoes, and then commanding him to stand. That bin Rasheed snapped to attention demonstrates that his **resistances** had been lowered in the moment, and that Gaudin had gained and was able to use some **authority** (a Cialdini **persuasion principle**) in the eyes of bin Rasheed. It further confirmed for Gaudin that bin Rasheed had military training. It was a satisfying **step forward**.*

The team declared a time out for prayer. When they resumed the interview, bin Rasheed sat back down in the chair with, it seemed, renewed energy. At the same moment, Bongardt knocked on the door, eager to question the suspect on the basis of information he had gathered at the hotel where bin Rasheed had been staying. Because the team members had not conferred among themselves prior to Bongardt's entrance, Bongardt was unaware of the progress that had been made. Gaudin later chided himself for neglecting to coordinate thoroughly with Bongardt.

Bongardt accused bin Rasheed of wearing new clothes, explaining that he knew someone had brought new clothes to bin Rasheed at the hotel and that the old clothes were put into a brown bag. Bin Rasheed remained silent, laughing.

*Teaching Note: This disorganized moment quickly led to a **step back**. Bin Rasheed regained some of his **information power**; he now knew the team had not coordinated, and that they did not in fact have his old clothes in their possession. Gaudin felt that he, or at least the team, had lost some of their **authority** in bin Rasheed's eyes.*

The team then called in John Anticev, an experienced FBI agent – they wanted his professional opinion given his legendary successes interviewing terrorists in the past. Anticev had worked the 1993 World Trade Center attack as well as the case against Omar Abdel-Rahman, the Blind Sheik. (As it happened, Anticev was leading an investigation of another suspect, Mohamed Odeh. Odeh had been picked up using a fake passport when he arrived in Pakistan on a flight from Kenya. He eventually confessed his role in the plot.) Based on his prior experiences, Anticev knew that a great deal could be learned from examining telephone records. He recommended to his colleagues, "Let's find out whom he has called."

In the presence of Gaudin and Parola, Anticev then began his discussion with bin Rasheed by asking him if he had had a chance to pray. With a calm demeanor Anticev had the suspect repeat his story, and asked bin Rasheed about persons he believed bin Rasheed knew. Bin Rasheed acknowledged that he knew them and seemed to enjoy lecturing a Westerner about the importance of these particular men. They chatted until late in the evening.

*Teaching Note: The intelligence interviewing professionals knew their own limits and sought to increase their **information power** by expanding their team. They sought out Anticev, an agent for whom they had great respect and whom they viewed as an **authority**. Anticev skillfully offered a powerful intangible **incentive** to bin Rasheed – rapt listening. It seems likely that bin Rasheed felt his **status** was acknowledged and his knowledge was **appreciated.***

"There's one other person we haven't talked about," Anticev observed. "Usama bin Laden." Bin Rasheed's eyes narrowed and he stopped talking. A small smile appeared on his face. Anticev, who had been listening like a captivated student, suddenly thrust a pen and paper into bin Rasheed's hand. "Write down the first telephone number you called after the bombing!" Bin Rasheed reported that he called Sameer al-Hada and relayed a phone number that translated from Arabic as 967-1-200578. After giving up the number, bin Rasheed stopped cooperating.

*Teaching Notes: The **information power** that Anticev had gained in previous terrorism-related cases allowed him to speak with **authority** on many topics and to seek **information** he knew would be of value to the team.*

*Why did bin Rasheed relay an accurate telephone number? One possible answer: According to Cialdini's **persuasion principle** of "**consistency**," people find it uncomfortable to feel they are being* *inconsistent, and getting caught up in many lies can bring on such a feeling. Bin Rasheed may have felt a sense of relief as a result of providing at least some accurate information, particularly if he thought the information was inconsequential or that he was just confirming information that Anticev already knew. Or he may have been on a roll, talking with Anticev relatively truthfully, for a long time.*

*It is possible that Anticev had successfully brought bin Rasheed into a train of thinking and a train of **memory** that pulled that phone number up to the "tip of his tongue." The suspect may just have been taken off guard – after a long period of talking authoritatively about people he knew, he may simply have continued, more or less without thinking. Or he may have been responding to Anticev's projection of **authority**. It is even possible that he was proud of having had access to such a number, and that giving such a number represented for him a small moment of **autonomy** and celebration of his **status**.*

The team then took custody of the clothes bin Rasheed was wearing, replacing them with a new button-down shirt and slacks. They also obtained a flight manifest indicating that bin Rasheed's flight to Nairobi had originated in Lahore, Pakistan, with connections in Karachi, Pakistan; Muscat, Oman; and Abu Dhabi, UAE. They learned that a return ticket had been issued for travel on August 10.

Gaudin, Parola, and the CID men also visited the hospital where bin Rasheed said he had been treated. Although no one remembered seeing the suspect, a janitor mopping the floor at the hospital approached the team. The janitor asked if they had come "for the keys and bullets." He said he had found keys and bullets in the hospital – on a window sill of the men's bathroom – and had called the police. The team retrieved these items from the Kenyan police, not knowing they would have any significance for the investigation.

The team then brought the phone number supplied by bin Rasheed to the telephone company. They asked for a list of all calls made to the Yemeni number from anywhere in Kenya during the first two weeks of August.

*Teaching Notes: The FBI agents worked in dual roles of intelligence interviewer and investigator, giving them an important **information*** *advantage. Because they were involved in the interviews they knew what to look for while gathering evidence. Their ability to obtain the bullets, the keys, and the flight manifest and to run down the list of calls continued to build **information power** in their favor.*

The Kenyans upgraded the charge against bin Rasheed from inability to provide identification to suspicion of murder. Bin Rasheed could now be held for fourteen days before being formally charged with murder. August 14

In the fourth interview, Parola told bin Rasheed, "Stop calling the explosions an 'accident.'" He showed him morgue photographs and asked, "Why did so many people have to die? If the real target was the embassy, why did so many innocent Kenyans have to die?"

*Teaching Notes: Parola addressed bin Rasheed's **resistance** but may have **side-stepped** just a bit, in an effective way. He addressed bin Rasheed's emotions by stepping into the **cross-cutting identity** of common humanity and related human loss.*

Provoked, bin Rasheed lectured on the injustices in Palestine and refugee camps in Southern Lebanon. He fumed, "Your embassy was attacked because of your foreign policy!"

*Teaching Notes: Bin Rasheed became emotional in the moment and responded. The team began to gain more **information power**: bin Rasheed was emotionally affected by the attack and cared enough to defend his position and his group's cause. He revealed a true **interest**: revenge on the United States. This **information** provided the intelligence interviewers more data on how to **persuade** bin Rasheed to continue to talk.*

For logistical purposes, on his third night of detention, bin Rasheed was moved to a private holding cell in the basement of Kenyan CID headquarters, where the interviews were taking place.

August 15

On day four, bin Rasheed asked, "Are we going to clear up my file today?" The team decided to leave the suspect alone in his cell. They did not want him to think he was especially important. They also needed time to run down leads, write reports, and digest what they had learned so far.

Teaching Notes: The team essentially ignored bin Rasheed's request to "clear up his file," and thus, for the time being, withheld meeting the **core concerns** *of* **status** *and* **role***. It is also possible that bin Rasheed greatly valued the attention he had been getting – viewing it as a kind of* **appreciation***. (Recall that people for whom attention represents* **appreciation** *may perceive even negative attention as better than no attention.) This can be an important point in intelligence interviewing: being "listened to" can be an important, albeit* **intangible, incentive***.*

This strategy showed bin Rasheed that the intelligence interviewers would not just continue to listen to his story, which they believed to be at least in part untrue. It sent the powerful message that the team had more valuable ways to spend its time. If relayed properly, such a message might also cause bin Rasheed to believe the team had another **source of power***: a* **fallback position** *should he continue to be uncooperative. Reflecting on his own strategy, bin Rasheed may have felt the need to provide at least some* **information** *of value in order to regain his importance to the interviewers. If he did not, some of his* **interests** *might go unmet, including his pride, his desire for attention, and perhaps his chance to be released from detention.*

Query: As an exercise, readers may wish to design a possible exchange between one or another of the intelligence interviewers and bin Rasheed that might have helped persuade bin Rasheed to believe that the interviewers indeed had a **fallback** *position should bin Rasheed not cooperate.*

August 16

Gaudin discreetly observed bin Rasheed reading an English-language magazine in his cell. When he inquired, the Swahili-speaking guards reported that they had been able to communicate with the detainee in English without difficulty. The guards confiscated the magazine without revealing that an interrogator had seen it.

Teaching Notes: This is a good example of the importance of attentive observation outside the interview format, and of communicating with *all persons involved with a detainee, in order to acquire **information**.*

Query: At this point in the detention, if the United States had had control of the facility, what would have been the best environment and the best plan to encourage bin Rasheed to provide more intelligence of value?

Gaudin entered the cell and asked bin Rasheed if he needed anything. Bin Rasheed requested some milk, which Gaudin delivered. Bin Rasheed thanked Gaudin for the milk.

*Teaching Notes: Gaudin continued to build **likeability** and perhaps feelings of **reciprocity**, believing this might help him persuade bin Rasheed in the coming days. Simply paying attention to bin Rasheed (taking note of his role as a possibly lonely detainee may have been an **intangible incentive**) likely helped Gaudin to continue to build an **operational accord**. Gaudin recalled that he was not giving in to frustration with bin Rasheed, even though he knew that bin Rasheed had been lying about his English language abilities and that his story was at least partially untrue. (This may be seen as a very professional response to **stress**.) Gaudin recalled how he kept his frustration in check – "I just reminded myself that I didn't want bin Rasheed to beat me."*

There was no interview on August 16.
August 17

The FBI brought in their own Lebanese-American interpreter, an older man named Mike Feghali whom Gaudin described as looking and acting like"your favorite uncle." Parola took the lead in the next interview. The interviewers brought in the morgue photos once again, since this had seemed to draw an emotional response from bin Rasheed in past interviews. They showed bin Rasheed a picture of a baby and mother fused together. Parola relentlessly repeated statements like, "This wasn't necessary." "Someone screwed up." "Why was the bomb put there?" "Why did so many innocent people have to die?" Bin Rasheed finally responded, "You're saying this is *my* fault? This is *your* fault. This is *America's* fault!"

Parola challenged bin Rasheed about some of the inconsistencies in his story, and bin Rasheed admitted to getting his cash via wire transfer from his friend Sameer al-Hada, whom he had called at the Yemeni number. The money was transferred to a shop in Eastleigh called Sheer Gold. Parola continued to confront bin Rasheed emotionally and relentlessly, and finally got him to admit that the U.S. embassy was the target of the attack. With emotions high, bin Rasheed launched into a tirade, shouting "If you put me on trial for this my tribe is going to kill you," and pushed Parola. He turned to Gaudin and threatened him and his family as well.

*Teaching Notes: After two days of no interviews – which bin Rasheed may have perceived as a loss of attention and an **intangible disincentive** for a detainee who had not been answering all their questions – the intelligence interviewers essentially picked up where they had left off. They had assessed that bin Rasheed had a feeling of guilt about the deaths in the attack. With this **information** the interviewers were quickly able to create an atmosphere of **stress** in the room in order to elicit an emotional response. Such a strategy likely **consumed** some of bin Rasheed's **resistances**, causing him to defend his position and his beliefs, and ultimately to provide more intelligence **information**.*

*As a result of this interchange bin Rasheed lost some of his **information power** to the interviewers. This loss of power, coupled with high emotions, appears to have elicited a desire for revenge, a powerful emotion that can often strain an **operational accord**. If future cooperation were important the interviewers needed to assess whether a change in tone would be beneficial in the next session, particularly given that they did not have a solid sense of bin Rasheed's ability to tolerate **stress**. They would also need to estimate the point at which a high level of **stress** would no longer be productive.*

August 18, 19, and 20
On August 18, bin Rasheed received medical attention from an FBI paramedic. His stitches were removed.

Teaching Notes: The paramedic checked bin Rasheed's wounds regularly. This may have met an emotional concern for an injured man in prison away from home (that is, communicating respect for bin

*Rasheed's **role**), in addition to the obvious humane necessity. Gaudin indicated that the medic performed all of his tasks with care. This type of treatment was likely helpful in terms of developing **accord**; it is difficult to steel oneself against feeling grateful for kind treatment. Cialdini's principles of **liking** and **reciprocity** may again have been activated, as well as feelings of **appreciation**. These feelings at this point in time may have been important, given the tone of the immediately previous interactions between bin Rasheed and the intelligence interviewers. For a man obviously sensitive to attention and emotions, positive attention may have been an important intangible **incentive**, and the loss of attention an important intangible **disincentive**.*

The U.S. team did not have access to the suspect on August 18 and 19. The Kenyan CID were preparing for an identification parade, a procedure similar to a police lineup in the United States. Previously hospitalized eyewitnesses were now ready to view the suspect. Kenyan law stipulates that a lineup be administered by police officers not affiliated with the investigation at hand. The identification parade was held at another police station miles outside the city on the morning of August 20. Eight stand-ins appeared in the lineup together with bin Rasheed. In Kenya, the witness must face the lineup without the protection of a one-way mirror and the witness must touch the shoulder of the accused to single him out. Out of six witnesses who claimed to have seen the persons involved in the attack, one identified bin Rasheed as the man who got out of the truck that had exploded. The rest of the witnesses failed to make any identification.

It had taken a little time to learn about calls made to the phone number, but on August 20 the team received the Kenyan reports on the phone number provided by bin Rasheed. Gaudin and Bongardt pored over the reports. The phone number was, in fact, a Yemeni number. Only two within-Kenya phone numbers had placed calls to that number: a call center situated near the Ramadah and IFTIN hotels, and a house in Nairobi.

In Kenya, the telephone company keeps a written record of the caller's name when collect calls are placed. The collect call log listed the caller as Khalid Salim. The call center fit with bin Rasheed's story, but the house clearly required further investigation. A series of other calls had also been made from the house before the bombing, the last of which had been initiated less than one hour before the attack.

Teaching Notes: These events provided new and important **information power***. The eyewitness identification and the matching of the telephone number constituted a turning point in Gaudin's mind: he was now convinced that bin Rasheed was directly involved in the attacks. Prior to these events Gaudin believed that bin Rasheed was hiding information, but he remained open-minded as to why. Gaudin recalled thinking that perhaps bin Rasheed was a drug dealer who did not want to get caught. The ability to remain open-minded and objective throughout the intelligence interview process is important, as it allows interviewers to continue to integrate various sources of data and not to be misled through selective perception. In this case it may conceivably also have served to contain some of the* **stress** *that comes from being lied to by a detainee.*

Further teaching note: While the telephone call connection was a solid, objective, verifiable point of reference, the eyewitness testimony might be considered less convincing. Considerable research demonstrates that eyewitness **memories** *are often faulty.*

The house was located at 43 Runda Estates. It was a nice villa with a two-car garage in a part of town where many embassy officials from various countries resided. The landlord described the tenant as "a local guy living with a bunch of Arabs." The tenant had a six-month lease and had paid the lease term and security deposit in cash in May. On the day of the bombing, it was reported, the tenant returned to pick up his security deposit and return the keys.

Bongardt took photos of the house. The FBI team was not able to get an Evidence Response Team (ERT) to the house right away. When they finally checked the villa, the ERT reported no evidence of explosive residue. Incredulous, Gaudin found out that the team had skipped the garage. D'Amuro sent the ERT back. This time they got a positive test. "The garage lit up like a Christmas tree," they said.

Teaching Notes: The results of good investigative work by U.S. and Kenyan law enforcement repeatedly provided **information** *power to the* *intelligence interviewing team. With this new knowledge about the house the interviewers were able to pursue their hypotheses with much greater vigor, demanding that the house be searched again. Their confidence and persistence paid off, and the intelligence interviewers were now better positioned to talk with bin Rasheed.*

At this point in the investigation, the team noticed a heightened interest in their case. Supervisors now asked regularly for status updates and reports.

On the night of August 20, the United States launched Tomahawk missile strikes against locations in Sudan and Afghanistan in retaliation for the embassy bombings. The al-Shifa pharmaceutical plant in Khartoum, alleged to be producing chemical weapons for al Qa'ida, was destroyed. In Afghanistan, terrorist training camps near Khost were targeted; however, bin Laden and his men had already fled in anticipation of U.S. retaliation.

Officials in Washington, considering the situation on the ground in Kenya to be too dangerous, started pulling the FBI out of Nairobi. D'Amuro recalled Parola first. Gaudin and Bongardt then focused on getting as much information as possible out of the suspect before they too would be pulled out.

August 21

On August 21, the Kenyan newspaper *The Nation* ran a short front-page article with the headline, "Face of the Grenade Thrower." Bin Rasheed, the paper reported, was accused of riding in the bomb truck and throwing a grenade at guards before the embassy blast. The story was complete with a picture of a smiling bin Rasheed with hands clasped together in a triumphant pose. Although the article included no statement by the suspect, it seemed clear that bin Rasheed must have cooperated with the photographer. It appeared that the photographer had paid someone off to get access to the detainee. Interestingly, the reported accusations had not come from the interrogation team. In fact, the team had yet to establish bin Rasheed's role in the blast –if any.

Teaching Notes: Gaudin recalls that while this article caught the team off guard it did not sway him in his understanding of bin Rasheed and his story. Gaudin believes that the results of the lineup had caused the newspaper reporter to assume that bin Rasheed was guilty. Gaudin, however, focused on the main issues still at hand: bin Rasheed had yet to confess, and he could probably provide more intelligence.

*Query: It would be interesting to know what happened between bin Rasheed and the journalist and the photographer. Did they convince bin Rasheed that the jig was up? Did they offer some **incentive**? How did they convince him to pose for the picture? Was it possible that bin Rasheed was at that point putting together a new **fallback** position – that is, that he would offer **information** in return for being able to speak for his cause worldwide?*

The Americans were told to wrap up whatever they could. They were to prepare to evacuate. The FBI team therefore had to deal with a likely deadline on their investigation. Gaudin fingerprinted bin Rasheed in his holding cell. Gaudin and Bongardt posed in a photo with the suspect so that they would have a means of documenting his height.

The team by now had accumulated a great deal of evidence that contradicted bin Rasheed's original story. They had the phone call records, the arrival card, the flight manifest, the explosives residue test results from the house, and the deception about clothes.

Gaudin began the next interview by saying, "Today you don't get to talk. You listen." Gaudin and Bongardt told bin Rasheed that they knew he was involved and could prove it, but all they really cared about was why all those innocent people had to die. They proceeded to place much of the evidence in front of him– the phone records, arrival card, and flight manifest. Gaudin said, "We found the house. Let me describe it to you. It's a big house with a terracotta roof and a number 43 on it." When shown the photo of the villa, bin Rasheed acknowledged that the intelligence interviewers seemed to know everything.

*Teaching Notes: Gaudin **indirectly** addressed possible **resistances** by stating up front that bin Rasheed was now in the **role** of a listener. (This could have made it less likely that the suspect would be mentally lining up his arguments.) Gaudin effectively used the position of **authority** he had built with bin Rasheed over the past nine days, and the **information power** that the team had systematically gathered. He put* *bin Rasheed into a situation where the detainee could no longer easily maintain* **consistency**.

With the original **fallback** *story demolished, bin Rasheed would have been hard pressed to continue this tactic of* **resistance***. He had to decide how to behave from this point forward. His decision may have been based on a mix of emotions, and his decision-making may have been less than fully conscious. It may have included a feeling of* **indebtedness** *and* **liking** *for the agents he had come to know, a sense of pride in his own accomplishments and a wish to talk about what happened, and a conscious weighing of options of how to best to pursue his own* **interests** *and those of his* **constituents** *– that is, his fellow jihadists. It is also possible that he had in fact prepared for this conversation and had constructed a new* **fallback position**.

Bin Rasheed said, "If you promise I'll be tried in the United States, I'll tell you everything. America is my enemy, not Kenya. I will tell you all about my involvement with the bombings, bin Laden, and al Qa'ida."His reasoning was that he wanted the United States to know why the bombing took place. He asked,"Will I be able to tell my story?" He wanted a guarantee from President Clinton.

Gaudin had never heard of al Qa'ida before.

Teaching Notes: Bin Rasheed's offer suggested that he might use one of his **sources of power,**namely **information***, as an* **incentive** *in exchange for a*tangible incentive*: going on trial in the United States. This is an interesting example of a detainee offering a deal to U.S. agents. Bin Rasheed's statements also provided the team with a valuable insight into one of his* **interests***: to have the cause he believed in, and his own* **status** *as an important enemy, known around the world (and, likely in his mind, validated.) If the team were able to meet or appear to meet this* **interest***, they would gain valuable* **power** *in the interview process, for they now possessed some* **incentive power** *to persuade bin Rasheed to provide more* **information**.

The team immediately relayed the request to Patrick Fitzgerald, the Assistant U.S. Attorney for the Southern District of New York (SDNY), who was in Kenya supporting the investigation. Bin Rasheed asked for time to pray the Istikhara, an Islamic prayer for guidance. He planned to sleep and wake up the next morning with his decision as to whether or not to cooperate with the Americans.

*Teaching Notes: Rather than try to pressure bin Rasheed to make an immediate decision, the team allowed him to have a sense of **autonomy** in making his own decision in his own way. They did this despite great time pressure. While some might view this as giving up control, a careful assessment suggests otherwise. The interviewers' **sources of power** were now greatly strengthened by **information, incentives,** and **relationship**. Bin Rasheed had lost his original **fallback** position and proposed a new **fallback** position, namely a public appearance in the United States to tout his cause. The **balance of power** for getting information seemed to be tipping toward the intelligence interviewing team. They hoped that bin Rasheed would continue to believe it was in his **interest** to provide **information**.*

*This kind of strategy – letting the detainee have time to make his own decision –is likely to increase cooperation, given that people are often more willing to cooperate if they feel they are doing so on their terms, and that they have not been coerced into acting against their own **interests**. Pausing for the evening also gave the team the time they needed to work out the details for bin Rasheed to be tried in the United States.*

August 22

With bin Rasheed's significance unfolding, Gaudin suggested to Fitzgerald and D'Amuro that they "bring in the A-team" to talk with the suspect. Gaudin had hoped that Doran and Anticev would take over.

They replied, "No, you got him to the table. You need to bring him the rest of the way."

*Teaching Notes: This seems to be a good example of an organization supporting its people. The leadership sent the message "We believe in you," a powerful **intangible incentive** for the intelligence interviewers. Further, they clearly seem to have recognized the **operational accord** that Gaudin had built with the detainee; **relationship** can be a very potent source of power.*

Fitzgerald then explained to bin Rasheed his full AOR, not the modified overseas version. The suspect was presented a Document of Understanding (DOU) stating the suspect's rights and his desire to be tried in the United States. The DOU further stated that law enforcement would make their best efforts to bring the suspect to the United States to stand trial. The interpreter orally translated both documents into Arabic. Gaudin said to bin Rasheed, "I've been with you for ten days. You know me now. I wouldn't go over this with you if I didn't think it could really happen." After two hours of discussion, the suspect agreed to sign the form without a full guarantee that his demands would be met. He trusted the Americans would do their best.

*Teaching Notes: This story presents a good example of the importance of **relationship power**. Despite still viewing Americans as "the enemy," bin Rasheed had come to see Gaudin as a person whom he could trust. It is also possible that the **incentive** to go to the United States, and to go public, was in fact quite powerful.*

However, the suspect stated, "I cannot sign this form. This is not my name. My name is Mohammed Rasheed Daoud al-'Owhali."

*Teaching Notes: Offering his true name was a good indicator that al-'Owhali's **resistances** had significantly lessened. Gaudin knew, however, that while this **step forward** was important, it did not mean that from this point on al-'Owhali would be fully cooperative on every topic and with every detail. The intelligence interviewers needed to continue to **persuade**, to build the **accord**, and to check out every bit of the **information**, throughout the process.*

A new form was typed up with the correct name and al-'Owhali signed it. The DOU text read as follows:

I ... have been fully advised of my rights, including my right to remain silent and my right not to answer questions without a lawyer present. As I have been previously told, I understand that anything I say or have said can be used against me in court in the United States. I also understand that if I choose not to answer questions my refusal to answer questions cannot be held against me in court. I further understand that if I choose to answer questions, I can always change my mind and decide not to answer any further questions. I understand that both Kenyan and American authorities are investigating the murder of the various American and Kenyan victims in and around the United States embassy in Nairobi.

I have a strong preference to have my case tried in an United States Court because America is my enemy and Kenya is not. I would like my past and present statements about what I have done and why I have done it to be aired in public in an American courtroom. I understand that the American authorities who are interviewing me want to know who committed the bombing of the embassy and how it was carried out.

I am willing to waive my rights and answer the questions of American authorities upon the condition that the undersigned law enforcement authorities make all best efforts to see that I am brought to the United States to stand trial. I understand that the undersigned prosecutor is only empowered to make recommendations to the Attorney General of the United States and other executive officials of the United States Government and I further understand that the United States Government only intends to act with the mutual agreement of the Kenyan government.

No other agreements or promises have been made other than as set forth in this document.

Al-'Owhali then explained,"I was willing to die in the execution of the plot, but not as a bystander." His mission was twofold: to force the embassy guards to lift the steel drop bar at the entrance to the underground parking garage, and to unlock the truck padlock should the detonator switch fail and throw a grenade into the truck to ignite the explosives. After he had jumped out of the truck, al-'Owhali realized he had left his pistol on the front seat. He threw a stun grenade at the guards who ran away in terror without lifting the drop bar. Al-'Owhali ran too because his mission was complete. To stay and be killed would be suicide, not martyrdom, he maintained. Martyrdom was acceptable, but suicide was against the teachings of Islam.

Teaching Notes: It might have been tempting to debate with al-'Owhali about whether or not this statement was accurate. While some might think that al'Owhali truly believed that his mission was complete, others might suspect that he did what most humans do in the face of *death – that is, to try save their lives. Al-'Owhali may also have fled instinctively, without much conscious thought. The important point to remember is that al-'Owhali was sharing his story, and that by listening intently – albeit critically – and choosing carefully when to intervene, the intelligence interviewers learned a great deal. "Just listening" may have been an important intangible **incentive**, showing **appreciation** and respect for al-'Owhali's **status**.*

Al-'Owhali wanted to tell his whole story from beginning to end. When he was done, the investigators could go back and ask questions. He warned that it was a very emotional story.

At this point, the tone of the discussion became similar to that of an after-action review. Like two soldiers comparing notes after a battle, Gaudin and al-'Owhali reviewed what went well and what went wrong in the operation.

*Teaching Notes: By respecting al-'Owhali's request, and his **autonomy**, the intelligence interviewers put al-'Owhali in the **role** of "storyteller" versus that of a detainee "giving up" what he knows. This informal style of "comparing notes" also capitalized upon a **cross-cutting identity**, building **affiliation**, showing respect for **status** and **role**, and in the process further **sidestepping** potential **resistances** at this critical time.*

August 23, 24, and 25

Once he had signed the DOU, al-'Owhali talked for three days about his role in al Qa'ida and the bombings. He provided the names, descriptions, and roles of his fellow cell members. At first he only supplied kunyas or nicknames, but if shown a photograph he relayed a great deal of information about the person pictured. He also provided details of the Dar es Salaam attack, unwittingly filling in gaps in U.S. knowledge.

Teaching Notes: The make-up of the intelligence interviewing team remained consistent and included Gaudin, Bongardt, Feghali (the interpreter), and Kenyan CID representatives. Gaudin reflected that while al-'Owhali was more cooperative, it "remained a chess match," as he would often only supply details if shown proof, such as a picture, *or if the interviewers could provide enough details so that al-'Owhali believed they already had the **information** he was about to tell them. They had no analytical support or reach-back capabilities at the time. Fortunately the interviewers were knowledgeable and could vet some of the information on their own.*

*One can imagine the increased effectiveness of these discussions had a good analytical team and more capability for vetting been available. Even at this point more **information power** might have been very useful.*

Al-'Owhali's Story: From Radicalization to Action

Mohammed Rasheed Daoud al-'Owhali was born in Liverpool on January 18, 1977, to devout and wealthy Saudi parents. His father had been studying for a master's degree in England. A year after his birth, al-'Owhali returned with his family to Saudi Arabia. Religion played a central role in his life. As a teenager, he read conservative religious magazines such as *al Jihad* and *al Mujahedeen*. He read books such as *Love and Hour of the Martyrs*, which glorified men who sacrificed their lives in jihad. He listened to cassette tapes of speeches by Sheik Omar Abdel Rahman, the blind Egyptian cleric later convicted for conspiring to blow up the Lincoln and Holland tunnels and other NY City landmarks.

Al-'Owhali was deeply troubled by Kissinger's Promise,which many in the Arab world considered a grand U.S. Government plan to occupy the Arabian Peninsula in order to control oil resources. The U.S. military had maintained a presence in Saudi Arabia since the 1990 Gulf War; this was seen as a threat to the holy cities of Mecca and Medina. In addition, the United States supported the Saudi government, viewed by many Arabs as corrupt and not true to the tenets of Islam).

While al-'Owhali was studying at Mohamed bin Saud religious university in Riyadh he met with a friend who had just returned from fighting on behalf of Muslims in Bosnia. Together they discussed joining the jihad in Bosnia, Chechnya, or Tajikistan. Al-'Owhali dropped out of the university after only his second year to join the fight.

The U.S. Government Case Study of Human Manipulation

Because he was underage al-'Owhali asked his father for permission to travel. Originally setting out for Tajikistan, al-'Owhali landed in Peshawar, a Pakistani town on the border of Afghanistan known for recruiting jihadists. In 1996 a recruiter sent him to the Khaldan training camp. The man in charge of hospitality at the camp gave al-'Owhali his first alias in what would be a series of aliases. He was told never to use his true name from then on, or to reveal his country of origin. He received basic military training and periods of instruction in religious ideology.

*Teaching Notes: Despite the past order to conceal his name, al-'Owhali provided his true name to the intelligence interviewers before telling his story, suggesting that his **interests** as a "jihadist" may have been lessened, if only for the time being. It may have been that the **authority** of his former leaders had lessened. It seems possible that other **interests** may have grown steadily during the discussions in Kenya, including the desire for attention, **appreciation**, and personal **status**.*

Based on his performance, al-'Owhali was chosen by the emir of the camp to have an audience with UBL. He asked UBL for a mission right away. UBL said that his time would come and encouraged him to get more training. Al-'Owhali then received advanced training at other camps, including al-Siddiq, al-Farouq, and a camp near Khost known as the Jihad Wal camp. He was trained in security and intelligence, how to kidnap, how to seize buildings, and how to hijack buses and planes. He also received intensive training in the management and operation of a cell.

Later al-'Owhali claimed not to have taken *bayat*, an oath of loyalty, to UBL. He explained that he had wanted a mission that would result in the death of Americans. If he pledged *bayat*, he explained, he risked having to accept a noncombatant or logistical assignment.

*Teaching Notes: It becomes clear that al-'Owhali viewed himself as a highly self-motivated, proud, independent, and goal-oriented person. This **knowledge** seems to have assisted the team in their **persuasion plans** as they continued to talk with al-'Owhali.*

Al-'Owhali became friends with Azzam, a young Saudi whom he met at the camps. Azzam nursed al-'Owhali back to health after a bout with tuberculosis.

Al-'Owhali asked UBL for permission to fight alongside the Taliban. He distinguished himself in what he called the "C Formation" battle in Kabul. Despite being outnumbered, he and five other men were able to repel enemy forces and hold their ground. For his loyalty and service, al-'Owhali was trusted to carry his rifle in the camps, even in the presence of UBL.

*Teaching Notes: This information affirms the hypothesis that al-'Owhali viewed himself as an important person in his social group. Reinforcing this sense of **status** was likely to appeal to al-'Owhali. When the team encountered more **resistances** as they talked with al-'Owhali, they realized that appealing to this sense of importance was likely to help in **persuasion**.*

Al-'Owhali's Timeline of the Nairobi Attacks

During his time in Afghanistan, Azzam recruited al-'Owhali for a suicide mission in East Africa.

With a clean shave, al-'Owhali traveled to Yemen on an Iraqi passport in the name of Abdul Jabbar Ali Abdul Latif. In Yemen he stayed with Sameer al-Hada, a fellow veteran of al-'Owhali's alleged victorious battle with the Taliban.

Al-'Owhali met with Azzam's cousin Bilal, who helped al-'Owhali secure a Yemeni passport in the name of Khalid Salim Saleh bin Rasheed. While in Yemen, al-'Owhali telephoned his parents in Saudi Arabia. His father visited him in Yemen.

When al-'Owhali returned to Pakistan, Khallad explained the upcoming mission as a suicide attack against a U.S. target in East Africa. He did not name the specific country. Al-'Owhali and Azzam were both instructed to make martyrdom videos. Khallad filmed al-'Owhali's video and even instructed him what to say in it. He told him to claim affiliation with the Third Martyr Barracks, First Squad of the El Bara bin Malik Division of the Liberation Army of the Islamic Holy Lands, a fictitious group. The video required five or six takes because al-'Owhali kept breaking into fits of laughter at his alleged group's name.

Al-'Owhali and Azzam were present in the background while John Miller of ABC News interviewed Osama bin Laden in Khost, Afghanistan, on May 28, 1998. UBL is positioned in front of a map of Africa. UBL warned of attacks against American targets.

On July 31, al-'Owhali left Lahore for Nairobi with stops in Karachi, Muscat, and Abu Dhabi.

On August 2, al-'Owhali arrived in Nairobi. He was one day late because he had missed a connecting flight. The delay caused al-'Owhali to miss the pre-arranged pickup at the airport. He had called Khallad to explain, and Khallad had immediately informed the cell in Kenya. Khallad had then called al-'Owhali back, and gave him detailed instructions to continue on to Nairobi, check into the Ramadah Hotel in Eastleigh, and wait to be picked up there. Harun arrived at the hotel later on that same day and paid the bill. Harun took al-'Owhali back to the rented villa in Nairobi where he resided with the other operatives.

Azzam arrived at the villa on August 3 from Mombasa. He was accompanied by the cell leader, Saleh. Saleh described the mission in more detail and revealed that there would be two bombings, one in Nairobi and one in Dar es Salaam.

A Toyota truck was loaded with twenty crates containing a mixture of TNT, aluminum nitrate, and aluminum powder. Al-Owhali went into the garage of the house at 43 Runda Estates to see the truck. He and Azzam were instructed how to ignite the bomb.

On August 4, Saleh took al-'Owhali on a walk-through of the embassy grounds to show where he wanted the bomb placed. Al-'Owhali tried to persuade Saleh to change the plan and relocate the truck from the back of the embassy to the front or to the underground parking garage. He wanted to minimize Kenyan casualties and maximize American deaths. Saleh told him the plan was already set. This was the location chosen and the plan would not be changed.

On August 5, Abdel Rahman wired the explosives to batteries in the back of the truck and an ignition switch on the dashboard.

The U.S. Government Case Study of Human Manipulation

The mission was scheduled for August 7. Friday morning was chosen because devout Muslims would be praying at their mosques.

On the day of the attack, al-'Owhali dressed in black shoes, baggy denim jeans, a short-sleeved collared shirt, and a blue cotton jacket. He placed a collect call to al-Hada in Yemen. He tucked four grenades into his belt and placed a pistol in his jacket pocket. He left the house with Azzam at 9:45 AM for the embassy.

Harun led the way to the target in a separate vehicle and waved the bomb truck on as they got close to the embassy.

Azzam instructed al-'Owhali to remove his jacket so he could better access the grenades. Al-'Owhali and Azzam listened to Islamic chants from the truck tape deck on the way to the target. "Will these two friends meet again in paradise?" the chanter asked.

The truck entered the rear embassy parking area and stopped at the drop bar. Another vehicle was exiting the parking garage. Al-'Owhali jumped out of the passenger seat, forgetting his gun. He yelled at the guards in English to lift the drop bar, and threw a stun grenade when the guards hesitated. The guards ran away. There was a great deal of confusion, but the drop bar remained down. Azzam began repositioning the truck so that it was parallel to the embassy building. He also fired a pistol out the window of the truck at the embassy. It was unclear to al-'Owhali what Azzam intended to do next. He felt he could serve no purpose by staying. He ran toward the Ufundi/Cooperative House. Azzam detonated the bomb.

Al-'Owhali was thrown to the ground by the force of the explosion, suffering several injuries. He lost two grenades. He walked to a local clinic for treatment. He disposed of the remaining grenade in a trash can at this location.

He was transferred by ambulance to MP Shah Hospital. After getting stitches, he reached into his pocket to see if he had any money. He found the extra bullets and the keys to the truck padlock. He washed these items in the men's bathroom sink to get rid of any fingerprints. After unsuccessfully trying to flush them down the toilet, he placed them on the bathroom window ledge and left the hospital.

He was unable to find his way back to the villa and instead took a taxi to the Ramadah Hotel. He convinced a sympathetic desk clerk to loan him the money to pay for the cab. He negotiated staying at the hotel without payment until he could contact his people in Yemen. The desk clerk secured some clean clothes for al-'Owhali from a Yemeni acquaintance.

On August 8, with no extraction plan, al-'Owhali made collect calls to al-Hada in Yemen asking for money and travel documents. He instructed al-Hada to tell Khallad that he "did not travel," a code phrase that Khallad would understand to mean that al-'Owhali was still alive.

Within a few days, al-'Owhali picked up the money transfer at a jewelry store near his hotel. He paid his bill at the Ramadah and checked out. He then checked into the nearby IFTIN Lodge.

The "Tone" of the Intelligence Interviews

With his interrogators, al-'Owhali talked about religion as much as he did about the bombing. Al-'Owhali explained that the Bible and the Qu'ran share a narrative history. The Qu'ran includes both a book devoted to Mary and the story of Noah's Ark. They discussed similarities among people of "The Book": Christians, Jews, and Muslims.

*Teaching Notes: The intelligence interviewers permitted al-'Owhali to discuss what was important to him, and to take on the **role** of teacher. In bringing up this comparison al-'Owhali may have been attempting to strengthen a feeling of **affiliation** with the intelligence interviewers. Continuing to **affiliate** with **crosscutting identities** may have allowed al-'Owhali to maintain his motivation to keep talking.*

Al-'Owhali explained that Muslims were allowed to marry people of the Book. He told Gaudin, "I could marry your sister. She could convert to Islam, but she wouldn't have to."

The discussions at times were deep and serious, and could invoke serious anger as well as more friendly discussion. For example, when Gaudin countered, "Then I could marry *your* sister," al-'Owhali became filled with rage. He stood up and said, "If you marry my sister, I have the right and duty to kill you. If she married you, then any children would be raised with your religion, not hers."

*Teaching Notes: Gaudin recalls that after this heated interchange they resumed their discussion with little difficulty. These dynamics actually reflect a well developed **operational accord,** permitting each party to debate, disagree, and even argue in the context of a working **relationship** without damaging the **affiliation** and the exchange of **information**.*

When asked what it would take to stop attacks against the United States, al'Owhali related a series of conditions. There should be no U.S. presence in Saudi Arabia; the United States would have to stop providing support to enemies of the Muslims – specifically Israel and the Serbs; and the United States should stop using its influence to support leaders in the Arab world who opposed implementation of sharia law.

On August 24 or 25, the team got photographs of Azzam and Bilal from the Saudis. Al-'Owhali identified both pictures. He kissed Azzam's photo and wept. Then he lapsed into a poetic chant, singing of someday joining Azzam in paradise.

When shown the morgue photos once again, al-Owhali explained, "This isn't the way it was supposed to be. I told them we should have attacked from the front."He claimed, however, that innocent people died because of U.S. foreign policy. The attack was necessary to broadcast the story of the injustice wrought on Muslims globally.

Teaching Notes: This fleeting admission of guilt confirmed that the team had accurately assessed al-'Owhali's feelings of guilt in the past.

*Query: How might an intelligence interviewer work with this sense of guilt to further develop more detailed information? One possible way is to heighten the sense of guilt by using statements such as those seen in this case:"Why did so many innocent people have to die?" There is another possible path:**resistances** can often be **sidestepped** by acknowledging and indirectly validating a person's emotions. In the case of al-'Owhali, the interviewers might have accomplished this by asking, "In your view, how could it have been done better?" or commenting "It must be difficult to feel that you needed to put people* *in harm's way simply to have your point heard."*

The Revelation of Actionable Intelligence

Al-'Owhali at a certain point claimed to have information on a matter of public safety. After receiving a written guarantee that the information would not be used against him, he warned the agents of future attacks. He told them that plans were in place to attack the United States inside its borders but that they weren't ready yet. Requesting that the Kenyan police not be present, he also told the Americans about a future attack in Yemen. He provided details, including that al Qa'ida would conduct the attack on a U.S. Navy ship while it was refueling in the port of Aden.

*Teaching Notes: The agents had no knowledge of this impending attack at the time of the interview, nor did they prompt al-'Owhali to provide this information. Gaudin believes that it was the **operational accord** that had developed between al-'Owhali and his interviewers that motivated al-'Owhali to provide this intelligence **information**.*

The Government of Kenya (GoK) considered their country to be a victim rather than a source of transnational terrorism. Because the U.S. embassy had been the intended target, GoK quickly agreed to hand over the prosecution to U.S. authorities, even though twenty times as many Kenyans as Americans had died in the attacks. The two countries worked well together on the joint investigation. Kenyan CID investigators were present at all interviews of al-'Owhali while he was in Kenya. The Americans and Kenyans also conferred as a team between interviews, and GoK supported the American investigation even after the United States withdrew its investigators.

Although the Pakistani authorities caught Odeh, several other operatives remain at large.

Teaching Notes: This case demonstrates the effectiveness of working with a "team," as the CID was able to provide a valuable perspective and cultural expertise throughout the interviewing process. It also shows the intelligence interviewers' flexibility. This case (like many others) shows that an interview can be effective with a variety of people present.

The U.S. Government Case Study of Human Manipulation

Prosecution and Aftermath

Al-'Owhali told Gaudin he expected to be released through a prisoner swap. He believed that his group would take hostages, including ambassadors, to exchange for him.

Teaching Notes: Bin Rasheed revealed another perceived **source of power** *—yet another* **fallback position***. His belief that he remained important to his group, that his group was powerful and would accept him back even though he had cooperated with the Americans, and that he would not suffer any personal consequences if released, likely reduced his* **resistances** *throughout the final days of the intelligence interviewing process. However, it does not explain why he provided unsuspected, potentially actionable intelligence that could have saved American lives. Again, this may have been due to the power of the* **relationship***, his pride in the agents'* **appreciation** *of his information, and the atmosphere of recognition of his* **status***.*

This case would mark the first time the FBI was sent abroad to investigate a bombing committed overseas, found the persons responsible, and brought them back to the United States to face trial. On August 26, just fourteen days after al'Owhali was picked up as "the man who didn't fit in," al-'Owhali was flown from Nairobi to New York, arriving early in the morning of August 27. He was accompanied by FBI personnel, primarily members of the Hostage Rescue Team, an elite group that provides force protection. He did not want to discuss the attacks during the flight. He was booked in New York and charged with murder. He listed "Mr. Steve" as his next of kin.

At the December 2000 hearing to suppress his confession, al-'Owhali and Gaudin were not permitted to speak. But Gaudin recalls that al-'Owhali looked pleased to see Gaudin, openly smiling in his direction. At subsequent legal proceedings, al-'Owhali made frequent eye contact with Gaudin.

The trial of al-'Owhali and his three co-defendants began on January 2, 2001. The court ruled that only the statements al-'Owhali had made after August 22, when he received his full AOR, would be admissible in court. On May 29, 2001, after a six-month trial, the jury returned its verdicts. All four defendants were convicted of all 302 counts in the indictment.

Fortuitously, on September 11, 2001, as it happened, al-'Owhali was in the Metropolitan Correctional Center, just six blocks away from the WTC. On October 18, 2001, all four men received the sentence of life in prison without the possibility of parole.

The United States built a new $68 million embassy building in Nairobi outside the downtown area. The Nairobi bombing site has become a memorial park.

In 2001, Stephen Gaudin was sent to language school in Vermont to learn Arabic. He was posted for two years in Yemen as a legal attaché at the U.S. embassy in Sana'a and still works for the FBI.

Mohamed Rasheed Daoud al-'Owhali is now serving his sentence at the federal Administrative Maximum Facility (ADX) (also known as the Supermax) in Florence, Colorado. He is currently appealing his conviction.

Questions for Consideration:

•*As you read through this case, were there points at which you wanted to add to the teaching notes? Or where you disagreed with some point of case analysis?*

•*Bearing in mind your own experience, what more did you want to know about this case? What additional facts and descriptions would you like to see in a teaching case of this kind?*

•*For example, suppose in the case of* al-'Owhali *there were hundreds of pages of his (the detainee's) account of the case, so that we would know, as we do with Tai, his own report of his thinking? How might information about al-'Owhali's thoughts and perspectives change your analysis of the case?*

•*Suppose in the case of* al-'Owhali *there had been access to Kenyan CID, and the guards, and perhaps other Kenyans on the scene, such as the man at the hospital? What might you have asked each of them?*

•*Suppose you could have talked with each of the other American agents; what might you have asked each of them?*

The U.S. Government Case Study of Human Manipulation

•*Research on neuroscience reveals that people gather much information below the level at which they are consciously aware. People process information emotionally as well as cognitively. What are the potential benefits – and pitfalls – of attending to and utilizing one's feelings and "intuition" when interacting with a detainee? What are some of the ways to ensure that an intelligence interviewer does not get sidetracked when responding to "gut feelings,"especially when working with a very persuasive detainee or a detainee who might be instinctively or deliberately provoking?*

•*Each source of power in interviewing can be either positive or negative. At what points during interviews of al-'Owhali does it seem that Gaudin developed relationship power? At what points does it seem that the agents either lost relationship power or could have lost such power? (Of course nobody can know for certain; the point is to consider the potential for gains and losses of each kind of power.)*

•*Research suggests that perceptions of the balance of power may affect an intelligence interview. What are your hypotheses about how the agents, and the detainee, may have perceived the balance of power between them at each point?*

•*Which of the principles of persuasion and which of the core emotional concerns seem to you to have been especially important at each point in the interview process? What sort of mental "picture" did you form of the detainee and his tangible and intangible interests (including his core concerns)? How did the interviewers engage those interests?*

•*Thinking in terms of incentives and disincentives, what kinds of tangible and intangible incentives and disincentives were helpful?*

The Man in the Snow White Cell

Merle L. Pribbenow
Limits to Interrogation
(2004). *Studies in Intelligence*, 48(1)

The war on terror is frustrating and confusing. It is a war of shifting targets and uncertain methods, a war that is unconventional in every sense of the word. One of the most difficult parts of the war for the average American to understand is the trouble we have had in obtaining information from some of the captured terrorists being held at Bagram Airbase in Afghanistan, Guantanamo Bay, Cuba, and other locations around the world.

A college classmate of mine, someone who knows I am a retired CIA operations officer, recently expressed to me his frustration with the pace of the war on terror. He said he believed that the terrorist threat to America was so grave that any methods, including torture, should be used to obtain the information we need, and he could not understand why my former colleagues had not been able to "crack" these prisoners.

Our current war on terror is by no means the first such war our nation has fought, and our interrogation efforts against terrorist suspects in the United States, Afghanistan, and Guantanamo Bay are (hopefully) based on lessons learned from the experiences of past decades. This article details one particularly instructive case from the Vietnam era.

Nguyen Tai

More than 30 years ago, South Vietnamese forces arrested a man who turned out to be the most senior North Vietnamese officer ever captured during the Vietnam War. This was a man who had run intelligence and terrorist operations in Saigon for more than five years, operations that had killed or wounded hundreds of South Vietnamese and Americans. US and South Vietnamese intelligence and security officers interrogated the man for more than two years, employing every interrogation technique in both countries' arsenals, in an effort to obtain his secrets.

Frank Snepp, the CIA officer who conducted the final portion of the interrogation, devoted a chapter in his classic memoir of the last years of the CIA station in Saigon to the interrogation of this man, whom he called the "man in the snow white cell."[22] Snepp thought that the South Vietnamese had killed this prisoner just before Saigon fell in April 1975 to keep him from retaliating against those who had tormented him in prison for so long.

Snepp was wrong. The prisoner survived. A few years ago, he published a slim memoir of his years of imprisonment and interrogation titled *Face to Face with the American CIA*.[23] It is an extraordinary book that describes how he resisted years of unrelenting interrogation by some of the CIA's most skilled, and South Vietnam's most brutal, interrogators. His book may provide some insights into the problems, both practical and moral, facing our interrogators today.

Early Nationalist

Like Osama bin Laden, Nguyen Tai was a sophisticated, intelligent, well educated man from a prominent family. His father, Nguyen Cong Hoan, was one of Vietnam's most famous authors. Tai's uncle, Le Van Luong, was a member of the Communist Party Central Committee and the second-in-command of the communist Ministry of Public Security (Vietnam's espionage, counterespionage, and security organization, patterned after the Soviet KGB).

Tai joined "the revolution"in 1944 at the age of 18. By 1947, when he was only 21, he was Chief of Public Security for French-occupied Hanoi city.[24]Throughout the war against the French, Tai operated inside Hanoi, behind French lines, directing communist intelligence collection activities and combating French efforts to penetrate and eliminate the communist resistance. This covert war was a difficult, dirty, "no holds barred"struggle that employed assassination and terror as its stock in trade.

Tai was ruthless in the conduct of his duties. According to a history of Hanoi Public Security operations, in April 1947, just after Tai took over command of security operations in the city, his office formed special assassination teams called "Vietnamese Youth Teams" [*Doi Thanh Viet*] to "eliminate" French and Vietnamese "targets." The Hanoi history devotes page after page to descriptions of specific assassination operations conducted by these teams.[4] In September 1951, as part of a classic operation run jointly by the national-level Ministry of Public Security and Tai's Hanoi security office, a woman pretending to be the wife of the leader of a pro-French resistance faction operating behind communist lines sank a French naval vessel with a 60-pound explosive charge she carried aboard in her suitcase. The woman kept the suitcase next to her until it exploded, thereby becoming perhaps the first female suicide bomber in history.

The U.S. Government Case Study of Human Manipulation

Following the communist victory at Dien Bien Phu in 1954 and the communist takeover of North Vietnam that followed, Nguyen Tai rose quickly in the hierarchy of the communist Ministry of Public Security. One aspect of his rise was said to have been his assistance in the prosecution of his own father for anti-regime statements.[5] In 1961, Tai was appointed director of the Ministry of Public Security's newly reorganized counterespionage organization, the dreaded KG-2 – Political Security Department II [*Cuc Bao Ve Chinh Tri II*].[6] In that capacity, he directed double-agent operations against South Vietnamese and American forces, including the successful effort to capture and double back US-trained spies and saboteurs dispatched into North Vietnam by parachute and by boat during the early-to-mid-1960s.[7]

Tai was also responsible for a ruthless crackdown on internal dissidents and directed the initial investigations that resulted in the infamous"Hoang Minh Chinh" affair, a purge of senior communist party"revisionists." The operation sought out allegedly pro-Soviet and pro-Vo Nguyen Giap elements –including members of the party's central committee and the cabinet, and several army generals – opposed to the policies of then-Communist Party First Secretary, Le Duan.[8]

Moving South

In 1964, leaving his wife and three young children behind, Tai was sent south to join the struggle against the Americans in South Vietnam. He became the chief of security for the Saigon-Gia Dinh Party Committee in 1966.[9]In one respect, at least, Tai's assignment made sense: He had extensive experience at running a similar clandestine security/intelligence/terrorist organization behind enemy lines from his work as Chief of Hanoi Public Security during the war against the French. However, Tai carried in his head some of North Vietnam's deepest, darkest secrets – including the fact that all the US and South Vietnamese "spies"in North Vietnam were now working for the North Vietnamese; the identities of communist spies in South Vietnam's leadership; specific points of friction in North Vietnam's relations with the Soviet Union and Communist China; and internal splits and factionalism within the North Vietnamese leadership. Therefore, sending him to operate covertly behind enemy lines was a tremendous risk for the Hanoi regime.

Tai immediately threw himself into his new assignment. One of his mission orders, contained in a 17 May 1965 memorandum from the Central Office for South Vietnam (COSVN) Security office, directed him to"exploit every opportunity to kill enemy leaders and vicious thugs, to intensify our political attacks aimed at spreading fear and confusion among the enemy's ranks, and to properly carry out the task of recruiting supporters among the lower ranks of the police."[10]

Tai attacked this mission with a vengeance, launching a program of bombings and assassinations against South Vietnamese police and security services and leadership figures. According to a Vietnamese Public Security press release in 2002, "Making great efforts, Public Security forces under Tai's command recruited agents, transported weapons into the city, and conducted many well known attacks that terrified enemy personnel. Of special note were the assassination of a major general assigned to the Office of the President of the Saigon government and the detonation of a bomb in the National Police Headquarters parking lot...."[11] Tai directed many other terrorist operations, including numerous bombing attacks against police personnel and locations frequented by police and security officers; the assassination of a senior member of the Vietnamese National Assembly; an assassination attempt against future South Vietnamese President Tran Van Huong; and assassinations of individual police officers and communist Viet Cong defectors.[12]

Capture

In 1969, Tai was forced to move his operations to a more secure area in the Mekong Delta, following the decimation of the communist infrastructure in the Saigon area by the Americans and South Vietnamese in response to the 1968 communist Tet offensive. While traveling to a political meeting in December 1970, he was arrested by South Vietnamese forces. The cover story and the identity documents carried by Tai and his traveling companions were quickly discovered to be false.

After an initial interrogation and physical beating by South Vietnamese security personnel, Tai shifted to his fallback position to avoid being forced to reveal the location and identities of his personnel in the area.

He "admitted" to being a newly infiltrated captain from North Vietnam. When the interrogation became more intense, he "confessed" that he was really a covert military intelligence agent sent to South Vietnam to establish a legal identity and cover legend before being sent on to France for his ultimate espionage assignment (which he claimed to have not yet been fully briefed on).[13]Each time he shifted to a fallback story, Tai made an initial show of resistance and pretended to give in only when his interrogator "forced"him to make an admission. He did this to play on the interrogator's ego by making him think that he had "cracked" his subject's story and to divert attention from the things that Tai wanted to protect--such as the location of his headquarters, the identity of his communist contacts, and his own identity and position.

Tai's effort succeeded in buying time for his colleagues and contacts to escape to new hiding places and in diverting his "enemy's" attention onto a false track. But his claim to be a covert military intelligence agent ensured that he would receive high-level attention. Instead of being detained and interrogated by low-level (and less well-trained) personnel in the Mekong Delta, Tai was sent to Saigon for detailed questioning by South Vietnamese and American professionals at the South Vietnamese Central Intelligence Organization's (CIO) National Interrogation Center (NIC).[14]

Counter-Interrogation Strategy

As any professional interrogator will tell you, the most important requirement for a successful interrogation is knowledge of your subject. The problem facing the interrogators at the NIC when Tai first arrived was that no one had any idea who he really was. Tai devised a cover story, complete with fake name, family and biographic data, and information on his work assignments. He pretended to be cooperative, but provided only information that was either already known or that could not be checked. To claim ignorance about the local communist organization and local contacts, he said he had just arrived from the North on an infiltration boat (one whose arrival was already known because the South Vietnamese had attacked and destroyed the boat when they discovered it at a dock in the Mekong Delta in November 1970). He stated he had been selected for the assignment in France because of his excellent French language skills and had been told that for reasons of security he would be informed of the precise nature of his mission in France only after he established a cover identity and received legal papers in Saigon for his onward travel.

The information Tai provided about his military intelligence training and instructors in North Vietnam was information he knew had already been compromised by communist agents captured previously. He was thus able to give his interrogators what seemed to be "sensitive"information they could confirm, thereby enhancing their belief in his story while at the same time revealing nothing that might cause further damage to his cause. The fact that he had initially "concealed" this information and only"confessed" after being beaten by South Vietnamese officers would, he knew, enhance the story's believability. Tai said his first CIA interrogators, an older man named"Fair" [sic] and a younger man named "John,"believed his story.

Suspicions began to surface about Tai's cover story. Tai claims that his story began to fall apart when members of his Saigon Security Office staff, desperate to find out what had happened to their boss, asked one of their agents inside the city to try to locate him, giving the agent his alias (but not his true name and identity) and the date and place he was arrested. When the South Vietnamese arrested this agent, Tai says that the South Vietnamese CIO began to wonder why an agent from Public Security would be trying to locate someone who claimed to be from military intelligence, an entirely separate organization.

Tai may believe this version of how his story began to come apart. But, in fact, he may not have been as successful at deceiving the Americans as he thought. According to former CIA officer Peter Kapusta, who told author Joseph J. Trento in 1990 that he had participated in Tai's interrogation,"John" quickly became suspicious of Tai's cover story and launched an investigation.[15]Tai admits that after the polygraph examination he had a confrontation with"John" when "John"tried to re-interview him about his biographic data.[16]Whatever the origin of the suspicions, Tai was turned back over to the South Vietnamese, who decided to conduct their own interrogation using their own methods.

Extracting a Confession

The South Vietnamese set to work to force Tai to admit his real identity, the first step in breaking him.

They began confronting him with gaps in his story and tortured him when he maintained he was telling the truth. They administered electric shock, beat him with clubs, poured water down his nose while his mouth was gagged, applied"Chinese water torture" (dripping water slowly, drop by drop, on the bridge of his nose for days on end), and kept him tied to a stool for days at a time without food or water while questioning him around the clock. But Tai held to his cover story.

After showing Tai's picture to the large number of communist Public Security prisoners and defectors then in custody, the South Vietnamese quickly learned Tai's true identity as the chief of the Saigon-Gia Dinh Security Section.

They began to confront him with informants, former security personnel who knew him and identified him to his face as the chief of Saigon Security. One of these informants was a female agent who, according to Tai's account, had planted a bomb at the South Vietnamese National Police Headquarters on Tai's orders.[17]Tai continued to maintain his cover story, and his attitude toward his confronters was so threatening (when combined with his past reputation) that he thoroughly terrified his accusers, one of whom reportedly committed suicide shortly afterward.[18]

The South Vietnamese tried a new ploy. They told Tai they were planning a secret exchange of high-ranking prisoners, but he would only be exchanged if he admitted to his true identity. They promised that he would not have to tell them anything else, but they could not exchange him if he did not confess his true identity.[19] They confronted him with captured documents he had written and with photographs of him taken years before when he served as a security escort for Ho Chi Minh during a state visit to Indonesia. Exhausted and weakened, both physically and psychologically, and comforting himself with the thought that, whether he confessed or not, the enemy clearly already knew his real identity, he finally gave in. Tai wrote out a statement admitting that, "My true name is Nguyen Tai, alias Tu Trong, and I am a colonel in the National Liberation Front of South Vietnam."[20]

No Respite

As Tai must have anticipated, his confession did not end his ordeal. After giving him a short rest as a reward, his South Vietnamese interrogators came back with a request that he provide details about his personal background and history. Tai refused, and the torture resumed. He was kept sitting on a chair for weeks at a time with no rest; he was beaten; he was starved; he was given no water for days; and he was hung from the rafters for hours by his arms, almost ripping them from their sockets. After more than six months of interrogation and torture, Tai felt his physical and psychological strength ebbing away; he knew his resistance was beginning to crack.

During a short respite between torture sessions, to avoid giving away the secrets he held in his head during the physical and psychological breakdown he could feel coming, Tai tried to kill himself by slashing his wrists. The South Vietnamese caught him before he managed to inflict serious injury, and then backed off to let him recuperate.[21]

Tai says he sustained himself during this period by constantly remembering his obligations to his friends and his family. At one point, when he was shown a photograph of his father, he swore to himself "that I will never do anything to harm the Party or my family's honor."[22]

Exactly what motivated him is difficult to say, but the key appears to be the reference to "my family's honor." As the educated son of an intellectual rather than a member of the favored "worker-peasant" class, it is likely that Tai's loyalties to the Party had been questioned many times. Tai does not disclose, nor does any outsider really know, what happened between Tai and his family when his father was criticized and fell out of favor with the Party shortly after the communist takeover of North Vietnam in 1954. He may have felt a need to prove his loyalty at that time. If, as Snepp wrote and Tai's interrogators believed, Tai helped prosecute his father during this period, his memoir suggests that he subsequently reconciled with his father and appears to have resolved never to cause such pain to his family again. Human psychology is a tricky business, of course, but in this case what appeared on the outside to be an exploitable weakness – Tai's apparent betrayal of his father– had been turned into a strength.

Lest anyone be too quick to condemn Tai's South Vietnamese interrogators, we should remember that the prisoner had just spent five years directing vicious attacks against these same men, their friends, their colleagues, and their families. They knew that if Tai escaped or was released, he would come after them again. During 1970, the last year of Tai's freedom, in spite of the losses his organization had suffered during the Tet offensive, communist accounts boast of at least three bombings and several assassinations conducted by Tai's personnel against South Vietnamese police and intelligence officers in Saigon.[23] It was as if members of the New York Police Department were suddenly handed Osama bin Laden and asked to extract a confession. If things got "a little rough," that certainly should not have come as a surprise to anyone.

In addition, accounts by US prisoners of war of their torture by North Vietnamese interrogators at the infamous "Hanoi Hilton" reveal that the methods of physical torture used on them were identical to methods Tai says were used on him. The war was vicious on all sides; no one's hands were clean.

The White Cell

What might have happened, if the torture had continued, can only be guessed. In the fall of 1971, Tai's superiors made a move that ensured his survival. On 9 October, US Army Sgt. John Sexton was released by his communist captors and walked into American lines west of Saigon carrying a note written by Tran Bach Dang, the secretary of the Saigon-Gia Dinh Party Committee. The letter contained an offer to exchange Tai and another communist prisoner, Le Van Hoai, for Douglas Ramsey, a Vietnamese-speaking State Department officer who had been held by the communists since 1966 and whom the communists believed was a US intelligence officer.[24] Tai's torture and interrogation immediately ended. Even though the negotiations for an exchange quickly broke down, Tai had suddenly become, as his communist superiors intended, too valuable for his life to be placed in jeopardy.[25] He was now a pawn in a high-level political game.

In early 1972, Tai was informed he was being taken to another location to be interrogated by the Americans. After being blindfolded, he was transported by car to an unknown location and placed in a completely sealed cell that was painted all in white, lit by bright lights 24 hours a day, and cooled by a powerful air-conditioner (Tai hated air conditioning, believing, like many Vietnamese, that cool breezes could be poisonous). Kept in total isolation, Tai lived in this cell, designed to keep him confused and disoriented, for three years without learning where he was.[26]

Tai's interrogation began anew. This time the interrogator was a middle-aged American whom Tai knew as"Paul." Paul was actually Peter Kapusta, a veteran CIA Soviet/Eastern Europe counterintelligence specialist with close ties to the famed and mysterious chief of CIA counter-intelligence, James Jesus Angleton.[27]Even by Tai's account, Kapusta and the other Americans who interrogated him ("Fair," "John," and Frank Snepp) never mistreated him in any way, although Tai was always suspicious of American attempts to trick him into doing something that might cause his suspicious bosses back in the jungle to believe he was cooperating with the "enemy." Kapusta and the other American officers tried to win Tai's trust by giving him medical care, extra rations, and new clothing (most of which Tai claims to have refused or destroyed for fear of compromising his own strict standards of "revolutionary morality"). They also played subtly on his human weaknesses--his aversion to cold, his need for companionship, and his love for his family.[28]

According to his memoirs, Tai decided he would shift tactics after learning that he was being returned to American control. Rather than refusing to respond with any answers other than "No" or "I don't know," as he had with the South Vietnamese, he now resolved: "I will answer questions and try to stretch out the questioning to wait for the war to end. I will answer questions but I won't volunteer anything. The answers I give may be totally incorrect, but I will stubbornly insist that I am right."[29]

In other words, Tai would engage in a dialogue, something he could not trust himself to do when being tortured by the South Vietnamese out of fear that his weakened condition and confused mental state might cause him to slip and inadvertently reveal some vital secret. He would play for time, trying to remain in American custody as long as possible in order to keep himself out of the hands of the South Vietnamese, whom he believed would either break him or kill him.

This meant he would have to engage in a game of wits with the Americans, selectively discussing with them things they already knew, or that were not sensitive, while staying vigilant to protect Public Security's deepest secrets: the identities of its spies, agents, and assassins. This was, however, a tricky strategy, and even Tai admits that it led him into some sensitive areas.

Interestingly, Tai blames the communist radio and press for broadcasting public reports on some sensitive subjects, thereby making it impossible for him to deny knowledge of such areas. Sounding not unlike many American military and intelligence officers during the Vietnam War, Tai wrote:

I had always been firmly opposed to the desires of our propaganda agencies to discuss secret matters in the public media....Now, because the "Security of the Fatherland" radio program had openly talked about the [Ministry's] "Review of Public Security Service Operations," I was forced to give them [the Americans] some kind of answer.[30]

Peter Kapusta worked on Tai for several months and apparently believed he was making progress. Then he was reassigned. Washington sent Frank Snepp to take over the case.

Snepp decided to try a new ploy to crack Tai's facade. Like other American officers who had interrogated Tai, Snepp did not speak Vietnamese. Interrogations were always conducted using a South Vietnamese interpreter, usually a young woman. Snepp decided to cut the South Vietnamese completely out of the interrogation to see if this might lead Tai to speak more freely. One day he brought in a

Vietnamese-speaking American interpreter to take over the duty.

Tai, ever suspicious, believed that as long as Vietnamese were directly involved in his interrogation, there was a chance that word about him might leak out to his "comrades" on the outside. If the Americans took over completely, Tai's superiors would have no chance of locating him, or of verifying his performance during the interrogation. Tai was always desperately concerned with leaving a clear record for his superiors to find that would prove he had not cooperated with his interrogators. He believed this was essential for his own future and that of his family. As a professional security officer, Tai was well aware of the Vietnamese communist practice of punishing succeeding generations for the sins of their fathers.

He decided to force the Americans to bring back the South Vietnamese interpreter by pretending not to be able to understand the American, whom he admits spoke Vietnamese perfectly well.[31]

The ploy worked in the end. Meanwhile, however, it led to the author's only involvement in this case. As Tai had planned, Snepp became angry and frustrated, blaming the American interpreter for the lack of results.

After the session, Snepp came to see me (we had become friends during his first tour in Vietnam), told me of his unhappiness with the"performance" of the interpreter (who was a close colleague of mine), and asked if I would be free to interpret for him in future sessions with Tai. As it happened, I was not available, and Snepp was forced to return to the use of an ethnic Vietnamese interpreter. I always wondered what could possibly have caused the problem that Frank described to me that afternoon. Thirty years later, when I read Tai's memoir, I finally understood.

Impact of the Paris Accord

On 27 January 1973, the Paris Peace Agreement was signed, calling for the release of all prisoners of war and civilian detainees. In compliance, Snepp, without obtaining prior authorization from the South Vietnamese CIO (which was still the organization officially responsible for Tai's detention), informed Tai and other communist prisoners of the agreement and its prisoner exchange provisions. Tai, totally isolated from information about the outside world, was suspicious at first. Finally, he managed to persuade one of his guards (who were under instruction not to talk to the prisoner unless absolutely necessary) to confirm Snepp's information.[32]

The American interrogation ended with the signing of the agreement in Paris, although he remained incarcerated in the snow white cell. Tai was able to use the information Snepp had given him about the prisoner exchange provisions to resist further efforts by the South Vietnamese to interrogate him. He was left isolated, but in peace, for the next two years, until Saigon fell in April 1975. He credits Snepp's information on the Paris accord with enabling him to resist and survive until his final release. Frank Snepp may have saved Tai's life.

According to his memoirs, Tai maintained his sanity and survived by reminding himself of his allegiance to his nation, his Party, and his cause, and by constantly thinking of his family. He followed a strict daily ritual of saluting a star, representing the North Vietnamese flag (a red flag with a single gold star in the center), that he had scratched on his cell wall and then silently reciting the North Vietnamese national anthem, the South Vietnamese Liberation anthem, and the Internationale, the anthem of the world communist movement.[33]

He wrote poems and songs in his head, memorizing them and reviewing them constantly to make sure he did not forget. While some of these poems were the obligatory paeans to the Party, most were about his love for his children and his family.[34]

Just before communist troops entered Saigon on 30 April 1975, a senior South Vietnamese officer ordered Tai's execution to prevent his release by victorious comrades. By some measure at least, it was not an unreasonable order--as Frank Snepp noted, "Since Tai was a trained terrorist, he could hardly be expected to be a magnanimous victor."[35]

The order came too late, however. All of the CIO's senior personnel were in the process of fleeing the country, and the junior enlisted men entrusted with the task of disposing of Tai, men who had no opportunity to escape, understandably decided that they might have more to gain by keeping the prisoner alive. They were afraid of retribution if the communist victors learned that they had killed him and they might even have hoped for some reward.[36]

Tai survived and returned to his family in Hanoi in the fall of 1975. Tai went on to other important positions, including a term as an elected member of the reunified nation of Vietnam's National Assembly. In June 2002, in a solemn ceremony held in Ho Chi Minh City (the former Saigon), Nguyen Tai was officially honored with Vietnam's highest award, the title of "Hero of the People's Armed Forces."

Reflections (by Merle Pribbenow)

What conclusions can we draw about the efficacy and appropriateness of the interrogation techniques used by the South Vietnamese and the Americans in the Tai case? While the South Vietnamese use of torture did result (eventually) in Tai's admission of his true identity, it did not provide any other usable information. The South Vietnamese played the key role in cracking Tai's cover story, but it was their investigation and analysis that put the pieces together to make a solid and incontrovertible identification of Tai, not their use of torture, that scored this success. A sensitive, adept line of questioning that confronted Tai with this evidence and offered him a deal – like the offer by his torturers to exchange admission of his identity for consideration in a notional prisoner exchange – would almost certainly have achieved the same result. Without doubt, the South Vietnamese torture gave Tai the incentive for the limited cooperation he gave to his American interrogators, but it was the skillful questions and psychological ploys of the Americans, and not any physical infliction of pain, that produced the only useful (albeit limited) information that Tai ever provided. This brings me back to my college classmate's question. The answer I gave him-one in which I firmly believe – is that we, as Americans, must not let our methods betray our goals. I am not a moralist. War is a nasty business, and one cannot fight a war without getting one's hands dirty. I also do not believe that the standards set by the ACLU and Amnesty International are the ones we Americans must necessarily follow. There is nothing wrong with a little psychological intimidation, verbal threats, bright lights and tight handcuffs, and not giving a prisoner a soft drink and a Big Mac every time he asks for them. There are limits, however, beyond which we cannot and should not go if we are to continue to call ourselves Americans. America is as much an ideal as a place and physical torture of the kind used by the Vietnamese (North as well as South) has no place in it. Thus, extracting useful information from today's committed radicals – like Nguyen Tai in his day – remains a formidable challenge.

Merle L. Pribbenow is a retired CIA operations officer.**Endnotes**

[22] Frank Snepp, Decent Interval, (New York, NY: Random House, 1977). Although I was assigned to the CIA's Saigon station at the time of Tai's arrest and interrogation, I knew little of his case. The material below is based almost entirely on public-source documents.

[23] Nguyen Tai, *Doi Mat Voi CIA My* [Face to Face with the CIA], (Hanoi: Writers Association Publishing House, 1999)

[3]*Bao Cong An Thanh Pho Ho Chi Minh* [Ho Chi Minh City Public Security], newspaper, 13 June 2002, accessed on 15 June 2002 at: http://www.cahcm.vnnews.com/1051/10510010.html Note: From the 1960s to the mid1990s, the Ministry of Public Security was called the Ministry of the Interior, even though it was still referred to officially as the "Public Security Service," and its officers were called "public security officers." For simplicity, I have used the term "Ministry of Public Security" throughout.

[4] Nguyen The Bao, Hanoi City Public Security Historical Research and Analysis Section,*Cong An Thu Do: Nhung Chang Duong Lich Su (1945-1954)* [Capital Public Security: A History (1945-1954)] (Hanoi, Vietnam: People's Public Security Publishing House, 1990), pp. 124–25, 132–33.

[5] Snepp, p. 35.[6] Lt. Col. Hoang Mac and Maj. Nguyen Hung Linh, Ministry of Interior Political Security Department II, *Luc Luong Chong Phan Dong: Lich Su Bien Nien (1954-1975); Luu Hanh Noi Bo* [Anti-Reactionary Forces: Chronology of Events (1954-1975); Internal Distribution Only] (Hanoi: Public Security Publishing House, 1997), p. 183.[7] *Nguyen Tai*, p. 157; Phung Thien Tam, ed., *Ky Niem Sau Sac Trong Doi Cong An*[Profound Memories From the Lives of Public Security Officers] (Hanoi: People's Public Security Publishing House, Hanoi, 1995), p. 71. For a detailed account of the successful North

Vietnamese effort to capture these spy/commando teams and redirect them

against US-South Vietnamese forces, see Sedgewick Tourison, *Secret War, Secret Army: Washington's Tragic Spy Operation in North Vietnam*(Annapolis, MD: Naval Institute Press, 1995), and Kenneth Conboy and Dale Andrade, *Spies and Commandos: How America Lost the Secret War in North Vietnam* (Lawrence, KS: University of Kansas Press, 2000).

[8.]The Hoang Minh Chinh Affair, still one of the Vietnamese communist party's darkest secrets, is referred to in: Public Security Science Institute, *Cong An Nhan Dan Viet Nam, Tap II (Du Thao); Chi Luu Hanh Noi Bo* [People's Public Security of Vietnam, Volume II (Draft); Internal Distribution Only] (Ho Chi Minh City, Vietnam: Ministry of Interior, 1978), p. 206; and in: Nguyen Tai, pp. 166–67. A fuller account of the Hoang Minh Chinh Affair can be found in: Bui Tin, *Their True Face: The Political Memoirs of Bui Tin* (Garden Grove, CA: Turpin Press, 1993), pp. 187–90, 370–87.

9.*Ho Chi Minh City Public Security* newspaper, 13 June 2002.10 Hoang and Nguyen, Ministry of Interior Public Security Department II, p. 229.11 *Ho Chi Minh City Public Security* newspaper, 13 June 2002. Note: According to the*New York Times*, 1 February 1969, the general involved, Maj. Gen. Nguyen Van Kiem of President Thieu's military staff, was wounded in this attack, but did not die.[12] Hoang and Nguyen, Ministry of Interior Public Security Department II, pp. 234–37; Ho Son Dai and Tran Phan Chan, War Recapitulation Section of the Ho Chi Minh City Party Committee, *Lich Su Saigon-Cho Lon-Gia Dinh Khang Chien (1945-1975)*[History of the Resistance War in Saigon-Cho Lon-Gia Dinh (1945-1975)], Ho Chi Minh City: Ho Chi Minh City Publishing House, 1994), pp. 575–76.

[13] Nguyen Tai, pp. 27, 32.

14 *Ibid.*, pp. 40–41.15 Joseph J. Trento, *The Secret History of the CIA* (New York, NY: Prima Publishing, 2001). On p. 352, the author writes: "In 1971, Peter Kapusta was the CIA's top hostile interrogator of non-military North Vietnamese intelligence officers at the National Interrogation Center in Saigon. His

colleague John Bodine handled military intelligence interrogations. One day, Bodine came to Kapusta with a plea for help. Something about a North Vietnamese captain he was interrogating did not ring true. Kapusta began to work on the case. It did not take him long to establish that the "captain" was in fact the North Vietnamese general in charge of counterintelligence. The general turned out to be one of the most important prisoners the United States ever captured in Vietnam."

[16] Nguyen Tai, pp. 71–73.

[17] A post-war communist account describes this woman as the daughter of a senior South Vietnamese police officer who had been seduced by one of Tai's Public Security assassins. *Ibid.*, pp. 105–06; Phung Thien Tam, pp. 224–28.

[18] Nguyen Tai, pp. 100–02; Snepp, p. 31.

[19] Nguyen Tai, p. 95. [20] *Ibid.*, p. 114.

[21] *Ibid.*, pp. 118–48. Tai says that when he was finally released in 1975 and told his story to his communist superiors, he was criticized for his suicide attempt, which some of the communist leaders viewed as a sign of weakness (p. 145).

[22] *Ibid.*, p. 88.

[23] Ho Son Dai and Tran Phan Chan, pp. 575–77. [24] Nguyen Tai, p. 145; Snepp, pp. 32–33; *New York Times*, 9, 10, 12 October 1971.

[25] Tai claims that North Vietnamese Minister of Interior Tran Quoc Hoan told him after the war was over that the leadership had realized that the chances for an actual prisoner exchange prior to a final peace agreement were poor, but their immediate objective was to "make it impossible for the Americans and their puppets to kill me" (Nguyen Tai, p. 145).

[26] Only when released in April 1975 did Tai discover that he was back at the National Interrogation Center in Saigon, the same place where American officers "Fair" and "John" had interrogated him a year earlier. Nguyen Tai, pp. 149–51; Snepp, pp. 31, 35.

[27] William Corson, Susan Trento, and Joseph J. Trento, *Widows* (London, UK: Futura Publications, 1990), pp. 98, 219, 260;

David Wise, *Molehunt* (New York, NY: Random House, 1992), p. 219.

28 Nguyen Tai, pp. 155-56, 182; Snepp, pp. 35–36.

29 Nguyen Tai, pp. 161–62. 30 *Ibid.*, p. 175.

31 *Ibid.*, pp. 203–04.

32 *Ibid.*, pp. 214–17; Snepp, pp. 36–37.

33 Nguyen Tai, pp. 70–71, 82. 34 *Ibid.*, pp. 24, 71, 186, 210–11.

35 Snepp, p. 37. 36 Nguyen Tai, pp. 243–44.

Nguyen Tai: Case Study with Teaching Notes

The case of Nguyen Tai is very unusual in its reconstruction of events long ago. As with many reports and stories captured in hindsight we cannot know what "really" happened at the time of the interrogation of Nguyen Tai. The events discussed below occurred between 1970 and 1975, and were reported by various persons involved in the case, including Tai, between 1977 and 2005. In addition, there are likely different "realities" in this case. Each of the actors will have viewed the events through their own set of perceptions, and may have remembered and recorded the events in a way that fit their perceptions. Finally, the source materials used for this case are not necessarily consistent with each other.

From the point of view of a teaching case, probably none of this matters. The retired CIA professional who wrote the case, contributions by one of the interrogators, and reports from Tai himself have made a poignant, provocative, and extraordinarily valuable contribution to the understanding of interrogation. It appears to be the only case of its kind.

The case illustrates:

- The extraordinary importance of understanding the real **interests** of a detainee

- The powerful, long reach of a detainee's pre-detention **social identities and constituencies** throughout years of detention

- The importance of **information**, and of expertise in the analysis and uses of information, for both detainee and intelligence interviewing professionals

- A detainee's intricate, years-long use of various, layered, **fallback** positions

- An array of attempts to confront and deal with a detainee's **resistances** with a variety of apparently inconsistent methods of **persuasion**, including years of severe physical abuse and proposed "deals"

- A detainee's skillful, highly self-disciplined and apparently largely effective efforts to maintain his **resistances**

- An unusual example of a detainee who appeared, often under severe duress, to understand and work to meet his own **core emotional concerns**

- An unusual example of a detainee who appears to have participated in a **limited operational accord** with an American interrogator —an interrogator who lawfully gave him **information** that may have helped to save his life

- The possible importance, although little is known, of the **relationships** between the detainee and various guards, apparently including exchange of **information**, some skillful **persuasion**, some discussion of **incentives** and **disincentives**

- A true conundrum: What might have been the outcome if the American interrogators had been able to apply insights from current behavioral science, from the successes of U.S. interrogation in WWII, and from expertise gained in non-coercive interviewing in the years since WW II, and if they had been able to interview Tai in an environment designed for promoting an **operational accord** with high-value detainees (including persons who had some **interests** similar to Tai's **interests**)?

As with the case study of al-'Owhali, the notes on the Tai case are intended to raise ideas, not to prescribe a "right way" to conduct intelligence interviews. Again, the original article appears in black text, the teaching notes in red, additional questions in blue, and key references from the teaching papers in bold italics. Readers who wish to learn more can turn back to the six papers to read about each of these ideas.

The Man in the Snow White Cell

Merle L. Pribbenow
Limits to Interrogation
(2004). *Studies in Intelligence*, 48(1)

The war on terror is frustrating and confusing. It is a war of shifting targets and uncertain methods, a war that is unconventional in every sense of the word. One of the most difficult parts of the war for the average American to understand is the trouble we have had in obtaining information from some of the captured terrorists being held at Bagram Airbase in Afghanistan, Guantanamo Bay, Cuba, and other locations around the world.

A college classmate of mine, someone who knows I am a retired CIA operations officer, recently expressed to me his frustration with the pace of the war on terror. He said he believed that the terrorist threat to America was so grave that any methods, including torture, should be used to obtain the information we need, and he could not understand why my former colleagues had not been able to "crack" these prisoners.

Our current war on terror is by no means the first such war our nation has fought, and our interrogation efforts against terrorist suspects in the United States, Afghanistan, and Guantanamo Bay are (hopefully) based on lessons learned from the experiences of past decades. This article details one particularly instructive case from the Vietnam era.

Nguyen Tai

More than 30 years ago, South Vietnamese forces arrested a man who turned out to be the most senior North Vietnamese officer ever captured during the Vietnam War. This was a man who had run intelligence and terrorist operations in Saigon for more than five years, operations that had killed or wounded hundreds of South Vietnamese and Americans. US and South Vietnamese intelligence and security officers interrogated the man for more than two years, employing every interrogation technique in both countries' arsenals, in an effort to obtain his secrets.

Frank Snepp, the CIA officer who conducted the final portion of the interrogation, devoted a chapter in his classic memoir of the last years of the CIA station in Saigon to the interrogation of this man, whom he called the "man in the snow white cell." Snepp thought that the South Vietnamese had killed this prisoner just before Saigon fell in April 1975 to keep him from retaliating against those who had tormented him in prison for so long.

Snepp was wrong. The prisoner survived. A few years ago, he published a slim memoir of his years of imprisonment and interrogation titled *Face to Face with the American CIA*. It is an extraordinary book that describes how he resisted years of unrelenting interrogation by some of the CIA's most skilled, and South Vietnam's most brutal, interrogators. His book may provide some insights into the problems, both practical and moral, facing our interrogators today.

Early Nationalist

Like Osama bin Laden, Nguyen Tai was a sophisticated, intelligent, well educated man from a prominent family. His father, Nguyen Cong Hoan, was one of Vietnam's most famous authors. Tai's uncle, Le Van Luong, was a member of the Communist Party Central Committee and the second-in-command of the communist Ministry of Public Security (Vietnam's espionage, counterespionage, and security organization, patterned after the Soviet KGB).

Tai joined "the revolution"in 1944 at the age of 18. By 1947, when he was only 21, he was Chief of Public Security for French-occupied Hanoi city. Throughout the war against the French, Tai operated inside Hanoi, behind French lines, directing communist intelligence collection activities and combating French efforts to penetrate and eliminate the communist resistance. This covert war was a difficult, dirty, "no holds barred"struggle that employed assassination and terror as its stock in trade.

Tai was ruthless in the conduct of his duties. According to a history of

The U.S. Government Case Study of Human Manipulation

Hanoi Public Security operations, in April 1947, just after Tai took over command of security operations in the city, his office formed special assassination teams called "Vietnamese Youth Teams" [*Doi Thanh Viet*] to "eliminate" French and Vietnamese "targets." The Hanoi history devotes page after page to descriptions of specific assassination operations conducted by these teams. In September 1951, as part of a classic operation run jointly by the national-level Ministry of Public Security and Tai's Hanoi security office, a woman pretending to be the wife of the leader of a pro-French resistance faction operating behind communist lines sank a French naval vessel with a 60-pound explosive charge she carried aboard in her suitcase. The woman kept the suitcase next to her until it exploded, thereby becoming perhaps the first female suicide bomber in history.

Following the communist victory at Dien Bien Phu in 1954 and the communist takeover of North Vietnam that followed, Nguyen Tai rose quickly in the hierarchy of the communist Ministry of Public Security. One aspect of his rise was said to have been his assistance in the prosecution of his own father for anti-regime statements. In 1961, Tai was appointed director of the Ministry of Public Security's newly reorganized counterespionage organization, the dreaded KG-2-Political Security Department II [*Cuc Bao Ve Chinh Tri II*].

*Teaching Notes: At least one of Tai's American interrogators, Frank Snepp, believed that this bit of **information** could afford him some **power** in the interrogation. He thought that Tai's betrayal of his father was a potential vulnerability to play on.*

*Query: As Tai's story unfolds below, with some discussion of Tai, his ways of thinking, and his use of **resistances**, would the use of this **information** have been an effective way to **persuade** Tai?*

In that capacity, he directed double-agent operations against South Vietnamese and American forces, including the successful effort to capture and double back US-trained spies and saboteurs dispatched into North Vietnam by parachute and by boat during the early-to-mid-1960s.

Tai was also responsible for a ruthless crackdown on internal dissidents and directed the initial investigations that resulted in the infamous"Hoang Minh Chinh" affair, a purge of senior communist party "revisionists." The operation sought out allegedly pro-Soviet and pro-Vo Nguyen Giap elements –including members of the party's central committee and the cabinet, and several army generals – opposed to the policies of then-Communist Party First Secretary, Le Duan.

Moving South

In 1964, leaving his wife and three young children behind, Tai was sent south to join the struggle against the Americans in South Vietnam. He became the chief of security for the Saigon-Gia Dinh Party Committee in 1966. In one respect, at least, Tai's assignment made sense: He had extensive experience at running a similar clandestine security/intelligence/terrorist organization behind enemy lines from his work as Chief of Hanoi Public Security during the war against the French. However, Tai carried in his head some of North Vietnam's deepest, darkest secrets – including the fact that all the US and South Vietnamese "spies"in North Vietnam were now working for the North Vietnamese; the identities of communist spies in South Vietnam's leadership; specific points of friction in North Vietnam's relations with the Soviet Union and Communist China; and internal splits and factionalism within the North Vietnamese leadership. Therefore, sending him to operate covertly behind enemy lines was a tremendous risk for the Hanoi regime.

*Teaching Notes: Tai possessed vital **information power**. He knew a great deal about interrogation and about Vietnamese and French interrogation methods. He may well have prepared himself for years, thinking, "What would I do if I were captured?" He knew a good deal about the geographic area he was in. He had learned much about several different adversaries and how they worked. He had detailed knowledge of some former comrades who had been captured and an idea of what they might have known and what **information** they might have given up. He knew some **information** that had in fact been compromised in the past. He also seems to have known a good deal about himself. He had been developing his own sense of his **moral authority** for years– he had a strong belief that his loyalties were correct. He apparently had very strong **relationships** with comrades and family. And he was used to operating in hightension situations.*

Tai immediately threw himself into his new assignment. One of his mission orders, contained in a 17 May 1965 memorandum from the Central Office for South Vietnam (COSVN) Security office, directed him to"exploit every opportunity to kill enemy leaders and vicious thugs, to intensify our political attacks aimed at spreading fear and confusion among the enemy's ranks, and to properly carry out the task of recruiting supporters among the lower ranks of the police."

Tai attacked this mission with a vengeance, launching a program of bombings and assassinations against South Vietnamese police and security services and leadership figures. According to a Vietnamese Public Security press release in 2002, "Making great efforts, Public Security forces under Tai's command recruited agents, transported weapons into the city, and conducted many well known attacks that terrified enemy personnel. Of special note were the assassination of a major general assigned to the Office of the President of the Saigon government and the detonation of a bomb in the National Police Headquarters parking lot...." Tai directed many other terrorist operations, including numerous bombing attacks against police personnel and locations frequented by police and security officers; the assassination of a senior member of the Vietnamese National Assembly; an assassination attempt against future South Vietnamese President Tran Van Huong; and assassinations of individual police officers and communist Viet Cong defectors.

Capture

In 1969, Tai was forced to move his operations to a more secure area in the Mekong Delta, following the decimation of the communist infrastructure in the Saigon area by the Americans and South Vietnamese in response to the 1968 communist Tet offensive. While traveling to a political meeting in December 1970, he was arrested by South Vietnamese forces. The cover story and the identity documents carried by Tai and his traveling companions were quickly discovered to be false.

Teaching Notes: Tai carried a mixture of official and forged identity documentation. While in North Vietnam Tai had worked hard to obtain official documents to back up his fictitious cover story, but after many *failed attempts he asked his organization to forge an ID card prior to his trip to South Vietnam. After Tai was arrested he anticipated that the forgery would be discovered. He prepared a cover story for the line of questioning to come. With this **information**, Tai then constructed another (**fallback**) cover story that he would "reveal" when pushed.*

After an initial interrogation and physical beating by South Vietnamese security personnel, Tai shifted to his fallback position to avoid being forced to reveal the location and identities of his personnel in the area.

*Teaching Notes: Tai's extensive **information** about interrogation and continuous analysis about how to **resist** providing valuable information enabled him to prepare layered **fallback** positions – layered cover stories. To construct these **fallback** stories he was able to build on his knowledge of North and South Vietnamese geography, intelligence information about the war, information about himself and his own resilience, an understanding of his constituents, and a good deal of information about his adversaries.*

He "admitted" to being a newly infiltrated captain from North Vietnam. When the interrogation became more intense, he "confessed" that he was really a covert military intelligence agent sent to South Vietnam to establish a legal identity and cover legend before being sent on to France for his ultimate espionage assignment (which he claimed to have not yet been fully briefed on). Each time he shifted to a fallback story, Tai made an initial show of resistance and pretended to give in only when his interrogator "forced"him to make an admission. He did this to play on the interrogator's ego by making him think that he had "cracked" his subject's story and to divert attention from the things that Tai wanted to protect – such as the location of his headquarters, the identity of his communist contacts, and his own identity and position.

*Teaching Notes: In the moment this (**fallback**) cover story seemed to make sense to Tai: he guessed that he had enough **information** based on events that took place prior to his arrest to make his story seem believable. He worked hard to calculate correctly his use of **information**. Tai could easily assess the value of his own information about North Vietnam. He had deduced at the beginning that his captors knew little about his true identity, and thus was able, for a short period,* *to reveal bits of a false story in order to prevent the discovery of his true identity.*

While Tai was able to disrupt the interrogator's line of questioning in the short term, he inadvertently raised his profile.

Tai's effort succeeded in buying time for his colleagues and contacts to escape to new hiding places and in diverting his "enemy's" attention onto a false track. But his claim to be a covert military intelligence agent ensured that he would receive high-level attention. Instead of being detained and interrogated by low-level (and less well-trained) personnel in the Mekong Delta, Tai was sent to Saigon for detailed questioning by South Vietnamese and American professionals at the South Vietnamese Central Intelligence Organization's (CIO) National Interrogation Center (NIC).

*Teaching Notes: The saga of Tai is an elegant example of using prepared, successive, **fallback** positions (or BATNAs) one after another. Tai prepared and prepared – to be flexible and to change tactics when needed. He apparently was thinking at each moment, "What is my **best alternative** if my captors take (this or that) action?" It also seems likely that Tai was prepared for death from the very beginning.*

As the story unfolds, it is clear that Tai did not want to die if he could preserve his information and his honor without dying. It also is clear that he understood and accepted the idea that death would protect his information. On the other hand, Tai seems to have been relatively confident that he could deceive his captors or withstand most interrogation methods he knew, at least for a while.

*Specifically, Tai developed and played the **role** of a detainee who is "capitulating." It is probable that all the while he was both consciously and intuitively assessing and attempting to manipulate **core concerns** of the interrogators. These were their **core concerns** to feel important (**status**) and to feel they were making progress in their **role** as interrogators. It appears that Tai was unusually skilled in his ability to observe and plan, and to use his own conscious **resistances** to stay focused. It is also likely that the abuse Tai experienced strengthened his own sense of his **identity** as a warrior and his resolve* *to protect his **information**.*

Counter-Interrogation Strategy

As any professional interrogator will tell you, the most important requirement for a successful interrogation is knowledge of your subject. The problem facing the interrogators at the NIC when Tai first arrived was that no one had any idea who he really was. Tai devised a cover story, complete with fake name, family and biographic data, and information on his work assignments. He pretended to be cooperative, but provided only information that was either already known or that could not be checked. To claim ignorance about the local communist organization and local contacts, he said he had just arrived from the North on an infiltration boat (one whose arrival was already known because the South Vietnamese had attacked and destroyed the boat when they discovered it at a dock in the Mekong Delta in November 1970). He stated he had been selected for the assignment in France because of his excellent French language skills and had been told that for reasons of security he would be informed of the precise nature of his mission in France only after he established a cover identity and received legal papers in Saigon for his onward travel.

The information Tai provided about his military intelligence training and instructors in North Vietnam was information he knew had already been compromised by communist agents captured previously. He was thus able to give his interrogators what seemed to be "sensitive"information they could confirm, thereby enhancing their belief in his story while at the same time revealing nothing that might cause further damage to his cause. The fact that he had initially "concealed" this information and only"confessed" after being beaten by South Vietnamese officers would, he knew, enhance the story's believability. Tai said his first CIA interrogators, an older man named"Fair" [sic] and a younger man named "John,"believed his story.

*Teaching Notes: For an intelligence interviewing professional, it is important to have more **information power** than the detainee – among other reasons, to enhance the ability to **persuade**. At this point in the case, the **balance of information power** seems to have been reversed. The interrogators appeared to have little **leverage**. Moreover, they were* *pitted against a skilled, calculating, prepared detainee who not only possessed intelligence of value, but also knew about **information** that had already been compromised, and therefore knew how to appear as if he were becoming more cooperative over time without actually betraying his comrades. Tai's writing also suggests that through acute observations of his surroundings, the movements of guards and other detainees, and some conversations here and there – combined with meticulous analysis of everything he observed – he continued to acquire much **information** in the early period of custody.*

*In summary, thus far, even in captivity Tai was able to develop some **information** about his interrogators' **interests and identities**, and a **fallback** position that he used as a platform to offer **intangible incentives** and maintain his **resistances**. These **intangible incentives** or rewards for the interrogators –the sense that they were making headway – apparently achieved Tai's short-term goals of buying time and staying alive.*

*Query: In this analysis, what resources might have been available to the interrogators that might have helped to tip the balance of **information power** to their favor? One possible answer: A team with an analyst or analysts who could carefully track the **information** Tai provided, compare it very quickly against other sources, and perhaps even notice the pattern of Tai's providing already known **information**. In addition, the team would want to observe and analyze Tai (much as he was doing himself). They would hypothesize about Tai's **core concerns**, his true **interests**, and how he might be **persuaded** to provide at least bits of a true story.*

Suspicions began to surface about Tai's cover story. Tai claims that his story began to fall apart when members of his Saigon Security Office staff, desperate to find out what had happened to their boss, asked one of their agents inside the city to try to locate him, giving the agent his alias (but not his true name and identity) and the date and place he was arrested. When the South Vietnamese arrested this agent, Tai says that the South Vietnamese CIO began to wonder why an agent from Public Security would be trying to locate someone who claimed to be from military intelligence, an entirely separate organization.

The U.S. Government Case Study of Human Manipulation

Tai may believe this version of how his story began to come apart. But, in fact, he may not have been as successful at deceiving the Americans as he thought. According to former CIA officer Peter Kapusta, who told author Joseph J. Trento in 1990 that he had participated in Tai's interrogation,"John" quickly became suspicious of Tai's cover story and launched an investigation. Tai admits that after the polygraph examination he had a confrontation with"John" when "John"tried to re-interview him about his biographic data. Whatever the origin of the suspicions, Tai was turned back over to the South Vietnamese, who decided to conduct their own interrogation using their own methods.

*Teaching Notes: Unfortunately there is little information in reference material on this case that explains why "John" became suspicious of Tai, or what type of investigation was launched. In Tai's memoirs, Tai was apparently confident that he had succeeded in deceiving his interrogators, including"John." This contradiction is a good example of differing perceptions, where more records are needed. One cannot know if these actually were each person's perceptions at the time, or if they possibly were reconstructed, later-reported **memories** – and the two relayed different interpretations of events.*

Extracting a Confession

The South Vietnamese set to work to force Tai to admit his real identity, the first step in breaking him.

*Teaching Notes: Tai was a highly intelligent and disciplined, sharply focused, very well prepared, and knowledgeable detainee with a long and proud allegiance to his cause and to his people. Given these qualities, the notion of getting Tai to "break" seems implausible. That he would willingly reveal his identity, and then all of what he knew, seems hard to imagine (see **Stress**).*

They began confronting him with gaps in his story and tortured him when he maintained he was telling the truth. They administered electric shock, beat him with clubs, poured water down his nose while his mouth was gagged, applied"Chinese water torture" (dripping water slowly, drop by drop, on the bridge of his nose for days on end), and kept him tied to a stool for days at a time without food or water while questioning him around the clock. But Tai held to his cover story.

*Teaching Notes: Torture appears to have kept Tai focused on his **role** as a "detainee" and the **relationship** between him and his captors as that of an "enemy." This dynamic appears to have served to sustain, or even increase, Tai's **resistances**. It is important to note that every kind of **power** in intelligence interviewing can be lost as well as gained. This appears to be an example of the potential to lose **power** because of a punitive **relationship**.*

After showing Tai's picture to the large number of communist Public Security prisoners and defectors then in custody, the South Vietnamese quickly learned Tai's true identity as the chief of the Saigon-Gia Dinh Security Section.

*Teaching Notes: The **information power** the interrogators obtained from other sources led to this vital **step forward**. In Tai's memoirs, he described his captors' attempts to have others identify him as quite obvious. So while this approach was effective for the interrogators, Tai was also able with this **knowledge** to plan his tactics, and possible changes in tactics, in his **resistance** strategy.*

Query: What might have been some possible ways to use the identifications made by other prisoners in future interviews with Tai?

They began to confront him with informants, former security personnel who knew him and identified him to his face as the chief of Saigon Security. One of these informants was a female agent who, according to Tai's account, had planted a bomb at the South Vietnamese National Police Headquarters on Tai's orders. Tai continued to maintain his cover story, and his attitude toward his confronters was so threatening (when combined with his past reputation) that he thoroughly terrified his accusers, one of whom reportedly committed suicide shortly afterward.

*Teaching Notes: Tai's **resistances** were **directly** confronted with powerful evidence against his cover story, yet Tai did not waver. In Tai's memoirs, Tai recalled that as his interrogators first confronted him with their **information** they made small errors, a fact that seems to have helped Tai to sustain his strength to **resist**. As they presented mounting evidence against him, however, he knew that his identity had* *indeed been exposed, and he now needed to determine how to behave.*

*Tai maintained his composure despite this shift in **information power**. It appears that he was able to keep his emotions under control and to continue to think through his options for **resistance**.*

*Pribbenow's case and Tai's memoir suggest both a powerful **charisma** and successful intimidation (**disincentive**) of those who confronted him. Tai's accusers may have been very afraid of Tai and panicked at the prospect of revenge from Tai's comrades (**disincentives**). It is also conceivable that the accuser who ended his life after witnessing Tai in his role as an unyielding detainee with ability to maintain his **resistances** experienced shame from the comparison with his own behavior, and turned to his own **fallback**. At the very least, Tai apparently used various aspects of negative **relationship power** very skillfully with those who confronted him.*

*For those who study intelligence interviewing, the question may arise as to whether a detainee can really possess "**disincentive**"**power**: that is, the power to threaten or punish his captors. This vignette in the Tai story is an interesting example of a detainee who apparently had an extraordinary **disincentive power** of intimidation and threats, and used this power, in this case against those who identified him. This topic also reappears at the very end of the Tai story. Tai apparently mobilized several sources of power with his last set of guards – probably including **incentives** and **disincentives** in the form of potential rewards or potential revenge from Tai's comrades and family.*

*Query: Review the ways to deal with **resistances** from the **Resistances teaching paper**. What would one or more of these strategies have looked like at this point in this case? Is it possible that the interviewers had alternatives that could have been more effective than **direct confrontation**? This is one of the central questions that arise from studying this case.*

The South Vietnamese tried a new ploy. They told Tai they were planning a secret exchange of high-ranking prisoners, but he would only be exchanged if he admitted to his true identity. They promised that he would not have to tell them anything else, but they could not exchange him if he did not confess his true identity. They confronted him with captured documents he had written and with photographs of him taken years before when he served as a security escort for Ho Chi Minh during a state visit to Indonesia. Exhausted and weakened, both physically and psychologically, and comforting himself with the thought that, whether he confessed or not, the enemy clearly already knew his real identity, he finally gave in. Tai wrote out a statement admitting that, "My true name is Nguyen Tai, alias Tu Trong, and I am a colonel in the National Liberation Front of South Vietnam."

Teaching Notes: The following may include a slightly different description of events from those above.

*According to Tai's memoir, after he was offered a deal (an **incentive**) – to be exchanged in return for providing his true name – Tai continued to maintain his then cover story (his **fallback** position) for many weeks. He withstood the interrogators' depriving him of water (a **disincentive**,) and in turn he also refused food. Tai's is a remarkable story of the use of **commitment** and **consistency**, which had the effect of his retaining the use of the **fallback cover story**. Tai also reminded himself of his ultimate **fallback**, death, which may have helped to sustain his **resistances**.*

*Noting that Tai was willing to die, the interrogators attempted to **persuade** him to provide his name, reminding him of his family and offering **incentives**, such as releasing him in exchange for admitting his true name. His interrogators were unsuccessful, and ultimately provided Tai with water and milk and temporarily ceased the line of questioning.*

*Tai was persistently confronted with more **information** about his true identity, and his interrogators continued in their efforts to **persuade** and to coerce. They tried to appeal to his **status** as an important person, but also threatened more torture (the worst of **disincentives**) if he did not admit his true identity. According to Tai's memoirs, he found the interrogators' arguments **unpersuasive**. His true **interests** lay in protecting his **information**, preserving his reputation and his honor for not turning traitor; at the time he was considering if death would be the only way to meet this need.*

Tai did listen carefully to the interrogators as they provided details *about his life, and determined that the interrogators' knowledge was superficial. He agreed to translate a French article at the request of the interrogators, given that in his identity as Hop he had claimed to know French. A couple of days later the interrogators showed Tai both his handwritten translation of the article and a letter he had written prior to his capture – the handwriting was indisputably the same. This appears to be an interesting example of a skillful plan to set a stage, and, with good timing, to use an unexpected "bolt" of **information**.*

*According to Tai, it was this source of **information power** – the handwriting comparison, coupled with a picture of Tai with Ho Chi Minh – that convinced Tai it was in his **interest** to provide his true name and rank to his interrogators, although nothing more. He reasoned that the evidence against him was irrefutable, and rationalized that if he died under their torture, he would die under his true name. Note that this point suggests that death under torture, so long as he was identified correctly, met his **interest** to maintain his reputation as a comrade loyal to the end.*

*When Tai did finally acknowledge his own identity, according to Tai's memoirs (that is, according to his own perceptions), he did so in a way that seems to have displayed and affirmed his own **autonomy**. He stated that he now chose to reveal this one bit of **information** because six months had passed since his capture. He had allowed "his people" who were not detained to take precautionary action since he had been arrested. Tai also purposely signed his admission using a signature that would alert those who truly knew him that something was not right – in accord with the powerful **interest** to maintain his honor and reputation. Tai appears to have **consistently** focused on how he could convince those in the outside world that he was not cooperating with the enemy.*

*Tai does not appear to have wavered at any time in his assessment of the **role** of his captors. If anything he methodically kept affirming to himself their **role** as the enemy, even when offered an **incentive** like food or the possibility of prisoner exchange.*

*Query: If there had been a team focused on analyzing all Tai's behavior, might they have figured out what his **interests** were, and how to use this **information** more effectively?*

The U.S. Government Case Study of Human Manipulation

No Respite

As Tai must have anticipated, his confession did not end his ordeal. After giving him a short rest as a reward, his South Vietnamese interrogators came back with a request that he provide details about his personal background and history. Tai refused, and the torture resumed. He was kept sitting on a chair for weeks at a time with no rest; he was beaten; he was starved; he was given no water for days; and he was hung from the rafters for hours by his arms, almost ripping them from their sockets. After more than six months of interrogation and torture, Tai felt his physical and psychological strength ebbing away; he knew his resistance was beginning to crack.

This insert into the Pribbenow case comes from a different article: In a Saigon Times Magazine (2001) article describing Tai's detention and the way in which Tai handled the physical torture, it is noted, "Tai spent several days thinking of a word to reply to enquirers automatically so that he could not be 'trapped.' Finally, he chose the word 'forget' for his answers. He was asked about the list of his leaders, the espionage base, the communications network, and his father's name, but he always said 'forget.'"

*Teaching Notes: The use of the term "forget" must certainly have raised suspicions about Tai's truthfulness and in that respect it would seem an unsophisticated "story." However Tai did not seem to care whether his interrogators believed him; his very focused **interest** was to protect his valuable information. Saying "forget" may have functioned like a mantra, allowing Tai to maintain a tight focus and to avoid the **depletion** of energies and **resistances**.*

During a short respite between torture sessions, to avoid giving away the secrets he held in his head during the physical and psychological breakdown he could feel coming, Tai tried to kill himself by slashing his wrists. The South Vietnamese caught him before he managed to inflict serious injury, and then backed off to let him recuperate.

*Teaching Notes: Months of torture (**disincentives**) seem only to have increased Tai's **resistances**. In fact, the torture seems to have confirmed Tai's determination to protect his information at all costs and forced him once again to consider his ultimate **fallback** position of death.*

The U.S. Government Case Study of Human Manipulation

*Tai's memoirs reveal that he believed his "forget" mantra was working effectively, but he became concerned when the interrogators began to focus their questioning on the secret agents in Tai's organization. He feared that the interrogators possessed drugs (**disincentives**) that could force a detainee to become delirious and reveal secrets. Fearing this loss of control, for the first time Tai began repeated attempts to end his life. He chose his method for suicide, a new **fallback**, with careful analysis. He reported that he attempted suicide for weeks, although at times he experienced some doubt about his actions. His behavior during this time suggests Tai's decision to die was not an impulsive act, but rather the only alternative he felt he possessed. The decision was particularly poignant, and must have been exceedingly difficult, because at the time his North Vietnamese comrades apparently viewed suicide as a "negative act."*

*After the guards discovered Tai's cuts they took away the means for Tai to hurt himself, and, according to Tai's memoirs, the interrogators once again offered Tai a deal – money, and exile abroad (**incentives**) – in exchange for his **information**. Tai's interrogators underestimated or misunderstood Tai's **interests** –to maintain his reputation and honor as a faithful comrade – and once again Tai indignantly rejected the offer.*

Tai says he sustained himself during this period by constantly remembering his obligations to his friends and his family. At one point, when he was shown a photograph of his father, he swore to himself "that I will never do anything to harm the Party or my family's honor."

*Teaching Notes: Tai made extraordinary efforts to stay mentally connected to the **social identities** of his pre-detention life – as a comrade and a loyal Party member and as a son, father, and husband. It also appears that he was able to concentrate, in a simple and powerful way, on the **interests** of "honor" and "loyalty."*

*These two concepts appear to have served as yet another and effective mantra that helped him to stay focused. This may also have been a way to distract himself from pain. The use of the two concepts may also perhaps have served as a way for Tai to comfort himself – to meet his own **core emotional concerns**. He seems to have provided for himself a sense of **appreciation** for his maintaining his honor and **affiliation** with* *his comrades. Holding out may well have enhanced his sense of **autonomy**. He maintained his own **status** as a North Vietnamese leader of high rank, and he devised a successful detainee **role**, by maintaining his silence even under extreme duress.*

Exactly what motivated him is difficult to say, but the key appears to be the reference to "my family's honor." As the educated son of an intellectual rather than a member of the favored"worker-peasant" class, it is likely that Tai's loyalties to the Party had been questioned many times. Tai does not disclose, nor does any outsider really know, what happened between Tai and his family when his father was criticized and fell out of favor with the Party shortly after the communist takeover of North Vietnam in 1954. He may have felt a need to prove his loyalty at that time. If, as Snepp wrote and Tai's interrogators believed, Tai helped prosecute his father during this period, his memoir suggests that he subsequently reconciled with his father and appears to have resolved never to cause such pain to his family again. Human psychology is a tricky business, of course, but in this case what appeared on the outside to be an exploitable weakness – Tai's apparent betrayal of his father– had been turned into a strength.

Teaching Notes: There is a little more information on this subject. In an interview published in the French newspaper L'Express shortly after South Vietnam was liberated, Frank Snepp stated,

*Because he (Nguyen Tai) could not stand cold, he was thrown into a cell belonging to the apparatus of powerful forces, and cold air was constantly blown into the cell, but he still refused to give in. I discovered one other weakness that he had. During the 1950s, he had tried to prove his loyalty to his superiors by disowning his father, a famous Vietnamese author who did not believe in communism. After we learned of the great importance of family in Vietnamese society, we endeavored to open up that painful wound. ... (We) could say that he was not completely true to his cause, and this wound might have caused a change in him. (*Vietimes, *online publication of Vinanet, 3 May 2008)*

Teaching notes: Snepp may have misinterpreted Tai's belief system and related emotions. He may have assumed that mentioning Tai's father *would cause Tai to be vulnerable, but in fact Tai appeared to have dealt with this issue and therefore used the line of questioning as a source of strength. This example highlights the importance of the interviewer remaining open-minded, and of continuously assessing a detainee's **interests and social identities** throughout the intelligence interviewing process.*

Lest anyone be too quick to condemn Tai's South Vietnamese interrogators, we should remember that the prisoner had just spent five years directing vicious attacks against these same men, their friends, their colleagues, and their families. They knew that if Tai escaped or was released, he would come after them again. During 1970, the last year of Tai's freedom, in spite of the losses his organization had suffered during the Tet offensive, communist accounts boast of at least three bombings and several assassinations conducted by Tai's personnel against South Vietnamese police and intelligence officers in Saigon. It was as if members of the New York Police Department were suddenly handed Osama bin Laden and asked to extract a confession. If things got "a little rough," that certainly should not have come as a surprise to anyone.

*Teaching Notes: While things getting "a little rough" may not be surprising to some people, an important question remains, "Was such treatment **effective**?" It takes great self-discipline for intelligence interviewing professionals to keep their own emotions under control during times of war, especially under the **stress** of extreme time pressure, and if comrades have been killed. In theoretical terms, intelligence interviewing professionals need constantly to assess their **own interests** to be sure that they can set aside the desire for immediate revenge and the urge to vent frustration and rage. This could be especially important if a detainee were goading the interviewers in an effort to distract them or provoke them into rendering him unconscious.*

*Intelligence interviewing professionals need to keep a constant eye on the true goal or "**interest**" of intelligence interviewing: to use strategies that will produce actionable intelligence in order to save lives. As an expert intelligence interviewing professional has said, "This is not about winning a fight or punishment. It is about getting information." It seems likely that self-discipline would be easier to* *maintain within the context of a well-trained, professional, intelligence interviewing team.*

In addition, accounts by US prisoners of war of their torture by North Vietnamese interrogators at the infamous "Hanoi Hilton" reveal that the methods of physical torture used on them were identical to methods Tai says were used on him. The war was vicious on all sides; no one's hands were clean.

*Teaching Notes: This point would seem to raise a question about what could have happened if Tai's captors had tried an entirely different approach. At the beginning, and here and there, there seem to have been sporadic attempts to use **incentives** with Tai, although not as part of a coherent strategy that he might come to trust. Apparently the captors also tried to manipulate the **context of captivity**, including an attempt to trap Tai with a stool pigeon. It appears, however, as if a major strategy of interrogation was **direct** confrontation of **resistances**, with intent to overwhelm Tai's **resistances**.*

*Query: Suppose from the outset it had been possible to construct a **tightly controlled interviewing context** like that of Fort Hunt during WW II? Suppose the strategy had been to **avoid resistances** as much as possible? Suppose skilled intelligence interviewing professionals who knew Tai's languages and constantly assessed Tai's **social identities**, likely **interests**, and perceptions of his experiences, had been involved from the beginning and throughout? Suppose these intelligence interviewing professionals, with the help of skillful analysts, had been able to construct their own **information** flow to Tai in his confinement, and **surprise and distract** him by not interrogating as he expected? Might they have been able to establish more of an **operational accord** with him, especially over a period of several years?*

The White Cell

What might have happened, if the torture had continued, can only be guessed. In the fall of 1971, Tai's superiors made a move that ensured his survival. On 9 October, US Army Sgt. John Sexton was released by his communist captors and walked into American lines west of Saigon carrying a note written by Tran Bach Dang, the secretary of the Saigon-Gia Dinh Party Committee. The letter contained an offer to exchange

The U.S. Government Case Study of Human Manipulation

Tai and another communist prisoner, Le Van Hoai, for Douglas Ramsey, a Vietnamese-speaking State Department officer who had been held by the communists since 1966 and whom the communists believed was a US intelligence officer. Tai's torture and interrogation immediately ended. Even though the negotiations for an exchange quickly broke down, Tai had suddenly become, as his communist superiors intended, too valuable for his life to be placed in jeopardy. He was now a pawn in a high-level political game.

In early 1972, Tai was informed he was being taken to another location to be interrogated by the Americans. After being blindfolded, he was transported by car to an unknown location and placed in a completely sealed cell that was painted all in white, lit by bright lights 24 hours a day, and cooled by a powerful air-conditioner (Tai hated air conditioning, believing, like many Vietnamese, that cool breezes could be poisonous). Kept in total isolation, Tai lived in this cell, designed to keep him confused and disoriented, for three years without learning where he was.

*Teaching Notes: This new environment was designed to take away almost all of Tai's feeling of **autonomy**: he no longer could watch other detainees to gather **information**, he could no longer track time or direction by observing the daylight, and he could no longer overhear his guards' discussions. In Tai's memoirs, he described his new surroundings as "too hard to comprehend." He now had no idea what his future held.*

*Query: How might a different type of environment from 1972 on have affected the Americans' ability to persuade Tai? One possible answer: placing Tai in a carefully thought-out environment designed to enhance the potential for an **operational accord**, as happened with some Japanese POWs during WWII. Entering into an environment that was the opposite of the previous detention center where Tai had been held might have been modestly effective. An unexpected decrease in physical and psychological pressure might also have been effective in gaining some power to persuade (see **Stress**). Under these conditions, might Tai conceivably have relaxed his vigilance in meeting his own **core emotional concerns**? Therefore, might there have been better opportunities to mobilize sources of **persuasion** such as **reciprocity**,* *social proof*, and various kinds of **authority,** along with the possible offer of **incentives**? As the story continues, it becomes clear that in fact some discrete attempts were made along these lines, although there was apparently no **integrated systems strategy**.

Tai's interrogation began anew. This time the interrogator was a middle-aged American whom Tai knew as"Paul." Paul was actually Peter Kapusta, a veteran CIA Soviet/Eastern Europe counterintelligence specialist with close ties to the famed and mysterious chief of CIA counter-intelligence, James Jesus Angleton. Even by Tai's account, Kapusta and the other Americans who interrogated him ("Fair," "John," and Frank Snepp) never mistreated him in any way, although Tai was always suspicious of American attempts to trick him into doing something that might cause his suspicious bosses back in the jungle to believe he was cooperating with the "enemy." Kapusta and the other American officers tried to win Tai's trust by giving him medical care, extra rations, and new clothing (most of which Tai claims to have refused or destroyed for fear of compromising his own strict standards of "revolutionary morality"). They also played subtly on his human weaknesses– his aversion to cold, his need for companionship, and his love for his family.

*Teaching Notes: While Tai's treatment by these interrogators appears to have been designed to build **operational accord,** his living conditions suggest otherwise. Tai once again showed his adeptness at sustaining his **resistances**: it seems he instinctively or consciously understood how to resist the strategies described in Cialdini's **principles of persuasion**, conceivably because he himself may have used these strategies on others in the past. Tai seems actively to have looked for **persuasive** attempts on the part of his interrogators and then labeled them in his mind as manipulative actions.*

*This cognitive, analytic process likely helped to limit the emotional power of the interrogators' **persuasion** strategies. For example, in Tai's memoir he describes refusing to use the **scarce** resources offered to him, such as two wool blankets to warm him in the cold cell, or to eat the "rich" food and the fruit he was offered, telling himself the Americans were only trying to "bribe"him. He labeled the medical care he was given as only a way to "win his sympathy," and believed* *his interrogators would use knowledge about his physical well-being to torture him. Tai would not permit himself to feel indebted to his captors. He refused to find any interrogator **likable**, and adamantly refused the attempts by any of his interrogators to establish **moral or "legitimate" authority**. The American interrogators seem not to have had skilled Vietnamese colleagues who, as imprisoned collaborators, could have helped them to mobilize a sense of **social proof**.*

*Query: The South Vietnamese had tried to place a collaborator next to Tai's cell, and while Tai did indeed engage with that person he maintained his cover story; he was always vigilant and skeptical. If the Americans had tried to use a collaborator, is there any way this could have been done that might have lessened Tai's **resistances**?*

*Query: In terms of **social identities** it seems clear that Tai worked hard to stay mentally connected and completely **committed** to his constituents at home. Would there have been any possible **cross-cutting identities** that one of the interrogators might have attempted to build with Tai in order to lessen Tai's focus on his pre-1970 loyalties, even if only for moments here and there?*

According to his memoirs, Tai decided he would shift tactics after learning that he was being returned to American control. Rather than refusing to respond with any answers other than "No" or "I don't know," as he had with the South Vietnamese, he now resolved: "I will answer questions and try to stretch out the questioning to wait for the war to end. I will answer questions but I won't volunteer anything. The answers I give may be totally incorrect, but I will stubbornly insist that I am right."

*Query: Is there any chance that Tai viewed it this way in hindsight? Perhaps Tai felt the wish to engage in conversation when treated like a human being with real needs. Or perhaps this new tactic was an example of Tai's skill in partially meeting the **interests** of Americans with **intangible incentives** (by talking.) It may well have been both.*

*Teaching Notes: In any case the tactics above appear to demonstrate Tai's skill in defending against Cialdini's **commitment/consistency** principle, perhaps in two different ways. First, Tai was explicitly prepared not to care about being accused of lying or looking* *inconsistent. (In effect, he arranged that he would not care what his interrogators thought of him, although this is ordinarily a very difficult stance to maintain when receiving treatment that meets **core concerns**.) Second, it also permitted Tai, when he wished, to adhere unshakably to a story that had been demonstrated to be false. It is easy to see how this might be relatively effective. Sticking to the same story is, in and of itself, a protection against distraction; it preserves more mental energy for sustaining **resistances**. This tactic is an interesting reprise of Tai's apparent skill in using simplicity to maintain focus and continue to protect his valuable knowledge.*

In other words, Tai would engage in a dialogue, something he could not trust himself to do when being tortured by the South Vietnamese out of fear that his weakened condition and confused mental state might cause him to slip and inadvertently reveal some vital secret. He would play for time, trying to remain in American custody as long as possible in order to keep himself out of the hands of the South Vietnamese, whom he believed would either break him or kill him.

Teaching Notes: Again, it is hard to imagine what would "break" Tai if he were to be tortured again. However, it is easy to imagine that Tai would have hoped still to live; that is, not to have to kill himself.

This meant he would have to engage in a game of wits with the Americans, selectively discussing with them things they already knew, or that were not sensitive, while staying vigilant to protect Public Security's deepest secrets: the identities of its spies, agents, and assassins. This was, however, a tricky strategy, and even Tai admits that it led him into some sensitive areas.

*Teaching Notes: It appears that when one talks at all, it is difficult constantly to filter and resist the dynamic that develops in an environment that encourages **operational accord**. It would also be more difficult to keep track of the stories and lies that one is telling. This may be one reason why, when he was being tortured, Tai chose just to say, "I forget." When talking, it is hard to maintain a constant, simple focus and clear boundaries, and to keep from experiencing the emotions that form, often below the level of conscious thought, and that might lead to unwittingly disclosing bits of information.*

The U.S. Government Case Study of Human Manipulation

Interestingly, Tai blames the communist radio and press for broadcasting public reports on some sensitive subjects, thereby making it impossible for him to deny knowledge of such areas. Sounding not unlike many American military and intelligence officers during the Vietnam War, Tai wrote:

I had always been firmly opposed to the desires of our propaganda agencies to discuss secret matters in the public media....Now, because the"Security of the Fatherland" radio program had openly talked about the [Ministry's] "Review of Public Security Service Operations," I was forced to give them [the Americans] some kind of answer.

*Teaching Notes: This story shows some of the power of **information**. But it is also puzzling. Tai had flatly denied allegations of his true identity and other sensitive topics when confronted in the past, even after being presented with information demonstrating he had lied. What dynamics were now in play that might have led Tai to feel that he was "forced" to supply an answer?*

Peter Kapusta worked on Tai for several months and apparently believed he was making progress. Then he was reassigned. Washington sent Frank Snepp to take over the case.

Teaching Notes: Tai's memoirs reveal that Kapusta attempted (through a translator) to keep a polite, conversational tone with Tai; to probe inquisitively; to confront him with detailed intelligence information that had been obtained from other sources; to revisit previously covered topics with different lines of questioning; and to provide Tai with books on various topics to encourage thought and conversation. He also offered various comfort items, such as candy, cigarettes, and soft drinks. Tai admitted that Kapusta was polite. However Tai recalled that he continued to lie about important facts, even in the face of contrary evidence; he refused to shake hands before and after sessions, reminding himself that his job was to defeat his enemy; and he refused comfort items. Tai wrote that he used his time and resources to his advantage (e.g., he read English books to improve his language abilities so that he could understand what the interrogator was saying instead of relying on the translator).

Query: If you had been an intelligence interviewing professional *during this period of time (but with your present knowledge), what strategy might you have taken in an attempt to **persuade**? Review in the six teaching papers the importance of **interests** and **social identities** in building an **operational accord,resonance**, meeting **core concerns**, building on various **sources of power**, Cialdini's **persuasion principles**, and methods to avoid **resistances**.*

Snepp decided to try a new ploy to crack Tai's facade. Like other American officers who had interrogated Tai, Snepp did not speak Vietnamese. Interrogations were always conducted using a South Vietnamese interpreter, usually a young woman. Snepp decided to cut the South Vietnamese completely out of the interrogation to see if this might lead Tai to speak more freely. One day he brought in a Vietnamese-speaking American interpreter to take over the duty.

Tai, ever suspicious, believed that as long as Vietnamese were directly involved in his interrogation, there was a chance that word about him might leak out to his "comrades" on the outside. If the Americans took over completely, Tai's superiors would have no chance of locating him, or of verifying his performance during the interrogation. Tai was always desperately concerned with leaving a clear record for his superiors to find that would prove he had not cooperated with his interrogators. He believed this was essential for his own future and that of his family. As a professional security officer, Tai was well aware of the Vietnamese communist practice of punishing succeeding generations for the sins of their fathers.

*Teaching Notes: The interrogator attempted to meet an **interest** he believed Tai held – the need for privacy – to persuade him to talk. Tai's true **interests**,however, lay in precisely the other direction. His **interest** was not to maintain privacy as conventionally understood, but to sustain his reputation and honor in the eyes of his **constituents** back home, together with the hope that he would be found. The whole Tai story shows the extraordinary power of **relationships and constituencies** – that is, his North Vietnamese relationships– in stabilizing and shielding Tai during years of duress. By reporting that Tai would have remembered: "the Vietnamese communist practice of punishing succeeding generations for the sins of their fathers" Pribbenow also suggests the very long reach of potential **disincentives*** *deriving from those same **relationships**.*

He decided to force the Americans to bring back the South Vietnamese interpreter by pretending not to be able to understand the American, whom he admits spoke Vietnamese perfectly well.

The ploy worked in the end. Meanwhile, however, it led to the author's only involvement in this case. As Tai had planned, Snepp became angry and frustrated, blaming the American interpreter for the lack of results.

*Teaching Notes: Tai was obviously convincing in his act, and was able through an extraordinary use of **information** power (and the powerful **disincentive** of essentially shutting down) to manipulate the interrogator in order to have a real **interest** met.*

*Tai may also, consciously or instinctively, have been playing to the American's weak **fallback** position. Recall that a **fallback** position is important not only for itself, but also for the **relative** power of one's **fallback** position compared with that of the other person. Snepp may have inadvertently signaled that he was under pressure, and Tai may have picked up that Snepp was under pressure to get results from him.*

*Query: What resources and type of assessment at this juncture might have been helpful in terms of understanding the motivation behind Tai's behavior? Possible answer: A team, including analysts, and another translator who could listen to the interchange and who could assist in assessing Tai's **interests** and **core concerns** and how to respond to them.*

After the session, Snepp came to see me (we had become friends during his first tour in Vietnam), told me of his unhappiness with the"performance" of the interpreter (who was a close colleague of mine), and asked if I would be free to interpret for him in future sessions with Tai. As it happened, I was not available, and Snepp was forced to return to the use of an ethnic Vietnamese interpreter. I always wondered what could possibly have caused the problem that Frank described to me that afternoon. Thirty years later, when I read Tai's memoir, I finally understood.

Teaching Notes: Snepp described in his book Decent Interval that he was under tremendous pressure from his organization to obtain information of "strategic value" from Tai, and to do so quickly. The CIA needed to justify why they had refused a prisoner exchange of Tai and American Foreign Service officer Douglas Ramsey; the CIA needed to create the perception that Tai was important and was cooperating. Unlike previous cases, where Snepp had taken weeks to read through a case and prepare his strategy, he was given almost no time to prepare for the interrogation once he landed in Saigon.

*Snepp wrote that he was able to obtain some information of value by raising the topic of Tai's wife and children. He described Tai as becoming very still, and stating, "I cannot think about my wife and children. The only way I can survive this is by putting all such hope aside. Then there are no illusions or disappointments." After learning this bit of **information**, Snepp continued to raise questions about Tai's family. Snepp wrote, "His [Tai's] dossier began to grow as he inadvertently let slip one detail after another in his helpless grasping after the one hope he knew he could not afford. I reported the progress to Washington. My superiors seemed satisfied." Unfortunately, Snepp does not write about the information Tai provided. It is possible that this is an example where important information was garnered by non-coercive methods in working with Tai.*

Impact of the Paris Accord

On 27 January 1973, the Paris Peace Agreement was signed, calling for the release of all prisoners of war and civilian detainees. In compliance, Snepp, without obtaining prior authorization from the South Vietnamese CIO (which was still the organization officially responsible for Tai's detention), informed Tai and other communist prisoners of the agreement and its prisoner exchange provisions. Tai, totally isolated from information about the outside world, was suspicious at first. Finally, he managed to persuade one of his guards (who were under instruction not to talk to the prisoner unless absolutely necessary) to confirm Snepp's information.

*Teaching Notes: It is instructive to try to imagine the sources of persuasion that Tai was able to use in talking with the guards: the hope of reward (**incentives**)? Playing on **moral authority** – the guard's respect for him? A fear of revenge (**disincentive**) after the war was over* *if the guard did not comply?*

This example highlights the importance of having a completely controlled environment for a high value detainee, where all the people who have access to the detainee are part of the team and interact accordingly. In this particular case it appears to have been the detainee who was able to learn from the guard, rather than the reverse.

The American interrogation ended with the signing of the agreement in Paris, although he remained incarcerated in the snow white cell. Tai was able to use the information Snepp had given him about the prisoner exchange provisions to resist further efforts by the South Vietnamese to interrogate him. He was left isolated, but in peace, for the next two years, until Saigon fell in April 1975. He credits Snepp's information on the Paris accord with enabling him to resist and survive until his final release. Frank Snepp may have saved Tai's life.

According to his memoirs, Tai maintained his sanity and survived by reminding himself of his allegiance to his nation, his Party, and his cause, and by constantly thinking of his family. He followed a strict daily ritual of saluting a star, representing the North Vietnamese flag (a red flag with a single gold star in the center), that he had scratched on his cell wall and then silently reciting the North Vietnamese national anthem, the South Vietnamese Liberation anthem, and the Internationale, the anthem of the world communist movement.

*Teaching Notes: This presents a powerful example of staying connected to outside **constituents** in order to sustain strength (see **interests and identities** and the **power of relationships**). This story also underscores that, time and again, Tai was sustained by thinking about various **fallback** positions – including the hope that the war would end. It also appears from Tai's memoirs that he may not really have been left in peace. During these months he reports continued attempts to trick him, a long period when his cell was permitted to become exceedingly hot, and a hunger strike by Tai. The memoirs report that he continued to **resist**.*

He wrote poems and songs in his head, memorizing them and reviewing them constantly to make sure he did not forget. While some of these poems were the obligatory paeans to the Party, most were about his love for his children and his family.

*Teaching Notes: Tai understood the potential implications of long-term isolation and the impact on one's emotional wellbeing (see **Stress**) and cognitive abilities (see **Memory**). Keeping one's mind active takes a good deal of energy, focus, and discipline. These mental exercises (as well as the physical exercises and a regimented daily schedule) almost certainly also helped him to maintain his **resistances**. (According to Snepp in Decent Interval, Tai woke up at 6 a.m. sharp every day and adhered to a strict schedule of exercise, reading, and eating throughout the day, and then went to bed automatically at 10 p.m., without ever seeing a clock or the sun.)*

An insert into the Pribbenow case from a different article: A Saigon Times Magazine article (Oct, 2001), written about Tai, described Tai's experiences during this time the following way:

People can hardly live without friends and fight without fellows. Tai is not an exception. In a white cold room that gives no feelings of space and time, he built friendship for himself by making a human puppet and a dog from paper and old clothes. He got the encouragement from these 'prison fellows' and shared feelings with them in silence, and cherished faithfulness and strong will. ....Tai says that in the prison, he could do what he had never done before. He used pieces of newspapers to make a chessboard, chess players and organize a match with his paper prisoner fellow. He maintained that habit to keep himself smart during the four years in jail.

*Tai's use of inanimate objects reflects the very real need for human interaction and speaks to the likely universality of **core emotional concerns**. Tai was not willing to have his interrogators meet these needs, and therefore worked to meet his own core concerns for **affiliation, appreciation,** and **autonomy** with these inanimate objects. These actions likely helped to insulate him somewhat from the interrogators' attempts to **persuade** him. They also affirmed for him a **role** as detainee that was very different than the one the interrogators were trying to get him to develop in him. And of course the chess games would indeed have fostered mental agility.*

Just before communist troops entered Saigon on 30 April 1975, a senior

The U.S. Government Case Study of Human Manipulation

South Vietnamese officer ordered Tai's execution to prevent his release by victorious comrades. By some measure at least, it was not an unreasonable order – as Frank Snepp noted, "Since Tai was a trained terrorist, he could hardly be expected to be a magnanimous victor."

The order came too late, however. All of the CIO's senior personnel were in the process of fleeing the country, and the junior enlisted men entrusted with the task of disposing of Tai, men who had no opportunity to escape, understandably decided that they might have more to gain by keeping the prisoner alive. They were afraid of retribution if the communist victors learned that they had killed him and they might even have hoped for some reward.

*Teaching Notes: The senior officers miscalculated the junior enlisted men's **interests** in this case. The senior personnel believed the men would follow their orders, but in reality the junior men quickly surmised that if they kept Tai alive and aided in his rescue they would be viewed more favorably by the North Vietnamese Liberation Army.*

Tai survived and returned to his family in Hanoi in the fall of 1975. Tai went on to other important positions, including a term as an elected member of the reunified nation of Vietnam's National Assembly. In June 2002, in a solemn ceremony held in Ho Chi Minh City (the former Saigon), Nguyen Tai was officially honored with Vietnam's highest award, the title of "Hero of the People's Armed Forces."

Reflections (by Merle Pribbenow)

What conclusions can we draw about the efficacy and appropriateness of the interrogation techniques used by the South Vietnamese and the Americans in the Tai case? While the South Vietnamese use of torture did result (eventually) in Tai's admission of his true identity, it did not provide any other usable information. The South Vietnamese played the key role in cracking Tai's cover story, but it was their investigation and analysis that put the pieces together to make a solid and incontrovertible identification of Tai, not their use of torture, that scored this success. A sensitive, adept line of questioning that confronted Tai with this evidence and offered him a deal – like the offer by his torturers to exchange admission of his identity for consideration in a notional prisoner exchange – would almost certainly have achieved the same result. Without doubt, the South Vietnamese torture gave Tai the incentive for the limited cooperation he gave to his American interrogators, but it was the skillful questions and psychological ploys of the Americans, and not any physical infliction of pain, that produced the only useful (albeit limited) information that Tai ever provided.

This brings me back to my college classmate's question. The answer I gave him– one in which I firmly believe – is that we, as Americans, must not let our methods betray our goals. I am not a moralist. War is a nasty business, and one cannot fight a war without getting one's hands dirty. I also do not believe that the standards set by the ACLU and Amnesty International are the ones we Americans must necessarily follow. There is nothing wrong with a little psychological intimidation, verbal threats, bright lights and tight handcuffs, and not giving a prisoner a soft drink and a Big Mac every time he asks for them. There are limits, however, beyond which we cannot and should not go if we are to continue to call ourselves Americans. America is as much an ideal as a place and physical torture of the kind used by the Vietnamese (North as well as South) has no place in it. Thus, extracting useful information from today's committed radicals – like Nguyen Tai in his day – remains a formidable challenge.

----

*Teaching Notes: This is the end of the Pribbenow article. Below are excerpts from other sources that may help the reader to understand the effect that Tai had on others. With respect to Frank Snepp it would appear that there was some **operational accord**, at least as perceived by Snepp.*

A section of Frank Snepp's memoir, Decent Interval, reads as follows:

Before North Vietnamese tanks swept into Saigon, a high-ranking CIA official suggested to a Saigon official that the best solution would be to make him disappear, because Tai was an experienced terrorist, so it was hard to expect that he would be a compassionate victor. The South Vietnamese official agreed. Tai was loaded onto a helicopter and thrown out over the South China Sea at an altitude of 10,000 feet. At this point he had endured four years of isolation in a snow white cell, and he had still never fully admitted who he really was. (Vietimes, online publication of Vinanet, 3 May 2008).

And from the Boston Globe in 2005:

After the war, Snepp left CIA, but, unable to get Tai out of his mind, he traveled to Paris specifically to pass the word through the Vietnamese mission that Tai had comported himself honorably and died bravely. (H.D.S. Greenway, Boston Globe, *May 2005)*

But that is not how the story ends. I am grateful to the BBC's Carol Hills, who informed me that Tai, unbeknownst to Snepp, managed to talk his South Vietnamese captors into releasing him once the last of the CIA had fled Saigon 30 years ago. Tai lives and wrote his own account of his interrogation. (H.D.S. Greenway, Boston Globe, *May 2005)*

Frank Snepp did not find out that Tai survived until years later. He says today that "for me, the interrogation of Tai brought into full focus the moral ambiguity of the war. There is no question that Tai would have shot me down on the street if he'd been given a chance at the time. And I would surely have returned the favor. But face to face across the interrogation desk, the 'despicable' persona of 'our enemy 'altered to reveal a deeply committed warrior enlisted in a cause he deeply felt. I could not but admire his strength, if not his ruthlessness, and wonder if his commitment might not have chastened other Americans so convinced of the righteousness of our own cause." (H.D.S. Greenway, Boston Globe, *May 2005)*

"Personally, the circumstances of the (CIA's) interrogation, veering so close as they did to psychological torture, eroded my own sense of certitude about my role in Vietnam," Snepp told me. "True, I always console myself that I treated Tai as well as I could. But confining Tai in that snow white room also made me realize how the war was compromising my own values. It was a catalyst to the disillusionment that would ultimately carry me out of the agency," but "I am greatly relieved that Tai was not part of the ghastly body count of that war."(H.D.S. Greenway, Boston Globe, *May 2005)*

Teaching Notes: From a Vietnamese reporter's description of his interaction with Tai, in a recent publication, there is a further affirmation of an extraordinarily self-disciplined Nguyen Tai.

He is a man who is very principled, who is very precise and meticulous, and he is a man who suppresses his feelings and emotions. During my conversation with him, although I asked him about many things, and I phrased my questions in ways that would lead others to get carried away with themselves so that they would just tell me everything and then, after they were finished, they would sit back and say to themselves, "Did I really tell him that?" He, however, was different. He spoke in a very measured tone, not open and easy but also not stern, not animated and enthusiastic but also not indifferent. Perhaps that quality helped him during the more than four years of constant interrogation that he endured in the solitary confinement cell of the puppet Central Intelligence Organization at 3 Bach Dang Street. (Vietimes, *online publication of Vinanet, 3 May 2008)*

Questions for Consideration:

•*As you read through this case, were there points at which you wanted to add to the teaching notes? Or where you disagreed with some point of case analysis?*

•*Bearing in mind your own experience, what more did you want to know about this case? What additional facts and descriptions would you like to see in a teaching case of this kind?*

•*Suppose in this case it had been possible to interview Nguyen Tai again about his early life and experiences and his belief system? What might you have wished to know?*

•*Suppose in the case of Tai there had been access to the South Vietnamese interrogators, and the guards, what questions might you have wished to ask? How might information about their thoughts and perspectives change your analysis of the case?*

•*Suppose it had been possible for the case writer to have included much of the information that the South Vietnamese and the American interrogators actually heard from Tai at each point during the years of Tai's confinement. Is it possible that this case might change in the light of such information?*

The U.S. Government Case Study of Human Manipulation